CHRIST HAVE MERCY

How to Put Your Faith in Action

Matthew C. Harrison

CHRIST HAVE MERCY
HOW TO PUT YOUR FAITH IN ACTION

MATTHEW C. HARRISON

Published 2008 by Concordia Publishing House
3558 S. Jefferson Ave., St. Louis, MO 63118-3968
1-800-325-3040 • www.cph.org
Text © 2008 Matthew C. Harrison

Library of Congress Cataloging-in-Publication Data
Harrison, Matthew C.
    Christ have mercy : how to put your faith in action / Matthew C.Harrison.
    p. cm.
    ISBN-13: 978-0-7586-1501-5
    1. Mercy. I. Title.
BV4647.M4H37 2008
241'.4--dc22

       2007047130

1 2 3 4 5 6 7 8 9 10   17 16 15 14 13 12 11 10 09 08

CONTENTS

Foreword

by Rev. Ray S. Wilke

I have waited thirty-eight years for this book to be published. We never learned the things presented in this book in the seminary in 1966. All of us suspected that there was some connection between the First and Second Tables of the Law given to Moses on Mount Sinai, but we didn't know how that connection played out in the Church and in the world. Nor could we put our fingers on the related theology presented in the Lutheran Confessions or the dogmatics books that we pored over in the seminary.

Seven years as a missionary in the Philippines taught me that the need for "Christ-style mercy" was to be found in the bulging, protein-deficient tummy of every child of the rice paddy. The need for "Christ-style mercy" was to be found in the furrowed brow of the typhoon-blown mother sitting amid the rubble of her nipa hut. The need for "Christ-style mercy" was to be heard from the lips of fathers walking in waist-deep water with a child on each shoulder, chanting his own version of the Kyrie as he pleaded for the thirty-one consecutive days of rain to stop. But we were evangelistic missionaries; our assigned task was to preach and teach the Gospel. It was not to become involved in social gospel. But then my Jeep stalled in four feet of water while delivering sacks of rice to people huddled in elevated huts, water all around. Right then and there I reasoned that there must be some good Lutheran theology somewhere to justify the compulsions of my heart in doing these things. I have finally found that theology in spades in Matt Harrison's comprehensive work *Christ Have Mercy*.

A dozen years ago over dinner and a nice glass of Chablis, the late Dr. Oswald Hoffman said to me, "We Lutherans have the best theology in the world, but we have yet to figure out how to pull it out of the pages of our theology books and down out of the airwaves and into the trenches of people's lives." Missouri Synod Lutherans need sound theology to function. We know no other way to present the Gospel.

Our presentation of the Gospel must be based on good scholarly theology or we cannot function. We dabble in feelings, but we don't trust them. We respect authority, but we don't submit to the "Vicar of Christ." We think logically, but we are suspect of "reason." What are we to do with all of Jesus' invitations to follow Him into the muddle and misery of people's lives? If it doesn't fit the formula of Word and Sacrament, we struggle. Well, perhaps there is more to Word and Sacrament ministry than we thought. What if the evidence was there all along, lying right there, undiscovered, in the Word, in the Confessions, in the writings of our revered Church Fathers? What if it could be proven from good sound theology that the urges of our heart to help the ones who have been beaten down sprang from Christ's own heart? These urges toward acts of human mercy are bound to the cross and to the cup and to the inviolable Word, even to the water poured over to vicariously make us righteous. The evidence of such things is all there, buried in the writings of Luther, the Confessions, and the Church Fathers, waiting to be translated and interpreted and arranged into what has become known as systematic theology.

Sometimes the tyranny of world affairs moves us toward unlikely behavior. The explosions among the relationships of nations and people present us with circumstances never seen before. Such was the case with Luther on the eve of the writing of the Augsburg Confession. He was beset, on the one hand, by the barbarism of the Turkish Islamic Empire and on the other hand by the unrest established between his own thinking and the teachings of the Roman Catholic Church. Beset by those conflicting interests, Luther invented a new application of the German word *Anfechtung*. This is what he wrote: "The Prince of Demons himself has taken up combat against me; so powerfully and adeptly does he handle the Scriptures that my scriptural knowledge does not suffice if I do not rely on the alien Word."[1] Luther defines this "alien word" as the Gospel, which must be spoken to us. Thus forgiveness comes from outside ourselves. That, Luther feels, is why I need the others, why I am dependent on the intercession and the community of the Church. So when Luther was asked to contribute to the Imperial Diet of Charles V, he set about to write what we now know as the Augsburg Confession. It was written to provide some mutual ground between the Roman Catholics and the Lutherans in their struggle against the Turks.

This is what Luther wrote in the Smalcald Articles: "We will now return to the Gospel, which does not give us counsel and aid against sin in only one way. God is superabundantly generous in His grace: First, through the spoken Word, by which the forgiveness of sins is preached in the whole world [Luke 24:45–47]. This is the particular office of the Gospel. Second, through Baptism. Third, through the holy Sacrament of the Altar. Fourth, through the Power of the Keys. Also through the mutual conversation and consolation of brethren."[2] How few Lutheran believers recall that Luther identified this consolation as an extension of the Gospel and therefore as a means of grace. How powerful has become this fireside/riverside/bedside/field and forest conversation among us, even while not being fully aware that it is truly a God-ordained conversation and consolation that we share.

Indeed, the "mutual conversation and consolation of brethren" might be overheard by a refugee mother and child who are waiting outside a portable LCMS World Relief and Human Care clinic in Malakal, Sudan. An Islamic tsunami widow in the east of India may hear with gladness the "mutual conversation and consolation of brethren" when it is served with bandages, food, and shelter for her fatherless children.

It is my prayer that you may devour this book with gladness. It is destined to become a staple on the shelves of students, scholars, and church leaders everywhere who thrill at the fresh/ancient logic of Jesus.

It is with gladness that Jesus still hears and responds to our Kyrie cry, "Christ, have mercy! Lord, have mercy." It is the cry that was heard in Eden and in Goshen and on Moriah's awful mountain. It is the cry that we hear around the world. Jesus deems it good to answer that cry today by means of His people.

NOTES

1   Heiko Obermann, *Luther: Man between God and the Devil*, trans. Eileen Walliser-Schwarzbart (New Haven: Yale University Press, 1989), 226.

2   SA III IV (*Concordia*, 278).

PREFACE

Our whole life is enclosed and established in the bosom of the mercy of God.[1] *Martin Luther*

Christ, have mercy! This is an unprecedented time of opportunity for the Church, and mercy is the key to seizing the moment. This book is written with the conviction that mercy—the mercy of Christ to and for us—and our demonstration of that mercy to those within and outside the Body of Christ is the key to the future of the Church. Mercy is the key to mission and stewardship. It is the key to living our Christian lives together in love and forgiveness. We desperately need to learn more deeply of the mercy of Christ so we may learn how to care for one another in the Church. Mercy is the key to moving boldly and confidently into the future with courage in the Gospel—a confidence and courage based on conviction.

I write as a convinced, convicted, and unapologetic clergyman of The Lutheran Church—Missouri Synod. The public confession of the Lutheran Church—most fundamentally stated in the Book of Concord—is my own, without equivocation. I believe C. F. W. Walther, the founder of the LCMS, explicated the faith correctly, also on the doctrines of church and ministry. These pages will show a side of Walther's doctrine of the ministry that is all but unknown—the pastor's divinely given role of care for the needy. Working with the writings of Martin Luther for this project has convinced me all the more that I am but a drop next to the ocean of insight into Christ that is the great reformer's. I find Luther's ability to state the truth with a unique turn of phrase particularly delightful and trust you will too.

Writing this preface, I am now happy to "free myself from the hames, bridle, saddle and spurs of the printers,"[2] though that metaphor, I must admit, hardly fits the wonderful and helpful staff at Concordia Publishing House!

Lord, have mercy! May He use my stammerings and nascent thoughts to spur on the work of mercy in the name of Christ and His Gospel! May others more talented and capable take up the cause! May

He grant us courage to seize the moment, the moment of mercy, for the sake of Christ and His Gospel.

_____ NOTES _____

1   AE 12:320.

2   Theodore G. Tappert, ed. and trans., *Luther: Letters of Spiritual Counsel*, Library of Christian Classics 18 (Philadelphia and London: Westminster Press and SCM 1945), 94–95.

Abbreviations

AC   Augsburg Confession

AE   Luther, Martin. *Luther's Works.* American Edition. General editors Jaroslav Pelikan and Helmut T. Lehmann. 55 vols. St. Louis: Concordia and Philadelphia: Muhlenberg and Fortress, 1955–86.

Ap   Apology of the Augsburg Confession

ELCA   Evangelical Lutheran Church in America

FC Ep   Formula of Concord, Epitome

FC SD   Formula of Concord, Solid Declaration

LC   Large Catechism

LCMS   The Lutheran Church— Missouri Synod

LSB   *Lutheran Service Book*

SA   Smalcald Articles

StL   Luther, Martin. *Dr. Martin Luthers Sämmtliche Schriften.* 2d ed. 23 vols. in 24. Edited by Johann Georg Walch. St. Louis: Concordia, 1881–1910.

Tr   Treatise on the Power and Primacy of the Pope

WA   Luther, Martin. *D. Martin Luthers Werke. Kritische Gesamtausgabe Schriften.* 68 vols. Weimar: Hermann Böhlau, 1883–1993.

1

Lord, Have Mercy
Christ, Have Mercy
Lord, Have Mercy

"DEAR GOD, I'VE GOT AN EMPTY SACK!"

What man can live and never see death? Who can deliver his soul from the power of Sheol? *Psalm 89:48*

For if sin and death did not exist, both world and flesh would have to leave us alone. These are the real enemies. They beset us the worst, and it is through them that the others oppress and harass us.[1] *Martin Luther*

Sound asleep for hours, I had been dead to the world. Then, suddenly, I was awakened by death. I fumbled for the phone, then held it to my ear.

"Hello?"

"Pastor?"

"What? Yes," I responded, neither awake nor asleep, groping for my glasses.

"Pastor, there's been an accident. Can you come to the Schmidt[2] farm right away? We have about thirty high school kids out here in a state of shock."

It was the call everyone dreads, but especially a young and inexperienced pastor. Within minutes I dressed and drove to a farmhouse a few miles from the small rural town that was home to my first parish. I saw the controlled chaos of the flashing lights of the emergency vehicles in the distance, jarring, even sickening, in the pitch black of the early hours. The flashing melee converged at a bridge not far from the house. I saw some men I knew well, guys who loved to play cards, drink coffee, and joke "up town." But here they bore a different countenance, dressed as volunteer EMTs and firefighters. I took a deep breath, then asked one of the men what had happened.

"Amy Schneider left the Schmidt place and lost control of her car. She hit the bridge. She didn't make it, Pastor." The man walked away.

LIFE'S LITURGY: THE BEADY EYES OF DEATH

The firefighters had removed Amy's body moments earlier. Her car lay impaled on the side of a concrete bridge. The water and the shattered glass in the creek below flickered in the moonlight. A few yards back, the flashing lights reflected in the eyes of the handful of teenagers standing in shock, weeping and shaking in the cool spring night.

Not an hour before, the house had been filled with the laughter and music of a high school graduation party. I encouraged the kids to return to the house, and, carrying my Bible, I followed them inside. Young people were huddled in small groups about the living room, faces reflecting shock and terror, holding one another, some shaking uncontrollably. A dear friend was dead. What they regarded as the most important event in their young lives—graduation from high school—had been marred forever by tragedy and death. I read them the resurrection story from St. Mark's Gospel, sang an Easter hymn, and remained with them until dawn. As I sat silently amid the weeping and the muffled attempts at consolation, I thought about the first Good Friday and Holy Saturday. Those days could not have been much different.

I walked toward my car as the sun rose, hues of red and blue on the horizon, chasing back the night. I stood again at the very spot where a young life had ended only hours earlier. The mangled hulk of Amy's car had been removed. I shook my head and turned as I tried to make out her tire tracks in the gravel of a washboard country road. Surveying the shards of wreckage in the stream below, I was torn by conflicting images. Where only hours before blood had flowed in the dark into an Iowa creek, the colors of the dawn now danced and shimmered with iridescent beauty. Gone, like the life now ended, was the drone of emergency vehicles. No more police radios interrupted the Iowa dawn; instead, birds sang in the morning with a cacophonous joy, just as they have been doing since the dawn of creation. The contradiction was stark.

Two hours later I stood in the pulpit, sermon manuscript cast aside, struggling to console the faithful of that small community. Life's liturgy—the disorder of this sinful life—is a liturgy unto death.

I had witnessed a foreshadowing of the Last Day. "Marrying and giving in marriage" (Matthew 24:38) (that is, the party) will be going on at the last. And then Jesus shall come "like a thief in the night" (1 Thessalonians 5:2). Every death, in fact, is a harbinger of that great and terrible day of the Lord. Every death is that thief in the night. Death stands over our shoulder, ever ready to steal us away. We avoid looking back, but occasionally we risk a glance into the dark, though we quickly return to the party. Death's beady eyes remain trained on us as we take our every breath, his steely stare like ice on our bare necks. When we refuse to acknowledge him, our consciences stir our stomachs with disquiet. Our discomfort with hospitals, our paranoia about cancer and other disease, our pain over loved ones lost—all are ways we admit that the Reaper stands closer than we care to acknowledge.

The Reaper manifests himself in other ways too. Broken relationships tear apart our consciences. Nagging guilt, anxiety, and fear overcome our lives. These are the faces of death avoided but unavoidable. The conscience knows what should and should not be. We know there must be an end, a resolution, a reckoning. God requires an accounting.

Death reveals what we seek desperately to deny. In our culture of death, disaffection, and anxiety, billboards and other media shout aloud "youth," "sexuality," and "no fear." We avoid the specter of death at all costs. The beautiful and famous tell us to rob life from the very youngest humans for the pursuit of cures to put off death. We try to prolong the last fleeting hours of life. We die in hospitals. We do not sit with the dead. We whisk bodies away to the funeral home for processing to make death tolerable, even "beautiful." Hollywood makes fortunes on our fear of death. Why all the fuss? Is it because death poses questions to us that we cannot answer, questions we do not want to hear?

Adam, where are you? Who told you that you were naked? Why are you afraid to see God face-to-face? Cain, where is your brother? What have you done? Why have you sinned? Why have you wasted your life on things that pass away? Why have you failed to show mercy to your neighbor? "Should not you have had mercy on your fellow servant, as I had mercy on you?" (Matthew 18:33).

Parish pastors stare death in the face regularly. The "order" is common. Family members ask, "How long, Doctor?" The family vigil continues as the final signs appear. The eyes glaze. Labored breathing weakens to a death rattle. The extremities cool. The family speaks its last good-byes. A last kiss. The last breath. The mouth drops open. The face distorts. "He's gone," whispers the nurse. Tears flow. The warm body quickly becomes cold. The family departs, but the march of death continues: the stench, rigor mortis, and quiet men in dark suits pushing a gurney do their work. Finally, the body bag. All these steps are unavoidable proof of the beady eyes of death, which are staring us down too.

"Wretched man that I am! Who will deliver me from this body of death?" (Romans 7:24). Lord, have mercy. Christ, have mercy. Lord, have mercy.

THE LITURGY OF LIFE: *KYRIE ELEISON!*

A Canaanite woman from that region came out and was crying, "Have mercy on me, O Lord, Son of David . . . . Lord . . . even the dogs eat the crumbs that fall from their masters' table." Matthew 15:22, 27

Let me, merely like a dog, pick up the crumbs under the table, allowing me that which the children don't need or even miss, the crumbs, and I will be content therewith. So she catches Christ, the Lord, in his own words and with that wins not only the right of a dog, but also that of the children. Now then where will he go, our dear Jesus? He let himself be made captive, and must comply. Be sure of this: that's what he most deeply desires.[3] *Martin Luther*

That mournful Sunday morning, the Kyrie was sung in Iowa just as it has been sung in the liturgy since the beginning of the Church. In fact, the Church retained this Greek liturgical response even when the Western Church switched to Latin as the language of the liturgy. Following the deacon's petitions "for the peace of the whole world," "for the well-being of the Church of God," and "for the unity of all," the congregation responded, "Lord, have mercy."[4] The petitions would vary in number, but the deacon continued the prayers of the Kyrie as the clergy moved in procession to their places around the altar. We can only imagine the cries for mercy from a congregation suffering persecution or facing the decimation of war or disease.

I am sure that you remember the Litany, the prayer that is more than three pages long in the hymnal.[5] The Litany, yet another ancient liturgical text, is an extended Kyrie. The Litany varied in length during the early centuries of the Church. Today, we may find the Litany to be unbearably long and tedious. Martin Luther encouraged the clergy at Lübeck that "the most prominent things that you will wish to impress upon yourselves as well as upon the people are the prayers and litanies . . . for the purity and fruit of the Word, for outward peace and government, and for all other things that you will read in the litany."[6] We are oblivious to the insecure existence of a medieval Church that found prayer a deep refuge. The people of the Middle Ages were beset by plague, crusade, and the probability of a miserable and short life. Fat and lazy in body and soul, we find it hard to cope with the briefest prayers and shortest liturgies. We pray that we enjoy times that do not call for a long Kyrie. Perhaps it is time to pray that the Lord would lengthen our Kyrie. Perhaps it is the chaotic nihilism of school shootings, crazed religious suicide bombers, and assassins by which the Lord shall again lengthen our Kyrie and strengthen our faith. According to Luther, "it takes more than milk-fed faith to await death, which terrified almost all the saints, and still does so."[7]

The Kyrie is both a confession and a proclamation of truth about us and the world in which we find ourselves. In the face of Paul's preaching, the ancient pagans shouted the acclamation "Great is Artemis of the Ephesians!" (Acts 19:28). That was a confession. However misguided, the festal throng in Jerusalem shouted the acclamation "Hosanna to the Son of David!" (Matthew 21:9). It was an acclamation of whom they thought Jesus to be and also a confession of the kind of salvation they thought they wanted.[8] Friedrich Lochner, an early Lutheran missionary from Germany (sent to North America by Wilhelm Löhe), described the Kyrie as the "humble confession of complete misery, the misery of a thousand plagues and great trials, which no mouth can adequately describe, and for the sake of which misery God's only Son was born . . . and greeted by the song of praise of the angels. However, freed from this curse, the redeemed of the Lord shall sing of this misery until the fullness of redemption shall have come."[9] Lochner knew misery and mercy. He sang his Kyrie. He married three times and outlived three wives. The Kyrie confesses misery and a world of hurt. It is a confession of our need. But the cry for mercy also confesses the One from whom mercy comes: "*Lord,* have mercy."

When the Syrophonecian woman laid her Kyrie before Jesus (Matthew 15:22), she knew Jesus was *Kyrios*, which is the Greek word we translate as "Lord." Most pleas for mercy in the Gospels acclaim Jesus as "the Son of David." But when the Church took the Kyrie into the liturgy, she knew exactly who the *Kyrios* was, it was her confession of faith, her creed. *Iesous Kyrios*, "Jesus is Lord," is the earliest confession of the Church. Consider the words of St. Paul: ". . . because, when you confess with your mouth that Jesus is Lord and believe in your heart that God raised Him from the dead, you shall be saved" (Romans 10:9–10, *author's translation*). According to the New Testament, confessing "Jesus is Lord" is not Law. This does not confess Jesus as Lord in the sense of that popular but misguided bumper sticker that asks: "Jesus is your Savior, but have you made him your Lord?" The Lordship of Jesus is not about what we do; it is about what God does. As Peter proclaimed on Pentecost, "God has made Him both Lord and Christ, this Jesus whom you crucified" (Acts 2:36). This statement is Gospel. Luther clarifies that "the little word *Lord* means simply the same as *redeemer*. It means the One who has brought us from Satan to God, from death to life, from sin to righteousness, and who preserves us in the same."[10] In Romans 10:13, Paul quotes Joel 2:32: "Everyone who calls on the name of the Lord ["Yahweh" in the original Hebrew] will be saved." *Iesous Kyrios* confesses that Jesus is Yahweh, that Jesus is almighty God in the flesh. As Luther writes, " 'Christ the Lord.' The sermon is short but it compresses the entire Holy Scripture in one bundle."[11] In the Kyrie, the Church confesses that Jesus, God in the flesh for us, is our source of mercy in an otherwise merciless existence. Luther states that "the Christian life is to be lived amid sorrows, trials, afflictions, deaths, etc."[12] According to one commentator on the liturgy, the "Kyrie represents our deepest spiritual longings and hopes, which can never be fully realized in this world. . . . the Kyrie is the song of the church in her exile . . . it is the *Maranatha* (Come O Lord!) of the primitive church."[13]

20

Mercy and the Empty Sack

The tax collector, standing far off, would not even lift up his eyes to heaven,
but beat his breast, saying, "God, be merciful to me, a sinner!" *Luke 18:13*

"Dear God, I've got an empty sack!" That is what the Kyrie confesses. The place to begin a book on mercy is at the Kyrie, which is an essential element of the Divine Service. Most people are convinced that the church service is about the Law. It is about what we give to God. All week long we give our labor to our employer. We give time to our children. We give charitably to or volunteer for our community. Thus on Sunday we set time aside and give something to God. We give a little money. We sing God's praises, give Him thanks, and head home. Jesus told a parable about a Pharisee with a similar view of worship. "Two men went up into the temple to pray, one a Pharisee and the other a tax collector. The Pharisee, standing by himself, prayed thus: 'God, I thank You that I am not like other men, extortioners, unjust, adulterers, or even like this tax collector. I fast twice a week; I give tithes of all that I get' " (Luke 18:10–12). Notice the subject of the verbs in the statements made by the Pharisee—each subject is the word "I."

Luther sided with the tax collector on the question of what the church service is. "The tax collector, standing far off, would not even lift up his eyes to heaven, but beat his breast, saying, 'God, be merciful to me, a sinner!' " (Luke 18:13). Notice who does the verb—the action—in the tax collector's brief prayer: it is "God." Following Jesus' lead in this parable, Luther stood the entire worship of the medieval Church on its head. In medieval Roman theology, worship was above all about the performance of the sacrifice of the Mass as a means to "secure an insecure existence."[14] The motion of the Mass was from man to God. The unbloody resacrifice of Christ in the Mass was an act by which temporal and eternal punishments were mitigated.

Before Luther began his program of liturgical and theological reform, the Castle Church at Wittenberg boasted no fewer than nineteen altars at which priests busily recited the Mass and offered the sacrifice of Christ's body and blood to placate God. Foundations and bequests had established these altars and others at church buildings throughout medieval Christendom at which the Mass was to be said for the dead in perpetuity. The action was all from man to God. Luther completely changed the trajectory. In the hymn Luther composed to teach the Ten Commandments, the Reformation Church sang, " 'You shall observe the worship day That peace may fill your home, and, pray, And put aside the work you do, So that God may work in you.' Have mercy, Lord!"[15] The movement is from God to man. It is Gospel!

Luther described the Divine Service as a man coming with an empty sack.[16] In the Invocation, the name of the triune God, the very name placed on us in our Baptism, is spoken on us again. That name is grace, mercy, and forgiveness dropped into our "sack." We add an "Amen," that is, a "Yes, it is so! It is in my bag." Then we confess our sins—"Dear God, my sack is empty"—and the pastor "in the stead and by the command of my Lord Jesus Christ" forgives us.[17] We say again, "Amen! It is in the bag." God gives more grace and mercy in the readings from Holy Scripture. The sermon is replete with the forgiveness of sins in Christ, the Gospel that "is the power of God for salvation to everyone who believes" (Romans 1:16). As the very words are heard, they do what they say. At the end of the sermon, the pastor speaks the apostolic blessing, and we say, "Amen! It is in the bag." The Lord's Supper is given, and the words spoken to us:

> Take, eat; this is My body, which is given for you. This do in remembrance of Me. . . . Drink of it, all of you; this cup is the new testament in My blood, which is shed for you for the forgiveness of sins. This do, as often as you drink it, in remembrance of Me.[18]

We receive Jesus' body and blood with a hearty, "Amen!" The sack continues to be filled right through the Aaronic trinitarian blessing: "The Lord bless you and keep you. The Lord make His face shine upon you and be gracious unto you. The Lord lift up His countenance upon you and give you peace."[19] And we respond, "Amen, Amen, Amen! Yes, it is in the bag!"

To be sure, in the Divine Service we thank God for His gifts. We praise Him. We confess Him to be the Lord. But the main thing is what *God* has done to fill our sacks with forgiveness, peace, love, and mercy.

We leave the Divine Service with the sack over our shoulders and quickly find ourselves in need of what the Lord has given us. Our spouse sins against us, and we sin against our spouse. What do we do? We open our sack: "Here, I have a sack full of grace, mercy, and forgiveness. Take some. In the name of Jesus take it." Our children sin against us; our co-workers frustrate us; our neighbors drive us up the wall. We respond, "Here, I have a sack full of forgiveness. Take it. It is yours." We encounter a person in need and cannot turn away. "Friend, I have received mercy from the Lord. Please receive the Lord's mercy and love from me." On Sunday, God calls us back to His gracious word of promise and presence to refill our bag and send us back into the world.

In those early morning hours, a small Iowa farming community drank deep of the "cup of suffering." That death drove a community to its knees only hours later as we sang our Kyrie, "Lord, have mercy." As Luther said, "Here is a case where mortals are bound to each other by a chain of misery. But mercy ought to break the fetters."[20] As Christians, we confessed our empty sacks in the face of our sin, this death, and the devil. And the Lord was pleased to fill our empty sacks yet again with "the cup of blessing that we bless" (1 Corinthians 10:16). And even under death's beady glare, we found mercy and resurrection hope. We prayed, "Father, if it be possible, let this cup pass from me; nevertheless, not as I will, but as You will" (Matthew 26:39). The cup of suffering remained, but the cup of blessing sustained. Thank God, "mercy is more comprehensive than sin."[21]

> Then take comfort and rejoice,
> For His members Christ will cherish.
> Fear not, they will hear His voice;
> Dying, they will never perish;
> For the very grave is stirred
> When the trumpet's blast is heard.
> (*Lutheran Service Book* 741:6)

> From all sin, from all error, from all evil;
> From the crafts and assaults of the devil;
> from sudden and evil death; . . .
> Good Lord, deliver us. . . .

O Christ, hear us.

O Lord, have mercy.

O Christ, have mercy.

O Lord, have mercy. Amen.

(The Litany, *Lutheran Service Book*, pp. 288–89)

NOTES

1 AE 28:135.

2 Names have been changed in this account.

3 Eugene F. A. Klug, ed., *Sermons of Martin Luther: The House Postils*, trans. Eugene F. A. Klug et al. (Grand Rapids: Baker Books, 1996), 1:325. Used with permission of Baker Publishing Group.

4 *Lutheran Service Book*, p. 152.

5 See *Lutheran Service Book*, pp. 288–89.

6 Theodore G. Tappert, ed. and trans., *Luther: Letters of Spiritual Counsel*, Library of Christian Classics 18 (Philadelphia and London: Westminster Press and SCM, 1955), 297.

7 Tappert, *Letters of Spiritual Counsel*, 231.

8 Peter Brunner, *Worship in the Name of Jesus*, trans. M. H. Bertram (St. Louis: Concordia, 1968), 208.

9 Friedrich Lochner, *Der Hauptgottesdienst der Evangelisch-Lutherischen Kirche* (St. Louis: Concordia, 1895), 111 (*author's translation*). Lochner wrote on the Church's corporate life of mercy in *Der Lutheraner* 32, no. 6 (March 15, 1876): 41–46.

10 LC II 31 (*Concordia*, 402).

11 Klug, *House Postils*, 1:119.

12 Tappert, *Letters of Spiritual Counsel*, 124.

13 Luther D. Reed, *The Lutheran Liturgy* (Philadelphia: Muhlenberg, 1947), 255.

14 Carter Lindberg, *Beyond Charity: Reformation Initiatives for the Poor* (Minneapolis: Fortress, 1993), 95.

15 *Lutheran Service Book* 581:4. Text copyright © 1980 Concordia Publishing House. All rights reserved.

16 See StL 19:802ff. as cited in C. F. W. Walther, *The Proper Distinction Between Law and Gospel* (St. Louis: Concordia, 1929), 19.

17 *Lutheran Service Book*, p. 185.

18 *Lutheran Service Book*, p. 162.

19 *Lutheran Service Book*, p. 202.

20 Tappert, *Letters of Spiritual Counsel*, 183.

21 Ap V 28 (*Concordia*, 106).

2

FATHER, SON, AND SPIRIT

WHO GOD IS AND HOW WE WILL BE

Be merciful, even as your Father is merciful. *Luke 6:36*

I must believe in Father, Son, and Holy Spirit, and then also love my neighbor. The Catechism teaches me this. Yet we minimize the importance of such doctrine today. How many of us pay heed to it?[1] *Martin Luther*

I thank God and Jesus Christ that someone has regarded us as human beings. *Eric, of Othoro Lutheran Rescue Center, Kenya*

Mercy is about who God is and who we are in Christ. To deny mercy is more than a mere transgression of particular laws. Denying mercy is a denial of who God is in Christ, a denial of the Holy Trinity. "And the catholic faith is this, that we worship one God in Trinity and Trinity in Unity . . . whoever does not believe it faithfully and firmly cannot be saved" (Athanasian Creed).[2]

Nearly 15 percent of the adult population of western Kenya is infected with HIV, the virus that causes AIDS.[3] The staggering infection rate gives one pause. Seeing a number in a book or in a newspaper article is one thing. It is quite another thing to see those who make coffins standing knee-deep in wood shavings, plying their honest but grim trade along every highway. A small, clear plastic panel is set in each coffin as a window, so mourners can see only the face of the deceased. Looking through that window provides a glance at the bitter harvest reaped from HIV/AIDS in Africa. The coffins witness to the story of death, but the problematic tale defies comprehension.

In 2003, I made my first trip to Nairobi, the capital city of Kenya. Two million of Nairobi's three million inhabitants live in hundreds of individual slums. Here, in the center of the country (the area surrounding Nairobi), the HIV infection rate is currently about 6 percent.[4] The sizable urban underclass lives daily to bury the dead and to die themselves. The bustling and exhaust-choked streets of Nairobi teem with life and movement, and a common sight are the *matutus* (small taxi vans) crammed full of mourners. Coffins strapped precariously to the tops of the vans sway as the vehicles navigate the round-abouts. The eyes of the passengers stare blankly, red-rimmed from tears. The *matutus* wend their way to vast urban burial grounds, making the trip again and again. The viral holocaust that is HIV/AIDS exterminates families, one person at a time.

Bishop Walter Obare, head of the Evangelical Lutheran Church in Kenya, recounted for me the deaths in his family that have been caused by HIV/AIDS. Bishop Obare has wonderful dark hands with a modest amethyst bishop's ring. I have seen those hands bless and absolve. I have seen them elevate the body and blood of Christ and proclaim God's peace to the gathered faithful. I have seen them hold the neck of a live chicken for auction to raise funds for a local congregation. I have seen them touch and bless little children in the Lutheran preschool located in Nairobi's Kibera slum. I have seen them clap a rhythm to teach a simple song about God's love in Christ. But it was striking to watch Bishop Obare count, finger by finger, his deceased loved ones. This man in his late fifties has lost six brothers and sisters to AIDS or, as he calls it, "the AIDS scourge." But the scourge affects children most vilely.

I am an Iowa kid, the son of the son of farmers from Sioux City. I didn't have the slightest idea or ever dream of seeing such places as I have seen in my travels. Although I have looked over the balcony of the Sunset Hotel of Kisumu near the Kisi hills of western Kenya many times, I never fail to be in awe. The Sunset is a first-rate second-rate hotel, but the view is priceless. Lake Victoria is always calm in the morning, and the white wings of pelicans flash brightly as they bank in loose unison into the eastern sunlight against the backdrop of the crystal blue sky. You can hear a hippo grunt and gurgle as early morning fishermen silently pole their craft in pursuit of fish. I have heard their nets slap the water at a distance of five hundred yards. Later in the morning small, protein-laden fish will fill buckets on the streets in the city market.

As one departs Kisumu, the ever-present smells of fish, charcoal, diesel, and sewage recede. To reach the orphanage in Othoro, we drive through the vast floodplain that rises into the Kisi hills. Although the valley floods often, the people continue to rebuild here, and I can see why. The maize grows tall and green, and the rice paddies are thick with plants. New galvanized and corrugated roofing material tops houses made using traditional mud-and-stick or baked-brick. Over the years that I have been passing through this place, the number of grass-roofed houses has dwindled, an indication of some prosperity.

The plain slowly elevates to the east, then the road climbs into the heart of the western rural highlands. Women with jars of this or that commodity perched atop their heads flank the road. Bicyclers by the hundreds transport vegetables, grain, woven mats, rope, and other products to town markets. Like ants, lines of pedestrians enter small towns, finding their way to open-air markets bustling with all manner of human activity. Well out in the countryside, but near this market road, is Othoro Lutheran Church.

My first visit to Othoro brought a "17-percent HIV/AIDS infection rate" jolt. I found a traditional mud-and-stick hut in pathetic disrepair about twenty yards from a modest church building. I had been in Masai cow-dung dwellings at the far edges of the Serengeti Plain. I had been in homes of mud construction that were beautifully painted, sporting marvelously troweled cow-dung floors, painted interiors, overstuffed chairs, and even doilies. However, the Othoro boys lived in squalor when compared to the standards of their own community. I have rarely beheld such lonely despair. Inside the little hut, which was not more than ten feet square, there was no furniture, not even a stool or bench. A scavenged rusted galvanized roof covered a mud floor. Two or three mats of elephant grass had been rolled and propped in the corner. Next to the mats were a half dozen worn plastic bowls of various shapes and colors.

As at many, perhaps even most, of the other Lutheran parishes across rural Kenya, the boys (and at least one girl) of Othoro had suffered the loss of both parents to AIDS. Without their little Lutheran parish, these children would even now face an unfathomable darkness. But the small congregation had mustered the mercy and means to provide a housemother to cook and look after them.

"What is your name?" I asked one of the boys standing near the hut.

"I'm Albert," came the reply.

"How long have you been here, Albert?" I inquired.

Albert craned his neck, listening intently to decipher my English. He replied, "I have been here eight years." His accent betrayed both his native tongue of Luo and Kenya's past as a British colony.

"Albert, where do you go to church?" I asked.

He shook his head slightly in mild consternation over my wasted verbosity and looked toward Othoro Lutheran Church a few yards away. "I go to Othoro Lutheran," he replied.

"How often do you attend church, Albert?" I asked.

"I go EE-very Sunday," he replied, jutting his chin slightly with a pride that bespoke his love for his church.

One by one the children told me how long they had been in this place. Responses varied from one to nine years. For some, memories of parents had all but faded.

I arrived at Othoro that first time with a promise in hand, a promise from a generous couple in Houston, Texas, to help build a home to serve these children and many more after them. "Do you boys want a new home?" I asked.

"Yes!" came the unanimous response.

"Bishop, let's build these boys a home!" I said, turning to Bishop Obare.

More than a year after my first visit to the children at Othoro, my anticipation peaked as we turned into the small compound already beginning to bustle with dedication day activity. There on the ground before me was the grassless spot where the hut had been. Behind were the magnificent new buildings of Othoro Lutheran Rescue Center—a facility planned, designed, and built by the Evangelical Lutheran Church in Kenya. To see what good $40,000 can do in Africa is breathtaking.

As I surveyed the new orphanage complex, I saw a number of children heading toward me. I thought they were one of the choirs that had come to the celebration. They were smiling broadly, dressed in gleaming white soccer shirts provided by the New England District of the LCMS (a tremendous supporter of Kenyan Lutheran orphans through LCMS World Relief). Just as I was about to ask, "Where are the children?" I looked into their faces and realized, here they were. They had all grown tremendously since my last visit. "It's you!" I shouted. "It's really you. Show me your new home."

With glee the boys and one little girl took me to the kitchen and explained each never-before-seen detail. Then it was on to the store-room and the dining hall. The sturdy metal chairs and tables had been built by the Lutheran trade school in Kisumu. Yes, the children were proud of the outhouses and, finally, the crown jewel of their excite-ment—the dormitory. The squalor of their former "home" flashed through my mind as I beheld twenty-four neatly made bunks. Our smiles simultaneously broke into tears of joy, and we stood together weeping silently. Finally, with tears streaming down my face, I broke the silence, "This gift has been given to you because this, the Othoro Lutheran community, loves you, and our Christians in America know about you and love you. All of this is because of Jesus' love. In this new home, we share His love with you."

Eric, a twelve-year-old boy whose life has been forged through years of deepest tribulation in the midst of a Christian community, was standing next to me. I asked him, "What do you think?"

Speaking with wisdom and faith well beyond his age, he offered these profound words, "I thank God and Jesus Christ that someone has regarded us as human beings."

WHO GOD IS AND HOW WE WILL BE

Mercy in Christ, before and above all else, is a matter of being. Well before doing, mercy is about who God *is* and who we *are*. The Lutheran Confessions state: "Faith that grasps mercy enlivens."[5] Denying mercy and compassion is a denial of both God and His cre-ation. We must know who God is to know who we are as human beings. God's very essence is mercy. Martin Chemnitz wrote: "Because [God's] mercy cannot be separated from His essence, it is greater in God than we can even imagine."[6] Apart from His clear revelation of Himself in Christ, all thoughts about God—even true inklings!—are at best the very dimmest indiscernible shadows of truth. In fact, as one theologian put it, knowledge of God apart from Christ is mere knowl-edge of a god not known.[7] We could just as well say that apart from what we know of mankind from God's Word, knowledge of mankind is knowledge of man not known. Philip Melanchthon, Luther's co-worker in the Reformation, wrote: "In this Word, like a fetus who draws nourishment in the womb of the mother through the umbilical cord . . . we sit enclosed, drawing our knowledge of God and of life from the Word of God, so that we may worship Him as He has revealed Himself."[8] God has revealed Himself in Christ as one, as tri-une, and as mercy. Only in the bright light of that revelation can we see who we are.

All Christian consideration of God begins and ends with Christ. "Long ago, at many times and in many ways, God spoke to our fathers by the prophets, but in these last days He has spoken to us by His Son . . . . He is the radiance of the glory of God and the exact imprint of His nature, and He upholds the universe by the word of His power. After making purification for our sins, He sat down at the right hand of the Majesty on high" (Hebrews 1:1–3). In his Gospel account, when St. John calls Christ the "Word," he establishes the apostolic faith that Jesus is the beginning and end of God's self-revelation of love and mercy. The voice from heaven at Jesus' transfiguration proclaims, "This is My beloved Son, with whom I am well pleased; listen to Him" (Matthew 17:5). St. Paul tells us that in Christ, God is "making known to us the mystery of His will, according to His purpose, which He set forth in Christ" (Ephesians 1:9). In Christ come the eternally prepared blessings of the Father, as the apostle tells the Ephesian Christians: "Blessed be the God and Father of our Lord Jesus Christ, who has blessed us in Christ with every spiritual blessing" (Ephesians 1:3).

The merciful Son of God has revealed a merciful Father. St. Paul writes: "I decided to know nothing among you except Jesus Christ and Him crucified" (1 Corinthians 2:2). There is no more groping for God's will. There is no more wondering about what God thinks of me or those around me. I am pleasing to Him by faith in His own beloved Son. My sin was taken by Christ to the cross. By faith Christ's righteousness before God is mine. St. Paul declares: "For our sake He made Him to be sin who knew no sin, so that in Him we might become the righteousness of God" (2 Corinthians 5:21). The merciful Son of God has revealed a merciful Father, who "in Christ . . . was reconciling the world to Himself, not counting their trespasses against them" (2 Corinthians 5:19). That revelation comes only by "the word of truth, the gospel of your salvation," by which we are "sealed" for our eternal "inheritance" by the Holy Spirit (Ephesians 1:13–14). Wilhelm Löhe wrote:

> Out of mercy the Son of God became man; He lived, died, rose, ascended into heaven, and lives forever to practice great mercy. The motive and purpose of all His works is mercy, and mercy is what He desires for those who are His. Because His love and His Father's and the Spirit's love can only be mercy, so our love for the brothers and all men should include nothing but mercy. The great basic command for our life is: "Be merciful, just as your Father in heaven is merciful" (Luke 6:36).[9]

The clearest and most direct revelation of the Trinity is in Christian Baptism, which shows God as mercy. According to Luther, "in baptism heaven is wide open and the Trinity is present to sanctify and save."[10] The apostle Paul writes: "He [the Father] saved us, not because of works done by us in righteousness, but according to His own mercy, by the washing of regeneration and renewal of the Holy Spirit, whom He poured out on us richly through Jesus Christ our Savior" (Titus 3:5–6). Although sinless, Jesus was baptized "to fulfill all righteousness" (Matthew 3:15). Christ mercifully "sinks and sticks Himself into the water" as though He were any ordinary sinner, so when we go into the water we may pull Him out with us.[11] We see in the account of Jesus' Baptism that the heavens are mercifully "torn open" (Mark 1:10 NIV) and the Father speaks. Luther states: "Heaven which before was closed, is opened by Christ's baptism and a window and door now stand open for us to see through. No longer is there a barrier between God and us, since God himself descends at the Jordan. The Father lets his voice be heard, the Son sanctifies baptism with his body, and the Holy Spirit descends in the form of a dove."[12] In this life we find sin, death, and misery. In Baptism we find God the Father, Son, and Holy Spirit as the triune God of mercy, life, and love, and we find that, mercifully, "heaven is nothing but windows and doors."[13]

The famous conclusion to Matthew's Gospel is likewise trinitarian and baptismal. Furthermore, in these words Jesus reveals His merciful presence: "I am with you always" (Matthew 28:20). God's name is no human attempt at description. When people say there is one god with many names and he is addressed in different ways by religions and cultures the world over, they know only a god of the laws of nature or of their own imagination. Their philosophy of god is smashed on the rock of Jesus' Baptism in Matthew 3. There, God reveals Himself as Father, Son, and Spirit—three persons yet one essence. "Go therefore and make disciples of all nations, baptizing them in the [*one*] name of the Father and of the Son and of the Holy Spirit" (Matthew 28:19). Luther writes:

> I, for one, must not let the name of God be such a minor thing. Where God's name is it makes all things pure and holy and makes and does all things in this regard. In short, God's name is nothing other than the almighty divine power, eternal purity, holiness, and life; and where it is used according to divine command, there it cannot be without fruit and benefit. Rather, it must work great unspeakable things and make such things as it itself is. Therefore in Baptism it must make pure and holy and throughout heavenly, divine men.[14]

Either the exclusive claims of the New Testament are true and "there is salvation in no one else, for there is no other name under heaven given among men by which we must be saved" (Acts 4:12), or all religion is a mere sociological construct of creative human speculation. There is no middle ground. The choice is either trinitarian orthodoxy or agnosticism, either Christ or the knowledge of a god not known. The gods of human speculation and imagination are no gods at all.

"SOMEONE HAS REGARDED US AS HUMAN BEINGS"

The New Testament is replete with texts that demonstrate that God's very nature and being is mercy. Mercy and compassion are explicitly revealed in each person of the Holy Trinity. Jesus tells us, "Be merciful, even as your Father is merciful" (Luke 6:36). The Father's mercy is manifest in the sending of His Son. Jesus is mercy incarnate. In his Gospel, Mark records that Jesus "had compassion on [the crowds], because they were like sheep without a shepherd" (Mark 6:34). From the cross Jesus prayed, "Father, forgive them, for they know not what they do" (Luke 23:34). And the Spirit is the spirit of mercy, as St. Paul writes to the Philippians: "If there is any . . . fellowship of the Spirit, if any affection and mercy" (Philippians 2:1 NKJV). *Koinonia* (the Greek word translated as "fellowship" or "communion") in the Spirit brings affection or compassion and mercy, which is worked by the same Spirit. Mercy is who God the Father, Son, and Holy Spirit is. This God defines who we *are*.

Numerous humanitarian and utilitarian reasons urge us to care about a twelve-year-old orphan half a world away. International responsibilities make it incumbent on developed nations to assist the developing world. Fundamental matters of human rights have been carefully defined and advanced by the United Nations, Western governments, and a host of nongovernmental organizations the world over. Global egalitarian and ethical reasons motivate democratic societies to offer aid because they "hold these truths to be self-evident, that all men are created equal, that they are endowed by their Creator with certain unalienable Rights." There are (sometimes misguided) missiological reasons for assisting the poor. Finally, there are self-serving motivations for aid that are often a prelude to exacerbating already complex and troubled circumstances.

However, for Christians, the bottom line is this: Who God is, is how we will be. Because we are God's very own in Christ, we reflect who He is. "I thank God and Jesus Christ, that someone has regarded us as human beings." The Holy Trinity shows His mercy and gives it to His people; thereby He makes us merciful people. As merciful people, God calls us to "regard as human beings" the most unlikely, lonely, unknown, and—to the world—insignificant. To God the poor are rich, the sick are healthy, the suffering are Christlike, the unlovable are loved. This is the nature of Christ. The apostle Paul writes that "God chose what is weak in the world to shame the strong" (1 Corinthians 1:27). The mercy of God is revealed in the death of God on the cross (Acts 20:28). The cross reveals the glory of God. Our calling to serve the lowly is our calling to be merciful as God is merciful. To fail to do so is to deny the Holy Trinity.

The Othoro orphans are a gift. The world and this sinful flesh might view them as a burden. However, they have become an opportunity for mercy and compassion. Their housemother cares for them.

Their pastor comforts them and administers God's Word of Law and Gospel. And these young people know the mercy of Christ. They may not have parents, but they do have a family in Christ, thanks to the love of that little Lutheran community. These children also serve one another in love, becoming channels for mercy themselves. And as Christian adults, they will never forget the love and mercy shown them as children, and they will reflect that love to others.

The promise Christ gave to His disciples holds good in Othoro, even as it does for you: "I will not leave you as orphans; I will come to you" (John 14:18). How wonderful that in one of the only passages in which Jesus speaks of orphans, He has just comforted His disciples with the doctrine of the Trinity. In Christ you, though once orphaned, have a heavenly Father. In Christ you have a beloved Brother who has borne your every burden in mercy (Hebrews 2:14). In the Holy Spirit you have eternal consolation and comfort. And like the Othoro children, you have a Church as your community of mercy. The Bride of Christ—the Church—is your "mother that conceives and bears every Christian through God's Word [Galatians 4:26]."[15] And you, too, have a shepherd after Christ's own heart, a pastor who every week in Word and Sacrament serves the mercy of the triune God. Through you all this mercy flows to others. Who God is, He makes us to be. Luther writes that "I must believe in Father, Son, and Holy Spirit, and then also love my neighbor"[16] as long as he lives.

> O let the people praise Thy worth,
> In all good works increasing;
> The land shall plenteous fruit bring forth,
> Thy Word is rich in blessing.
> May God the Father, God the Son,
> And God the Spirit bless us!
> Let all the world praise Him alone,
> Let solemn awe possess us.
> Now let our hearts say, "Amen!"
> (*Lutheran Service Book* 823:3)
>
> God the Father in heaven, have mercy.
> God the Son, Redeemer of the world, have mercy.
> God the Holy Spirit, have mercy. . . .

We implore You to hear us, good Lord.

To grant all women with child, and all mothers with infant children, increasing happiness in their blessings; to defend all orphans and widows and provide for them . . . and to have mercy on us all:

We implore You to hear us, good Lord.

(The Litany, *Lutheran Service Book*, pp. 288–89)

_____ NOTES _____

1   AE 22:443.

2   *Lutheran Service Book*, pp. 319–20.

3   See "Kenya: HIV/AIDS a Major Health Issue in Western Region" http://www.irinnews.org/report.aspx?reportid=57405 (accessed 28 September 2007).

4   See Charlene Porter, "Local Organizations Contribute to U.S. AIDS Relief," http://usinfo.state.gov/xarchives/display.html?p=washfile-english&y=2006&m=August&x=20060817160729cmretrop0.3556787 (accessed 28 September 2007).

5   Ap XXIV 73 (*Concordia*, 231).

6   Martin Chemnitz, *Loci Theologici*, trans. J. A. O. Preus (St. Louis: Concordia, 1989), 1:61.

7   Heinrich Schlier, *Internationale Zeitschriftenschau für Bibelwissenschaft und Grenzgebiete*, Band XI (Duesseldorf: Patmos, 1964–65), 177.

8   Philip Melanchthon, *Loci Communes*: 1543, trans. J. A. O. Preus (St. Louis: Concordia, 1992), 21.

9   Holger Sonntag, trans., *Löhe on Mercy*, ed. by Adriane Dorr and Philip Hendrickson (St. Louis: LCMS World Relief and Human Care, 2006), 22.

10   StL 10:2082.58; WA 37:649.5ff. (*author's translation*).

11   StL 10:2080.53; WA 37:647.13 (*author's translation*).

12   Eugene F. A. Klug, ed., *Sermons of Martin Luther: The House Postils*, trans. Eugene F. A. Klug et al. (Grand Rapids: Baker Books, 1996), 1:218. Used with permission of Baker Publishing Group.

13   StL 10:2081.56; WA 37:648.17ff. (*author's translation*).

14   StL 10:2074.40; WA 37:642–43 (*author's translation*).

15   LC II 42 (*Concordia*, 403–4).

16   AE 22:443. "Christian love is not a human possibility. Initially, it has nothing to do with the idea of humanitarianism, with feelings of sympathy, with eroticism or compassion. It is possible only through faith in Christ and through the work of the Holy Spirit" (Dietrich Bonhoeffer, *Sanctorum Communio: A Theological Study of the Sociology of the Church*, trans. Joachim von Soosten, Dietrich Bonhoeffer Works [Minneapolis: Fortress, 1998], 1:167–68).

3

MERCY INCARNATE

HAVE THIS MIND IN YOU

Let each of you look not only to his own interests, but also to the interests of others. Have this mind among yourselves, which is yours in Christ Jesus.
Philippians 2:4–5

Our Lord and Savior Jesus has left us a commandment which applies equally to all Christians, namely, that we are to render . . . the works of mercy [Luke 6:36], to those who are afflicted and in a state of calamity, and that we are to visit the sick, try to free the captives, and do similar things for our neighbor so that the evils of the present may be somewhat lessened. Our Lord Jesus Christ himself gave us the brightest example of this commandment when . . . he descended from the bosom of the Father into our misery and our prison, that is, into our flesh and our most wretched life, and took upon himself the penalty for our sins so that we might be saved.[1]
Martin Luther

COMPASSION IS A "VISCERAL" BUSINESS

In Christ, compassion means action because of who He is. In Christ, God acted and acts for the temporal and eternal blessing of the world. When we are in Christ, we can do nothing other than act for the well-being of others.

"Follow your gut!" Well, not in determining matters of the Christian faith and life, or at least not until your "gut feeling" has been thoroughly informed by and subjected to the Word of God. However, we all would do well to follow Christ's "gut"! Jesus Christ is the embodied, incarnate, enfleshed mercy of God (John 1:14). Because of who He is, He acted mercifully in time, took on our flesh, and bore our sin to death on a wretched cross in the supreme act of mercy. Because Christ is who He is (Mercy Incarnate), He does what He does (mercifully saves) and He makes us after His own image (merciful people)! When a person or a congregation rejects mercy, the individual or congregation is rejecting Christ. It is that simple. It is that radical! Jesus tells us, "As you did not do it to one of the least of these, you did not do it to Me" (Matthew 25:45). And according to Martin Luther, "these words of Christ bind each of us to the other. No one may forsake his neighbor when he is in trouble."[2] Mercy is about the incarnation of Christ.[3]

Splanchnon[4] has to be one of the all-time great Greek words in the New Testament. You will not find more incarnational, enfleshed talk about Christ than in this word. I am convinced the word is an example of New Testament onomatopoeia, that is, a word that sounds like what it denotes. Repeat *splanchnon* a few times at a low decibel, smile inverted, and lips pursed, and you will know what it means even without Greek 101. As you repeat the word, you can almost imagine a pagan priest removing these organs from a sacrificial animal and casting them on a surface to be "divined" to predict the future. Say the word and you are back in Old Testament times, watching the priest removing the bowels of the sacrificial animal and casting them aside—*splat!*—to be burned or hauled out of the city. *Splanchnon* sounds like a verbal *splat!* You can all but hear the word used in this most base and concrete meaning in Acts 1:18: ". . . falling headlong [Judas] burst open in the middle and all his bowels [*splanchnon*] gushed out."

In ancient pre-Christian usage, the Greek word *splanchnon* denoted the "inward parts" of a sacrifice, such as the "liver, lungs and spleen." It also denoted the lower half of the body—the womb or the loins.[5] In more figurative usage, and for obvious reasons, the word meant "the seat of 'impulsive passions.'" In pre-Christian use, *splanchnon* is never used for mercy.[6] In the Septuagint, the Greek edition of the Old Testament (ca. 100 BC), *splanchnon* began its journey toward its significant and sacred use in the Gospels (see, for example, Proverbs 17:5, "To be merciful"), particularly in association with Jesus and His actions.

Study of the word *splanchnon* in reference to Jesus reveals something extraordinary about our Savior's compassion. For Jesus, compassion is literally "visceral." The verb is used eleven times in the Gospels. Seven times the verb appears as an action attributed to Jesus. Twice the verb is used as an action attributed to characters in parables told by Jesus. Given the origin and development of the use of the word, we might think that in the Gospels it came to mean simply "to have compassion" or "mercy," and it does. However, each time *splanchnon* occurs as a conviction or sentiment or emotion in Christ (or of characters in parables), there is consequent merciful *action*. Compassion *begets* action. Mercy *makes* something *happen*. For Jesus, *splanchnizomai*, the verb form of *splanchnon*, is always "compassion giving birth to action." Take a look at the following.

1. MATTHEW 9:36–38

Compassion: "When [Jesus] saw the crowds, He had compassion [*splanchnizomai*] for them, because they were harassed and helpless, like sheep without a shepherd" (v. 36).

Action: "Then [Jesus] said to His disciples, 'The harvest is plentiful, but the laborers are few; therefore pray earnestly to the Lord of the harvest to send out laborers into His harvest'" (vv. 37–38).

2. MATTHEW 14:13–21 (JESUS FEEDS 5,000)

Compassion: "When [Jesus] went ashore He saw a great crowd, and He had compassion [*splanchnizomai*] on them" (v. 14).

Action: Jesus healed their sick, and when evening came and the disciples wanted Jesus to send the people to buy food, He replied, "They need not go away; you give them something to eat" (v. 16). The disciples answered that they had only five loaves of bread and two fish. But Jesus said, "Bring them here to Me" (v. 18).

3. MATTHEW 15:32–39 (JESUS FEEDS 4,000)

Compassion: "Then Jesus called His disciples to Him and said, 'I have compassion [*splanchnizomai*] on the crowd because they have been with Me now three days and have nothing to eat'" (v. 32).

Action: Jesus continued, "And I am unwilling to send them away hungry, lest they faint on the way" (v. 32).

4. MATTHEW 18:21–35 (PARABLE OF THE UNMERCIFUL SERVANT)

Compassion: "So the servant fell on his knees, imploring him, 'Have patience with me, and I will pay you everything.' And out of pity [*splanchnizomai*] for him . . ." (vv. 26–27).

Action: ". . . the master of that servant released him and forgave him the debt" (v. 27).

5. MATTHEW 20:29–34 (JESUS HEALS TWO BLIND MEN)

Compassion: "And stopping, Jesus called [the two blind men] and said, 'What do you want Me to do for you?' They said to Him, 'Lord, let our eyes be opened' " (vv. 32–33).

Action: "And Jesus in pity [*splanchnizomai*] touched their eyes, and immediately they recovered their sight and followed Him" (v. 34).

6. MARK 1:40–45 (JESUS CLEANSES A LEPER)

Compassion: "And a leper came to [Jesus], imploring Him, and kneeling said to Him, 'If You will, You can make me clean.' Moved with pity [*splanchnizomai*] . . ." (vv. 40–41).

Action: "[Jesus] stretched out His hand and touched him and said to him, 'I will; be clean.' And immediately the leprosy left him, and he was made clean" (vv. 41–42).

7. MARK 8:1–10 (JESUS FEEDS 4,000)

Compassion: Jesus said, "I have compassion [*splanchnizomai*] on the crowd, because they have been with Me now three days and have nothing to eat. And if I send them away hungry to their homes, they will faint on the way" (vv. 2–3).

Action: "And [Jesus] asked them, 'How many loaves do you have?' They said, 'Seven.' And He directed the crowd to sit down on the ground. And He took the seven loaves, and having given thanks, He broke them and gave them to His disciples to set before the people" (vv. 5–6).

8. MARK 9:14–29 (JESUS HEALS A BOY WITH AN UNCLEAN SPIRIT)

Compassion: "Jesus asked his father, 'How long has this been happening to him?' And he said, 'From childhood. And it has often cast him into fire and into water, to destroy him. But if You can do anything, have compassion [*splanchnizomai*] on us and help us" (vv. 21–22).

Action: "And Jesus said to him, 'If You can! All things are possible for one who believes.' Immediately the father of the child cried out and said, 'I believe; help my unbelief!' And when Jesus saw that a crowd came running together, He rebuked the unclean spirit, saying to it, 'You mute and deaf spirit, I command you, come out of him and never enter him again.' And after crying out and convulsing him terribly, it came out" (vv. 23–26).

9. LUKE 7:11–17 (JESUS RAISES A WIDOW'S SON)

Compassion: "As [Jesus] drew near to the gate of the town, behold, a man who had died was being carried out, the only son of his mother, and she was a widow, and a considerable crowd from the town was with her. And when the Lord saw her, He had compassion [*splanchnizomai*] on her and said to her, 'Do not weep'" (vv. 12–13).

Action: "Then [Jesus] came up and touched the bier, and the bearers stood still. And He said, 'Young man, I say to you, arise.' And the dead man sat up and began to speak, and Jesus gave him to his mother" (vv. 14–15).

10. LUKE 10:25–37 (PARABLE OF THE GOOD SAMARITAN)

Compassion: "But a Samaritan, as he journeyed, came to where he was, and when he saw him, he had compassion [*splanchnizomai*]" (v. 33).

Action: Jesus said, "He went to him and bound up his wounds, pouring on oil and wine. Then he set him on his own animal and brought him to an inn and took care of him. And the next day he took out two denarii and gave them to the innkeeper, saying, 'Take care of him, and whatever more you spend, I will repay you when I come back.' Which of these three, do you think, proved to be a neighbor to the man who fell among the robbers?" The lawyer said, "The one who showed him mercy." And Jesus said to him, "You go, and do likewise" (vv. 34–37).

11. LUKE 15:11–32 (PARABLE OF THE PRODIGAL SON)

Compassion: "And [the prodigal son] arose and came to his father. But while he was still a long way off, his father saw him and felt compassion [*splanchnizomai*]" (v. 20).

Action: "And [the father] ran and embraced him and kissed him. And the son said to him, 'Father, I have sinned against heaven and before you. I am no longer worthy to be called your son.' But the father said to his servants, 'Bring quickly the best robe, and put it on him, and put a ring on his hand, and shoes on his feet. And bring the fattened calf and kill it, and let us eat and celebrate. For this my son was dead, and is alive again; he was lost, and is found.' And they began to celebrate" (vv. 20–24).

Why is Jesus' compassion invariably followed by action? Jesus' compassion results in action because of who He is. There is one other use of *splanchnon* in the Gospels. It is in the Song of Zechariah: "And you, child [John the Baptist], will be called the prophet of the Most High; for you will go before the Lord [Christ] to prepare His ways, to give knowledge of salvation to His people in the forgiveness of their sins, because of the tender [*splanchnon*] mercy [*eleous*] of our God" (Luke 1:76–78). The *splanchnon*, the compassion of God the Father, results in the sending of John followed by the sending of the Lord Jesus Christ. Christ is the *splanchnon eleous*, the compassionate mercy (literally, the "bowels of divine mercy"), of God Incarnate, according to Zechariah.

As we might expect of trinitarian theology, *splanchnon* is used of God the Father (Luke 15:20), God the Son (Luke 10:33ff.), and of God the Holy Spirit (Philippians 2:1). We know God as merciful only in Christ and His work. Luther writes in his Large Catechism: "There was no counsel, help, or comfort until this only and eternal Son of God—in His immeasurable goodness—had compassion upon our misery and wretchedness. He came from heaven to help us [John 1:9]."[7]

IT IS NOT ABOUT ETHICS!

I do not wish to give you the impression that the important or decisive thing about Jesus is His ethics—His example of or directives (Law) to care for the needy. The ethical teaching Jesus presents offers nothing that cannot be found in other religions. The attempt to follow the example of Jesus as the means to gain God's favor merits nothing but hell.[8] Even Jesus' miracles are not the center of our confession of Jesus Christ as Savior. These compassionate actions are significant because they flow from and point to Jesus as God Incarnate and Savior. "The gospel everywhere shows Christ to be a merciful, gracious man, ready to help everyone by word and action in body and soul."[9] Indeed, Christ came as "someone humble and plebeian, one of the people (*hoi palloi*)."[10] In Christ's compassionate actions (His miracles and ultimately His suffering and death on the cross), this mercy is a revelation of the Father.[11] God "hides" Himself, as it were, in the man Jesus Christ. He is hidden under a virginal conception, an ignominious birth, a childhood, a carpenter's trade, a completely human countenance and person, and finally under suffering and death. God and man are united in the one person of Christ. Christ's birth is the birth of God—for us. Christ's death is the death of God in the flesh to pay for the sins of the world (Mark 15:39; 2 Corinthians 5:19; Acts 20:28). Only the gift of faith can grasp the unfathomable truth of the death of God in the person of Jesus Christ. The sinless one dies for sinners.

The coming of God into the flesh is Gospel. It is God's gracious act to accomplish our salvation. Luther writes that Jesus "became incarnate to comfort."[12] Jesus is mercy incarnate. Christ's life is filled with compassion and compassionate action for those in need. Christ's life is more than an example for our living. The incarnation of Christ is the strongest and most powerful Gospel gift. He was the sacrifice that earned salvation for us. In Word and Sacrament, the Church delivers what Christ obtained on Calvary—forgiveness of sin. In Word and Sacrament the Christian is born again. Raised to walk in newness of life (Romans 6), the believer demonstrates compassion for those in need, the lowly, the suffering, the orphan, etc. However weakly and imperfectly, our compassion reflects the compassion of God Himself. God accepts our daily acts of compassion as our daily and holy worship because of Christ. Philippians 2:5–8, the great Pauline hymn of the incarnation, teaches us the key motivation for divinely wrought mercy:

> Have this mind among yourselves, which is yours in Christ Jesus, who, though He was in the form of God, did not count equality with God a thing

to be grasped [as did Satan!], but made Himself nothing, taking the form of a servant, being born in the likeness of men. And being found in human form, He humbled Himself by becoming obedient to the point of death, even death on a cross.

Luther echoes the thought in a sermon for Christmas Day based on the familiar passage in Luke: "For unto you is born this day in the city of David a Savior" (2:11).

> Unto you is born a Savior[.] Whoever is not changed for the better by this word and made more godly, praising and thanking God; whoever does not relish this heavenly wine, nor have his heart warmed by this fire, to become kinder and gentler to his neighbor, him will the judge and hangman make more pious, for he's beyond reprieve. The fact that he's not set ablaze by this fire nor drawn by this heavenly wine—that Christ is our brother, yes, has become flesh and blood with us—plainly shows that he is a lost and condemned man.[13]

We cannot repeat or imitate the incarnation of Christ per se (that is, "have this mind among yourselves" does not mean that we are to become God in the flesh). The incarnation, servanthood, self-humbling obedience, and finally death on a cross on our behalf—the Gospel—creates Christ's attitude in us. We are baptized by Christ into merciful compassion for those in need around us. In this way we indeed become "incarnate" to our neighbor. Luther nailed it when he wrote:

> Therefore, if we recognize the great and precious things which are given us, as Paul says [Rom. 5:5], our hearts will be filled by the Holy Spirit with the love which makes us free, joyful, almighty workers and conquerors over all tribulations, servants of our neighbors, and yet lords of all. For those who do not recognize the gifts bestowed upon them through Christ, however, Christ has been born in vain . . . . Just as our neighbor is in need and lacks that in which we abound, so we were in need before God and lacked his mercy. Hence, as our heavenly Father has in Christ freely come to our aid, we also ought freely to help our neighbor through our body and its works, and each one should become as it were a Christ to the other that we may be Christs to one another and Christ may be the same in all, that is, that we may be truly Christians.[14]

Because of Christ's incarnation, we are freed and sent by God as "incarnate" christs to one another. As Luther said, we "clothe ourselves in our neighbor's flesh."[15] We have compassion (*splanchnon*) enlivened by Christ, and that compassion takes action. To refuse to "have this mind in you" is to refuse mercy. It is worse than a mere transgression of the Law; it is a denial of the very incarnation of Jesus Christ in the flesh. Thus John the apostle could write:

> By this we know love, that He laid down His life for us, and we ought to lay down our lives for the brothers. But if anyone has the world's goods and sees his brother in need, yet closes his heart [*splanchnon*!] against him, how does God's love abide in him? Little children, let us not love in word or talk but in deed and in truth. *1 John 3:16–18*

> Love divine, all loves excelling,
> Joy of heav'n to earth come down!
> Fix in us Thy humble dwelling,
> All Thy faithful mercies crown.
> Jesus, Thou art all compassion,
> Pure, unbounded love Thou art;
> Visit us with Thy salvation,
> Enter ev'ry trembling heart.
> (*Lutheran Service Book* 700:1)

> God the Son, Redeemer of the World, have mercy . . .
> By the mystery of Your holy incarnation; by Your holy nativity;
> By Your baptism, fasting, and temptation; by Your agony and bloody sweat;
> By Your cross and passion; by Your precious death and burial;
> By Your glorious resurrection and ascension; and by the coming of the Holy Spirit, the Comforter:
> Help us, good Lord.
> (The Litany, *Lutheran Service Book*, p. 288)

NOTES

1   AE 42:121–22.

2   Theodore G. Tappert, ed. and trans., *Luther: Letters of Spiritual Counsel*, Library of Christian Classics 18 (Philadelphia and London: Westminster Press and SCM, 1955), 233.

3   AE 42:121–22.

4   The plural of this Greek word, *splaxna* is translated in the New Testament as "bowels."

5   Gerhard Kittel and Gerhard Friedrich, *Theological Dictionary of the New Testament*, trans. and ed. Geoffrey W. Bromiley (Grand Rapids: Eerdmans, 1971), 7:548.

6   Kittel and Friedrich, *Theological Dictionary of the New Testament,* 7:549.

7   LC II 29 (*Concordia,* 402).

8   See Galatians 3.

9   WA 37:507.17 as cited in Ian D. Kingston Siggins, *Martin Luther's Doctrine of Christ* (Eugene, OR: Wipf & Stock, 2003), 37.

10 WA 10.1/2:150; 13:626.21 as cited in Siggins, *Luther's Doctrine of Christ,* 36.

11 WA 46:101.14 as cited in Siggins, *Luther's Doctrine of Christ,* 43.

12 Tappert, *Letters of Spiritual Counsel,* 98.

13 Eugene F. A. Klug, ed., *Sermons of Martin Luther: The House Postils,* trans. Eugene F. A. Klug et al. (Grand Rapids: Baker Books, 1996), 1:119. Used with permission of Baker Publishing Group.

14 AE 31:367–68.

15 Joel R. Baseley, trans., *Festival Sermons of Martin Luther: The Church Postils, Winter and Summer Selections* (Dearborn, MI: Mark V Publications, 2005), Winter Section, 117.

4

The Heart of Mercy's Heart

JUSTIFICATION

For by grace you have been saved through faith. And this is not your own doing; it is the gift of God . . . . For we are His workmanship, created in Christ Jesus for good works. *Ephesians 2:8–9*

You are white as snow [Isa. 1:18], pure from all sins. But you must wear this red dress and color now, and remember to love your neighbor. Moreover, it should be a fervent love, not a pale-red love . . . . For this is the way sins are covered, even a multitude, a heap, a sea, a forest of sins.[1] *Martin Luther*

Modernism and Postmodernism: The End of Justification?

The modernist interpreters of the Bible labored to salvage some existential meaning in antiquated texts. They viewed the Scriptures as the product of bygone cultures that spoke the language of mythology— and such a perspective is no longer palatable in this scientific age. Many scholars distilled the meaning of the New Testament down to ethics or human religious experience. Like peeling back the layers of an onion, they shed the "myth," layer after layer. The modernist creed quickly became:

And I believe in Jesus Christ, God's only Son, our Lord, who was

not conceived by the Holy Spirit,

not born of the virgin Mary,

probably suffered under Pontius Pilate,

perhaps was crucified, died and buried,

but certainly did not descend into hell,

did not rise again on the third day,

did not ascend into heaven, and

will by no means come again to judge the living and the dead.

However, these modernist scholars viewed themselves as Christian apologists, defenders of the "faith" in an era spooked by, or even increasingly confident in, the notion that there is no God at all. Moving beyond the ancient dogma that "there is no salvation outside the Church"[2] (that is, no salvation without faith in Christ, which lands one in the Church) was easy, once these modernist scholars concluded the New Testament teachings on the sacrifice of Jesus, "the divine Christ," belonged on the pile of ancient cultic mythology, whether Greek or Jewish. They determined that the earliest believers had squeezed Jesus through the sieve of cultic religion and added a twist of Pauline Pharisaism. Finally, the Early Church displaced the "real" (and merely) human Jesus. These so-called apologists alleged that Jesus had a simple religion of the Fatherhood of God and a corresponding emphasis on ethical behavior, that is, the brotherhood of mankind. Some scholars even asserted that beyond the Lord's Prayer and the Beatitudes, all other words and deeds in the New Testament attributed to Jesus were likely words and events invented by zealous and misguided disciples.

Modernism made the study of the Scriptures a cold scientific endeavor carried out in the ivory tower. It drove a wedge between the (alleged) Jesus of history and the Christ of faith, as though each were quite different from the other. Marxism was the ultimate political child of modernism. Based on Georg Wilhelm Friedrich Hegel's dialectics, Marxism explained all of history as a purely natural progression of conflicting human forces.

At approximately this same time, science discovered microbiology and Charles Darwin posited a process of "natural selection" to explain all of life and its illnesses or successes, without recourse to divinely wrought causes. The late nineteenth century solemnly released itself from original sin and the divine curse of Genesis 3. A radically optimistic view of human nature was matched by atheistic fervor. God and the riddle of divine fate were no longer in the way. Rising confidence in human autonomy and advancement had been on a two hundred year advance, winning "its complete victory in German idealism . . . established . . . primarily through Hegel, and even after the collapse of the school of Hegel it continues to be operative in the subsequent epoch of evolution in the fields of natural science and history."[3]

World War I buried European optimism for one hundred years, as well as launching a century of the worst butchery in the history of humankind. Released from the shackles of a transcendent God and His universal Law, Communists and Marxists set about building utopia and eventually murdered tens of millions. Likewise, Nazism sought to "renew culture" while denying the Christian God. The Nazi Party used the technology at its disposal to advance a radically romantic return to paganism. Nazi leaders held that "God" is completely immanent, that is, found in blood, race, country, the victor, the powerful. Millions of Jews, dissenters, and others deemed unworthy were gassed. Although Nazism's true "god" shot himself in the head in a Berlin bunker, its rejection of a transcendent and universal God who has delivered a universally applicable Law lives on, strangely enough, in the intelligentsia's liberal left[4] and in the tenets of postmodernism. Deconstructionists pull trigger after trigger in a game of Russian roulette with Western Christian culture.

The fall of Communism coincided with a religious resurgence. Behind the Iron Curtain, churches became the bright torch for political liberation as revolutionaries found within the Church the platform to effect change. Sadly, the spiritual awakening did not continue in European Protestant denominations. Again church buildings sit empty and pose no threat to established authority. Yet this does not mean there is no reestablishment of religion in Europe; rather, it is taking place in European mosques. Since 9/11, conflict with the West has brought a resurgence of Islam, even in countries such as Kyrgyzstan that formerly were only nominally Islamic. As an example of this rise in Islamic enthusiasm, on a recent trip to Sumatra, the number of veiled women begging alms from passing motorists amazed me. Were they begging for money for food or clothing? No, the money they received will build new mosques along every mile of the road.

Europe is not the only area of the world undergoing changes to the religious culture. In the West, mainline Protestantism continues its free fall, even as Evangelicals and Roman Catholics experience steady growth and fervor among the faithful. Africa is burgeoning with Christian conversion and growth. In Sudan, Ethiopia, Uganda, and elsewhere, Christians and Muslims struggle to the death. And a militant form of Hinduism (an oxymoron!), intense in its hatred of

Christianity and the West, is on the rise in India.

So, is God dead? Has science and reason relegated religion to the ash heap of history? Hardly! Modernism's idealistic quest for a godless society is at least temporarily exhausted. Its replacement is postmodernism. Unlike modernism, which believed only man/science could discover the truth, postmodernity declares there is no universal truth. The cacophonous chaos of conflicting religious, cultural, and philosophical worldviews—thrown into the space of an ever-shrinking world—comprise the elements of the postmodern phenomenon.

Postmodernism frees "truth" from its shackles of exclusivity, allowing the individual and/or the community to define it. Thus truth is radically subjective and contextual. Texts and words only gain meaning imported by the reader. We hear repeatedly, "That might be your truth, but it isn't mine" or "What does that mean to you?" Postmodernism has made its way deep into the Church, robbing her of the truth and security in the work and word of Jesus. When there are one hundred languages and nearly that many religions in Manhattan, how can a Christian possibly confess that "this has been decided by the Father from eternity: whom He would save He would save through Christ. Christ Himself says, 'No one comes to the Father except through Me' (John 14:6). And again, 'I am the door. If anyone enters by Me, he will be saved' (John 10:9)"?[5] What of the rest of the Lutheran confession of the true faith in Christ?

CAN JUSTIFICATION MEAN ANYTHING TODAY?

Can the central message of the Bible make any possible sense in this context? Is God's Word still an inclusively exclusive message? How can we possibly believe it to be the absolute universal truth? Is there any meaning in the following article of the Augsburg Confession?

> Our churches teach that people cannot be justified before God by their own strength, merits, or works. People are freely justified for Christ's sake, through faith, when they believe that they are received into favor and that their sins are forgiven for Christ's sake. By His death, Christ made satisfaction for our sins. God counts this faith for righteousness in His sight (Romans 3 and 4 [3:21–26; 4:5]).[6]

Many authors and sometimes even church leaders assert that such a confession is meaningless to postmodern ears. A host of political theologies attempt to explain reality from the subjective experiences of various individuals or groups. Many are convinced they must recast the Gospel into languages and contexts that are "meaningful" today, for example, a feminist or transgender interpretation.

How did this happen? Clearly there is a struggle against all authority, including that of the "divine" Scriptures. Happily and safely tenured, the revisionists rewrite history while teaching in seminaries and other institutions. Then newly trained clergy go forth, spouting their favorite theology of liberation to congregants who stare at such preachers like a cow stares at a new barn door (a phrase Luther supposedly used to describe those who deny that Baptism works forgiveness). The focus changes from Christ to the needs of man, which are not seen in the context of sin and grace. Thus mainline denominations are dying and dying quickly.

Other cultures have much to teach us, even in the ways they interpret the Scriptures. There are unique cultural gifts for understanding particular aspects of the Bible. For example, African tribal societies are much closer to New Testament culture than we are, thus these groups have greater insight into particular aspects of the biblical message. But the divine authority of the Bible and the Church's clear confession limit such interpretation. Step outside those boundaries, and the result is what Amos prophesied:

> "Behold, the days are coming," declares the Lord GOD, "when I will send a famine on the land—not a famine of bread, nor a thirst for water, but of hearing the words of the LORD. They shall wander from sea to sea, and from north to east; they shall run to and fro, to seek the word of the LORD, but they shall not find it." *Amos 8:11–12*

THE UNIVERSAL NEED FOR SELF-JUSTIFICATION

Traveling the world, I have seen the best and the worst of humanity. I have seen the oppressed and the oppressor. I have met Hindus, Buddhists, Muslims, Protestants, Catholics, Animists, and tribe after indigenous tribe. There is no more fundamental desire of the human race than justification, that is, to justify one's being and existence. It is a human universal. I justify my wealth. I justify the time spent working away from family. I justify the approach I have taken toward my children. I justify the treatment of my wife. I justify my value to my employer. I justify my right to pennies from a wealthier man. I justify my right to your money. I justify my callousness toward my neighbor. I justify my lack of charity. I justify my plea for various commodities or humanitarian aid. I justify my lethargy. I justify my thievery by lying to others and believing the lies myself. I justify my tribe's hatred of "those people." Universally practiced and understood, the language of "justification" is a fundamental phenomenon of life in society.

Not far from the Ethiopian boarder with Kenya lies the remote oasis of Marsabit. I first came upon this outpost during a trip to visit a far-flung congregation of Lutherans in a desert sea of Islam and Somburu animism. After nearly two hundred kilometers on a terrible road (eight hours of kidney-battering ruts and two flat tires), we finally pulled into Marsabit, which is only the halfway point on the road to Nairobi. As happens in any Kenyan town on a well-traveled route, the "street boys" crowded around the vehicle carrying white people from the West. In the dust and the heat I did not have the energy to roll up the window. The boys crowded closer. "Watch your things," the Kenyans with us said. "These boys will steal anything."

I have heard the warning dozens of times and not experienced a theft yet. These boys typically have lost their parents to HIV/AIDS and have taken to the streets. In Kisumu there are 2,500 such street boys, ranging in age from two or three years old to young men in their mid-twenties. These street boys taunt tourists and refuse to back away from vehicles. They are disrespectful of elders. Shooed away like so many flies, the boys retreat slightly, then return again and again until they exhaust their hope of reward.

"Give me a dollar! Give me a dollar! Give me that pen!" cried eight or ten boys as they crowded the window, pressing their bodies and faces against the door or glass. Covered in the filth of the street, their clothes bear a brown film of African dirt, pant legs ragged at the knees. Some eyes were red and glazed from sniffing glue or other substance abuse.

I pulled two hundred shillings (a couple dollars) from my pocket and held it firmly in my hand. Before I could say anything, the boys made a mad rush for the cash. Ten hands descended upon mine like so many vultures on a carcass, squabbling and jerking and jockeying. "I will give you this," I shouted, "but it is for sodas for all of you. Every boy gets one."

My friend John, a Kenyan, stepped in with stern Kiswahili, scolding the boys and chastising them. Then he entered a small storefront market and purchased a carton of milk for each of the dozen or so boys. Each boy laughed, strutted, and swaggered as if the small carton of milk was a winning lottery ticket. Some returned to the car to say thanks. Others did a victory dance with the carton of milk in hand. I watched as they moved on to the next vehicle to repeat the spectacle. Ultimately, what were they doing?

These street boys merely reveal each of us for what we are and seek. The families, communities, and even the world have condemned these children to meaninglessness and apparent nonexistence. The verdict has been rendered upon them publicly: they are worthless, and they know it. In a pathetic frenzy over pennies, striving for attention and affirmation, they seek acknowledgment and recognition as human beings in the only way they know how. Oswald Bayer wrote about this:

> There is no escaping the questions and evaluations of others. If one accepts and welcomes the other or not, if one greets the other or not, if one acknowledged the other—either through praise or reproach, affirmation or negation—or if one does not acknowledge the other and regards the others as worthless, a decision is made concerning our being or non-being. Only a being that is recognized and acknowledged is a being that is alive. If no one were to call and greet me by name, if no one were ready to speak to me and look at me, then I would be socially nonexistent.[7]

The street boys remind me of the fundamental need for recognition and justification. Most attempts at self-justification are more refined, more "suburban." I am thankful to see the great slums of the world, the street boys, and the victims of AIDS. I loved being an inner-city pastor, dealing with schizophrenic street people, addicts, or the mother who sneaked into the balcony of the sanctuary and dangled her baby over the edge until the police arrived. These behaviors seem so much more honest to me—more honest than the sins hidden in suburban subdivisions. Where sin is understood as sin, justification will never lose its significance. In fact, the fundamental dilemma of the human being in postmodernity is not new. Bayer points out:

> Modernity and post modernity each presuming their situation to be entirely new, are merely recycling the basic situation of the human being, who, oscillating between defiance and despondency, pride and desperation, cannot ultimately know himself. . . . The human being audits and judges the world from this perspective until he becomes his own angel of death and the angel of death for others existing with him.[8]

BY GRACE FOR CHRIST'S SAKE THROUGH FAITH

By nature, every person knows something of God's Law (Romans 2:14), and each person knows just enough to think he can justify himself. However, justification and the peace it brings is a gift. God strikes down every attempt at self-justification with a damning and universal, "No! It's not enough! All are condemned!" The New Testament puts forth an unavoidable, universal, and unalterable truth: "Now we know that whatever the law says it speaks to those who are under the law, so that every mouth may be stopped, and the whole world may be held accountable to God. For by works of the law no human being will be justified in his sight, since through the law comes knowledge of sin" (Romans 3:19–20). Repeatedly the New Testament blankets "all" with condemnation under the Law of God: "None is righteous, no, not one" (Romans 3:10); "all who rely on works of the law are under a curse" (Galatians 3:10); "in Adam all die" (1 Corinthians 15:22). As Lutherans we confess, "Our churches teach that people cannot be justified before God by their own strength, merits, or works."[9]

Although every attempt at self-justification before God is futile and damning, there is justification, there is a declaration and counting of a person as righteous unto eternal blessedness. It is by God's act, not ours, as the Lutheran Confessions declare: "People are freely justified for Christ's sake . . . . By His death, Christ made satisfaction for our sins. God counts this faith for righteousness in His sight."[10]

We are justified freely. Grace is a gift—undeserved, unearned, unexpected, and unbelievably generous. St. Paul writes: "But the *free* gift is not like the trespass. For if many died through one man's trespass, much more have the grace of God and the *free* gift by the grace of that one man Jesus Christ abounded for many. . . . If because of one man's trespass, death reigned through that one man, much more will those who receive the abundance of grace and the *free* gift of righteousness reign in life through the one man Jesus Christ" (Romans 5:15, 17, *emphasis added*).

We are justified "for Christ's sake," not because we changed something within ourselves. It may be easy to conclude that we are better people under the Law because faith does create love and motivate good works. However, though we do grow in grace, no matter how we grow, "the Law always accuses us, always presents an angry God to us. . . . Afterward, we begin to keep the Law. . . . In the flesh we never satisfy the Law."[11] Thus justification is not a one-time event. God "justifies the ungodly" (Romans 4:5). To be just, we must also always be "ungodly" under the Law. And the text that demonstrates this dual saint/sinner, justified/condemned, Gospel/Law nature of being a Christian is Romans 7, which is presented by the apostle Paul in the present tense: "I do not do the good I want, but the evil I do not want is what I keep on doing. . . . So I find it to be a law that when I want to do right, evil lies close at hand. . . . Wretched man that I am! Who will deliver me from this body of death? Thanks be to God through Jesus Christ our Lord!" (Romans 7:19, 21, 24–25).

We are justified not because of something that has changed within us. Adolf Köberle's book *The Quest for Holiness*[12] demonstrates how perpetual attempts at self-justification occur along three persistent paths: attempts at perfecting the mind, the will, and the emotions. In real life, it works out this way: The intellectual seeks to comprehend and define the divine. The moralist strives to possess pure moral thought and action. The mystic seeks to empty himself of everything that is not "god" and seeks to feel god by his ecstatic presence. All three of these are fruits from the same tree.

All of this is the antithesis of grace. "For Christ's sake" we are just. The definitive work in justification is outside us, not inside us. This work was performed by Jesus Christ, not us, and it occurred on Golgotha more than two thousand years ago. "It *is* finished!" Jesus cried out from the cross (John 19:30). The apostle Paul explains: "In Christ God was reconciling the world to Himself" (2 Corinthians

5:19). This act transcends all of history. It was justification for me and for everyone who ever lived before and after Jesus. Peter testifies, "There is no other name under heaven given among men by which we must be saved" (Acts 4:12).

We are justified by grace *through faith*. In justification (God declaring me not guilty) *faith* is passive; it only receives the gift. If salvation is by grace, then it is free and not our doing. If salvation is for Christ's sake (because of His work), then its cause and source are outside of us, that is, apart from us. Faith is nothing in and of itself. It merely lays hold of Christ, His accomplished work, and the forgiveness of sin. There is no stepping forward in the glare of the Almighty and pleading, "Look at my faith! I have faith. I have made a decision to believe." If that were so, then justification would no longer be free and *by grace*. St. Paul writes: "For by grace you have been saved through faith. And this [faith] is not your own doing; it is the gift of God" (Ephesians 2:8–9). To plead that one *has Christ* is very different than to say that faith *lays hold of Christ*. No faith, no Christ. His promised grace is itself a gift, and because it is a gift, it is sure.

George Spenlein had been in the monastery with Luther for four years. In April 1516, Luther wrote to him because Spenlein was suffering under the weight of his own sin to the point of despair:

> My dear brother, learn Christ and him crucified. Learn to pray to him and, despairing of yourself, say: "Thou, Lord Jesus, art my righteousness, but I am thy sin. Thou has taken upon thyself what is mine and hast given to me what is thine. Thou has taken upon thyself what thou wast not and hast given to me what I was not." Beware of aspiring to such purity that you will not wish to be looked upon as a sinner, or to be one. For Christ dwells only in sinners.[13]

There is no middle ground. Justification by grace for Christ's sake through faith—or self-justification. Wilhelm Löhe wrote, "Where there is a false security and the illusion of self-righteousness, there the gruesome air of death blows across deathbeds."[14] Again, we recall Luther's words: "Christ dwells only in sinners." Without this understanding of justification, there is no Christian, no Christian life, no Church. Where there is no Christian or the Church, there is no divine mercy. God's gift of mercy, justification for Christ's sake, animates the

Church's work of mercy. According to Luther, "a justified person loves his neighbor and does the works of love."[15] Justification by grace for Christ's sake through faith is the heart of mercy's heart.[16]

> Oh, how great is Your compassion,
>
> Faithful Father, God of grace,
>
> That with all our fallen race
>
> In our depth of degradation
>
> You had mercy so that we
>
> Might be saved eternally!
>
> (*Lutheran Service Book* 559:1)
>
> *Kyrie eleison.*

NOTES

1   AE 51:297.

2   See LC II 45 (*Concordia*, 404): "For where Christ is not preached, there is no Holy Spirit who creates, calls, and gathers the Christian Church, without which no one can come to Christ the Lord."

3   Werner Elert, *The Structure of Lutheranism*, trans. Walter A. Hansen (St. Louis: Concordia, 1962), 475.

4   See Gene Edward Veith, *Modern Fascism: The Threat to the Judeo-Christian Worldview* (St. Louis: Concordia, 1993).

5   FC SD XI 66 (*Concordia*, 611).

6   AC IV (*Concordia*, 33).

7   Oswald Bayer, *Living by Faith: Justification and Sanctification*, trans. Geoffrey W. Bromiley (Grand Rapids: Eerdmans, 2003), 1. Bayer is a retired professor of systematic theology at the University of Tübingen in Germany.

8   Oswald Bayer, "Justification: Basis and Boundary of Theology," in *By Faith Alone: Essays on Justification in Honor of Gerhard O. Forde*, ed. Joseph A. Burgess and Marc Kolden (Grand Rapids: Eerdmans, 2004), 76.

9   AC IV 1 (*Concordia*, 33).

10   AC IV 2–3 (*Concordia*, 33).

11   Ap V 174–75 (*Concordia*, 128).

12   Adolf Köberle, *The Quest for Holiness* (New York: Harper & Brothers, 1936).

13   Theodore G. Tappert, ed. and trans., *Luther: Letters of Spiritual Counsel*, Library of Christian Classics 18 (Philadelphia and London: Westminster Press and SCM, 1955), 110.

14   Holger Sonntag, trans., *Löhe on Mercy*, ed. by Adriane Dorr and Philip Hendrickson (St. Louis: LCMS World Relief and Human Care, 2006), 6.

15   AE 29:53.

16   See AE 51:271, 297.

5

BAPTIZED FOR THIS MOMENT

WATER OF LIFE IN A WORLD OF HURT

We were buried therefore with Him by baptism into death, in order that, just as Christ was raised from the dead by the glory of the Father, we too might walk in newness of life. *Romans 6:4*

When Christians are baptized, they give ear to the Gospel, read Holy Scripture, partake of Holy Communion, and love their neighbor.[1] *Martin Luther*

"It's right on top of New Orleans," the nameless voice intoned as we stood mesmerized by a weather monitor deep within a U.S. State Department building in Washington DC. I was in the capitol for meetings with United States Agency for International Development (USAID).[2] Within seventy-two hours, thanks to generous donors I was heading for Baton Rouge on a private jet stuffed with chainsaws. I was filled with nervous anticipation, mentally preparing to get a handle on the situation. I needed to stand beside my Lutheran brothers and sisters and hold up their arms as they formulated plans for rescue and response. I would determine what needed to be done in St. Louis, Missouri, to bring the resources of the LCMS to bear for the sake of her people on the front lines in Louisiana, Mississippi, and Texas in the wake of Hurricane Katrina.

Upon our arrival, the surreal calm of Rev. Kurt Schultz, president of the Southern District of the LCMS, simultaneously bespoke shock, personality type, and faith—saint and sinner, or saint and person suffering severe trauma. For a time, the district's treasurer could not be found and was feared dead (thankfully he was located a couple of days later). Fourteen feet of water from Lake Pontchartrain covered the road to the district's headquarters; sporadic cell phone service was the only mode of communication.

As if to acknowledge his personal loss and compress his mourning into a manageable space before addressing the needs of a thousand others, President Schultz took me to his home in Slidell, the fruit of a couple's labor over thirty years. It was devastated: The water had risen about six feet inside the house, then slowly receded to leave thick black mud on everything. A cherished grand piano was eight inches deep in swamp mud. The house's contents were in total disarray; much was completely destroyed. We helped President Schultz salvage some clothing and a few personal effects for himself and his wife. Then he asked me to pray for him, so we stood on the street in front of the house as I said, "The Lord gives and the Lord takes away. Blessed be the name of the Lord. Grant Your servant Kurt, O Lord, the strength to bear up under this challenge in the name of Christ." We took a deep breath and turned toward the car. Thus began LCMS involvement in the heroic recovery effort of the Southern District.

Four days into the chaos, we were traveling with Pastor Scott Schmieding of Trinity Lutheran Church, Baton Rouge. With great concern, we had been monitoring a situation in New Orleans in which nearly one hundred people were trapped near the French Quarter, too scared to leave the basement of St. Paul Lutheran Church on Burgundy Street. Armed looters were marauding through the streets, pillaging and firing at will. The LCMS World Relief and Human Care office in St. Louis had been in touch sporadically with Pastor David Goodine. Barbara Below, a licensed clinical social worker and director of Social Ministry Organizations with LCMS World Relief and Human Care, had burned up the phone lines to get the group noticed. She also called me, pleading for us to do something, anything, to get these people out immediately—a couple individuals were in danger of death from illness and dehydration.

As Pastor Schmieding drove us toward command central for the state of Louisiana, I called Tim Goeglein, a former parishioner from my years in Indiana who is now a special assistant to President George W. Bush. I asked for his help with the situation at St. Paul, and he contacted the Department of Homeland Security. I also called Chaplain Steve Lee, executive director of Peace Officer Ministries, who was as deep inside New Orleans as possible. I asked if he could get close to the church building and help with the situation. Meanwhile, Pastor Schmieding and I sailed into Louisiana Katrina Command Central, where the governor's husband determined the nature of our concern and took us to the command center for the Louisiana State Police. We were told the group would be out in two hours.

We left to attend to other matters, but a few hours later we heard the good news that a convoy of state and local police and the National Guard had rescued the group from St. Paul.

This was only one of many amazing rescue efforts that took place in the hours and days following Katrina. But I was most amazed by the worship service at Trinity, Baton Rouge, the Sunday after the hurricane hit. Refugees had inundated the church's facilities, and Pastor Schmieding was running on empty, so he asked if I would preach. By this time I also had been several days with minimal sleep (on a couch in spare property owned by Trinity). I was quickly realizing my ability to think clearly and strategically was becoming exhausted as I managed the collection and distribution of resources from St. Louis, where the LCMS World Relief office had gone into full disaster/crisis overload. (The amazing cooperation that occurred at LCMS headquarters is another great story.) I preached on Romans 8:28, "All things work together for good . . ." I preached on the cross and the hidden way God so often works His good will. I will never forget the families, whose homes lay submerged thirty miles to the south, weeping and holding on to one another.

At the end of the service, Pastor Schmieding outlined the emerging rescue and relief efforts. He looked to the congregation and asked for volunteers who were willing to participate. Then it hit me. I was still looking at this community—even Baton Rouge—as one devastated and in need of *outside* assistance. But the people of God had stepped forward en mass, prepared to show God's mercy to others. I realized at that moment how I had underestimated the Body of Christ *there*, at the point of duress. They confidently chose to act in mercy for their neighbors. God baptized and preached them into one body through Pastors Schmieding and David Buss and countless others. They responded as "one body" because they had "one Lord, one faith, one baptism" (Ephesians 4:5). Truly, they "were baptized for this moment."

ONE BODY . . . ONE BAPTISM

The damage water can do is beyond calculation, but water works blessings too. Baptism is a hurricane of grace and mercy in Christ. Martin Luther points out that "this baptism is a deluge of grace, just as that one [the flood] was a deluge of wrath."[3] The New Testament teaches clearly that Baptism is God's action, and it works the forgiveness of sins. Baptism *is* the Gospel. To say *no* to Baptism is to say *no* to Christ's mandate, gift, and person. It is to say *no* to "the entire divine majesty."[4] It is to say *no* to the Gospel. To turn Christ's Gospel gift (God's gracious action to forgive) into our act of devotion (Law) is works-righteousness. As St. Paul writes, "All who rely on works of the law are under a curse" (Galatians 3:10). And Jesus said, "Truly, truly, I say to you, unless one is born of water and the Spirit, he cannot enter the kingdom of God" (John 3:5). Luther clarified that "although it [Baptism] is performed by human hands, it is still truly God's own work"[5] and that "in Baptism God speaks."[5] The Sacrament of Holy Baptism involves water, word, and God's command.[7] We see in Christ's great mandate of Baptism for all (Matthew 28:19) that the Lord—Father, Son, and Holy Spirit—lays His name upon us and claims us as the object of His mercy.

BAPTISM MEANS WE ARE IN THIS TOGETHER

One does not choose to be born. It is the same with being born again.[8] Jesus Himself teaches that Baptism is a "passive" activity, mandating in Matthew 28 that "all nations" should be baptized. Baptism is passive; its gifts are received by faith. It is the Gospel in action. St. Paul writes: "For in Christ Jesus you are all sons of God, through faith. For as many of you as were baptized into Christ have put on Christ" (Galatians 3:26–27). Thus Luther writes in his explanation of Baptism in the Large Catechism: "So you see plainly that there is no work done here by us, but a treasure, which God gives us and faith grasps [Ephesians 2:8–9]."[9]

Nowhere does the Bible teach that Baptism is symbolic. It is never called a "sign" of something else. It is a gift that effects forgiveness of sin, life, and salvation. Luther writes: "Baptism is not only natural water, but a divine, heavenly, holy, and blessed water, and whatever other terms we can find to praise it. This is all because of the Word, which is a heavenly holy Word, which no one can praise enough. For it has, and is able to do, all that God is and can do [Isaiah 55:10–11]."[10] The biblical texts in support of this are overwhelming: "Repent and be baptized every one of you in the name of Jesus Christ for the forgiveness of your sins" (Acts 2:38; see also Acts 22:16). Titus 3:4–8 is striking:

> But when the goodness and loving kindness of God our Savior appeared, He saved us, not because of works done by us in righteousness, but according to His own mercy, by the washing of regeneration and renewal of the Holy Spirit, whom He poured out on us richly through Jesus Christ our Savior, so that being justified by His grace we might become heirs according to the hope of eternal life.

"He saved us, *not because of works* . . . *but* according to His own mercy, *by the washing*"—our Lord is doing the work. God is the subject of the verbs. We are the subject of the verb only in the negative, that is, *not* by works done by us! The phrase "washing of regeneration and renewal of the Holy Spirit" is a direct reference to Jesus' teaching on Baptism in John 3, where He tells Nicodemus, "unless one is born again . . . . Unless one is born of water and the Spirit, he cannot enter the kingdom of God" (vv. 3, 5). In his Epistle to the Romans, St. Paul repeatedly demonstrates the real results of Baptism: "We were buried therefore with Him by baptism into death, in order that, just as Christ was raised from the dead by the glory of the Father, we too might walk in newness of life" (Romans 6:4). Baptism connects us with Jesus; by Baptism, His death becomes our death and His life becomes our life (Romans 6:5). Baptism is where we are "crucified with [Christ]" (Romans 6:6). In Baptism we "have died with Christ," so "we believe that we will also live with Him" (Romans 6:8). Baptism is not an act by which one works oneself into the Church. It is God's act of mercy by which we are joined to Christ. In Baptism, all that is His becomes ours.

BAPTISM AND MERCY

What does Baptism, as God's act of mercy, have to do with the corporate life of mercy of the Church? Baptism creates the Church. Luther writes that "baptism is our only comfort and admits to every blessing of God and to the communion of all the saints."[11] Baptism defines who we are. Again from Luther: "When Christians are baptized, they give ear to the Gospel, read Holy Scripture, partake of Holy Communion, and love their neighbor."[12]

By Baptism, one is brought into a communion, a body of the baptized. The corporate nature of Baptism, however, usually receives little attention. The section on Baptism in *Luther's Small Catechism with Explanation* explicates Baptism wonderfully as far as it goes, but this section offers little on the corporate and ethical ramifications of the Sacrament. However, Luther's treatment in the Catechism uses the plural nearly throughout. And the New Testament describes Baptism, like all the great events in the life of a Christian, in the plural. When we are baptized "into Christ," we are baptized into a body, Christ's body, and therefore "into" one another.

The plurals of Romans 6 jump off the page. Paul uses a number of words that clearly express the *togetherness* and *plurality* that Baptism brings about among those who receive it.[13] The following Greek words can only be translated by using several English words:

ebaptistheemen = as many as "were-baptized-together-in" Christ (6:2)

sunetapheemen = we "together-were-buried-with" Christ (6:4)

sunestauroothe = our old self "was-crucified-together-with" Christ (6:6)

suzeesomen = we "together-will-be-made-alive-with" Christ (6:8)

Thus we have the following plurals in this key Pauline passage on Baptism:

How can *we* [plural] who died to sin still live in it? (6:2)

Do you not know that all of *us* [plural] who have been baptized into Christ Jesus were baptized into His death? (6:3)

In order that . . . *we* [plural] too might walk in newness of life. (6:4b)

If *we* [plural] have been united with Him in a death like His, *we* [plural] shall certainly be united with Him in a resurrection like His. (6:5)

We [plural] know that *our* [plural] old self was crucified with Him. (6:6a)

Now if *we* [plural] have died with Christ, *we* [plural] believe that *we* [plural] will also live with Him. (6:8)

This is not symbolic language. The Church really and truly is the Body of Christ. Baptized into Christ and made members of His Body, because we are in Him, we become ever more what He is—merciful one to another. Luther writes: "Thus we Christians, through our rebirth in baptism, become children of God. And if we pattern ourselves after our Father and all his ways, all his goods and names are likewise our inheritance forever. Now, our Father is and is called merciful and good, as Christ says, 'Be merciful, even as your Father is merciful' [Luke 6:36]."[14]

To deny mercy—even worse, to reject the demonstration of mercy and care to those in need—is more than breaking God's Law. Denying mercy denies and rejects the Gospel of Holy Baptism. It denies the mercy of God in Baptism. It denies the triune God, who is named in Baptism. It denies the gracious word of the Father ("This is My beloved Son," Matthew 3:17). It denies the Son who undergoes and opens Baptism to us. It denies the Spirit, who descends also upon us in Baptism. It denies the gifts of that same Spirit, among which are charity, mercy, humility, and love. Denial of mercy to the unbaptized fails to recognize that we, too, were once outside the Church, outside of Christ. We, too, were brought into the Body of Christ through mercy, despite ourselves.

Infant baptism beautifully demonstrates this. Born into the flesh, we are children of the flesh, "dead in our trespasses" (Ephesians 2:5). God's mercy seeks and creates the object of its love—though that object is quite unlovable! Denial of mercy to needy Christians in particular is a denial of Christ's Body, the Church. It is a denial of Christ in my neighbor, as we read in Scripture: "For as many of you as were baptized into Christ have put on Christ" (Galatians 3:27) or "As you did it to one of the least of these My brothers, you did it to Me" (Matthew 25:40). So Luther can say that Baptism (like the Lord's Supper) makes us all, with Christ, "one loaf."[15] Denial of mercy, even to non-Christians, is a denial of the way the Lord has sought and claimed us who were unlovable and condemned sinners. Baptism *is* mercy.[16] No Baptism, no mercy. Commenting on 1 Peter 1:22, Luther began with Baptism and ended with the responsibility to love even beyond the brotherhood of faith:

> Thus in Baptism we Christians have all obtained one brotherhood. From this no saint has more than I and you. For I have been bought with just as high a price as he has been bought. God has spent just as much on me as He has spent on the greatest saint. . . . Love, however, is greater than brotherhood; for it extends also to enemies, and particularly to those who are not worthy of love. For just as faith is active where it sees nothing, so love should also not see anything and do its work chiefly where nothing lovable but only aversion and hostility is seen. . . . And this, says St. Peter, should be done fervently and with all one's heart, just as God loved us when we were unworthy of love.[17]

In Baptism our lives are "hidden with Christ in God" (Colossians 3:3). In Baptism we know that all our sins are forgiven and covered by Christ, in whom we are "clothed." According to Luther, life becomes, then, a joyful daring, that is, a daring to believe that because of Jesus we are wholly pleasing and acceptable to God.[18] And it becomes daring to live life outside ourselves and in and for others: "The Father of infinite mercies has by the gospel made us daring lords."[19]

The baptized still endure crosses and live in a real world of hurt. Because Baptism unites us with Christ and His cross, we should not be at all surprised when we bear a splinter or two of that cross in this life.[20] Hurricanes and tornados still come. Cancer and Alzheimer's disease plague family members. As St. Paul informs us, "We are being killed all the day long" (Romans 8:36). Our lives in Christ are hidden under trials and temptations, the challenges of sin and death, and, finally, the power of the devil. These threaten and beset us in this world. But we can say with Luther, "Nevertheless, I am baptized. And if I am baptized, it is promised to me that I shall be saved and have eternal life, both in soul and body."[21]

The terrible death and destruction brought by Hurricane Katrina changed people's lives forever. The water brought both sad and courageous stories of families, friends, and neighbors striving to survive, clean up, and move forward. Christians found strength to endure amid suffering from another death by water: Baptism. In Baptism's new birth there welled up a confidence and courage in the Gospel to forge ahead. Amid the deluge, the people of God have been blessed to be a blessing. Baptized for this moment, they have lived and are continuing to live Titus 3:

> When the goodness and loving kindness of God our Savior appeared, He saved us, not because of works done by us in righteousness, but according to His own mercy, by the washing of regeneration and renewal of the Holy Spirit, whom He poured out on us richly through Jesus Christ our Savior, so that being justified by His grace we might become heirs according to the hope of eternal life. The saying is trustworthy, and I want you to insist on these things, so that those who have believed in God may be careful to devote themselves to good works. These are excellent and profitable for people. *Titus 3:4–8*

> I [Christ] have imposed the Gospel, Baptism, and the Sacrament on you. And . . . it is your treasure, which I have given you gratis. . . . But now, since you have all received the treasure that you should have, do just this one thing: be joined together in the bonds of love.[22] *Martin Luther*

> I bind unto myself today
> The pow'r of God to hold and lead,
> His eye to watch, His might to stay,
> His ear to hearken to my need,
>
> Against the demon snares of sin,
> The vice that gives temptation force,
> The natural lusts that war within,
> The hostile foes that mar my course.
> (*Lutheran Service Book* 604:3–4)

> O Lord, have mercy.
> O Christ, have mercy.
> O Lord, have mercy. . . .
> Be gracious to us.
> Spare us, good Lord. . . .
> From lightning and tempest; from all calamity by fire and water; and from everlasting death:
> Good Lord, deliver us.
> (The Litany, *Lutheran Service Book*, p. 288)

NOTES

1   AE 22:197.

2   USAID has provided economic and humanitarian assistance worldwide for more than forty years.

3   WA 2.727ff. (*author's translation*).

4   StL 10:2095.87 (*author's translation*).

5   LC IV 10 (*Concordia*, 424).

6   StL 10:2065.21 (*author's translation*).

7   StL 10:2059.8.

8   John 1:12; John 3:1–8; and John 15:16: "You did not choose Me, but I chose you."

9   LC IV 37 (*Concordia*, 427).

10 LC IV 17 (*Concordia*, 425).

11 AE 53:103.

12 AE 22:197.

13 AE 24:226.

14 AE 42:28.

15 AE 24:226.

16 See Titus 3:5: "according to His own mercy, by the washing . . ."

17 AE 30:42–43.

18 AE 42:164.

19 AE 48:390.

20 See AE 27:404.

21 LC IV 44 (*Concordia*, 427).

22 AE 24:252–53.

6
SPOKEN FREE AND
LIVING MERCIFULLY

And seizing [his fellow servant], he began to choke him, saying, "Pay what you owe." *Matthew 18:28*

After [confession and absolution] we can do a lot of good [works]—to the glory of God alone and to the benefit of our fellow-men . . . . For God gives us his grace freely and without cost; so we should also serve him freely and without cost.[1] *Martin Luther*

"BUT DO YOU FORGIVE ME, DAD?"

Living mercifully is a high holy art of faith. A couple years ago, my two boys were racing home on their bicycles from the neighborhood swimming pool. They had come down the fairly steep hill to our home, the youngest, Mark, was in the lead, big brother Matthew hot on his trail. As they neared our driveway, Matthew's front wheel inching toward the lead, the fatal error occurred that now lives in familial infamy. Matthew's front wheel rubbed the left side of his sibling's rear wheel. At the same time, like a slow-motion replay, Mark darted to the left toward the driveway, crossing the trajectory of his mischievous sibling.

I was cleaning the garage, oblivious to the world, when I heard the unmistakable sound of bicycles tumbling and scraping over the pavement. Then there was a split second of silence followed by the wailing of two boys. This was not the normal cry of children who have been told that it is past their bedtime. No, this was weeping-and-gnashing-of-teeth wailing. It is the sound I have always associated with the grotesque figures of the damned, mouths gaping, in the painting by Lucas Cranach on the back of the altar in St. Mary's Church in Wittenberg, where Martin Luther preached.

I raced to find two scraped and bloodied bodies sitting upright. My Boy Scout first-aid merit badge training kicked in. Mark needed Mom's attention to doctor the wounds on knees, elbows, and face.

Matthew, the perpetrator, sat on the driveway crying, waiting for my inspection. As I assessed his condition, I began the interrogation: "What happened? *What happened?*"

As every parent knows, such incidents are rarely purely accidental. As a true believer, Matthew has a special gift of the Holy Spirit—he cannot hide his guilt. And this child had that "I don't want to tell you what I did—but I know I'm caught red-handed" look on his face. He held his hand limply for my inspection as he began to 'fess up. Matthew admitted that he had intentionally made contact between the bikes and caused the whole thing. As he spoke, I literally watched his hand swell out of shape.

"Oh no, it's broken," I grumbled through clenched teeth in parental disgust, the whole affair quickly making hay with my sinful flesh. "Get in the car. We need to go to the emergency room."

A flood of anger filled me—more medical bills, another four-hour wait for treatment. The poor kid lay on the back seat of the car, crying. I was vacillating between anger and worry, and the worry made me angrier. The in-car conversation went like this:

Perpetrator, crying: "What are they going to do to my hand, Dad?"

Irate parent: "They are going to put the broken bones back in place and put a cast on your hand for a number of weeks. You are going to miss most of baseball season."

Loud bawling.

Son: "Dad, will it hurt?"

Irate parent, gruffly: "Yes! It's going to hurt."

More loud bawling.

Son: "But, Dad ... Dad ..."

Irate parent, sharply: "What?!!"

Son, stammering through his tears: "Dad ... Dad ... Do ... Do you forgive me, Dad? Do you forgive me?"

Ouch! My son's words had "grabbed my neck" and cut me to the quick. Luther wrote that when the Canaanite woman said to Jesus after His intense rebuff that "even the dogs eat the crumbs that fall from their masters' table" (Matthew 15:27), "she catches Christ, the Lord, in his own words and with that wins not only the right of a dog, but also that of the children."[2] Jesus could not refuse her plea for mercy. He had come to have mercy. He wants nothing more than to have mercy. He delights in being asked for mercy. Moreover, Jesus actually is mercy.

My son, knowing Christ and believing exactly what I had taught him about living a merciful life, had "caught me in my own words."

"Yes. Yes, Matthew, I forgive you. I *do* forgive you."

A pause.

"Matthew?"

"Yes, Dad?"

"I'm sorry I lost my cool and yelled at you."

"I forgive you, Dad."

I will always treasure that moment. Both of us will treasure it together in eternity. My son knows something of being spoken free and living mercifully.[3]

DIVINE WORDS DO WHAT THEY SPEAK

As with all words, divine words mean something. Divine words perform the power and mercy of God. They create what they speak by God's will and promise. What's more, the Lord actually places His divine words on human lips. We are "spoken free" in the Gospel.

God's Word does what it says. When God said, "Let there be light," there was light (Genesis 1:3). When Jesus said, "Lazarus, come out," the man who had been dead and shut in the grave came out (John 11:38–44). When Jesus said, "The words that I have spoken to you are spirit and life" (John 6:63), they are.

God's Word comes to us as Law and Gospel. God's Law condemns the sinner as it "not only identifies sin but also, like a swift kick to a sleeping dog that arouses the animal to bark and bite, the Law stirs up the power of sin (Romans 7:7–9)."[4] The Law makes sin utterly sinful. Because in this life we always retain the old sinful nature "about our necks," the Law repeatedly, constantly, unendingly unveils our sin, makes us angry, then brings us to our senses (Luke 15:17ff.). The Law of God drives us back to Christ in repentance. Then we hear the Good

News, God's Gospel promise fulfilled in Jesus Christ, our only Savior from sin. According to the apostle Paul, the Gospel "is the power of God for salvation to everyone who believes" (Romans 1:16).

The Lutheran Church confesses what God's Word speaks in the Gospel according to St. John, which records Jesus' words: "If you forgive the sins of anyone, they are forgiven; if you withhold forgiveness from anyone, it is withheld" (John 20:23). In these words, Jesus Himself created the Office of the Holy Ministry and gave it to the Church. C. F. W. Walther, the first president of the LCMS, pointed out in a sermon on John 20:19–31 "that in these words the power to remit and retain sins on earth ascribed to the church and her ministers is so plain and obvious that it requires no argumentation."[5] At Christ's behest and mandate, pastors are "to preach the Gospel, to forgive and retain sins, and to administer Sacraments."[6] In a sermon on Matthew 16:13–19, Walther stated that "the congregation, the original possessor of the keys, has transferred them to her preacher according to the institution of God, that he should administer them not in his own, but in Christ's and in her name."[7]

The Lutheran Confessions also teach that an Office of the Keys for opening and closing heaven through the proclamation of Law and Gospel is "given to the entire Church."[8] The "entire Church" encompasses both pastors and hearers (Matthew 18:15–20). The Bible, Luther, and the Lutheran Confessions say the same thing. Pastors have an office, which is on behalf of Christ. The following question related to the Office of the Keys is typically included in Luther's Small Catechism, even those editions published during his lifetime: "*What do you believe according to these words [John 20:23]?* I believe that when the called ministers of Christ deal with us by His divine command . . . this is just as valid and certain, even in heaven, as if Christ our dear Lord dealt with us Himself."[9]

Does this mean only pastors forgive sins? No! Every Christian is able to speak forgiveness when sin besets us in our unique vocations and stations of life. According to Luther not only can every Christian do this, but every Christian *should* do this.[10] There is *never* a shortage of sin! But a word of Gospel, a word of forgiveness—even spoken by the humblest child ("Yes, I forgive you, Dad")—is divine and effective. The

Lutheran Confessions call such words "mutual conversation and consolation of brethren."[11] Luther calls this lay absolution "confidential."

> Besides this public, daily, and necessary confession, there is also the confidential confession that is only made before a single brother. If something particular weighs upon us or troubles us, something with which we keep torturing ourselves and can find no rest, and we do not find our faith to be strong enough to cope with it, then this private form of confession gives us the opportunity of laying the matter before some brother. We may receive counsel, comfort, and strength when and however often we wish. . . . The origin and establishment of private Confession lies in the fact that Christ Himself placed His Absolution into the hands of His Christian people with the command that they should absolve one another of their sins [Ephesians 4:32].[12]

To forgive is the vocation of all Christians.

Living Mercifully

Immediately following Christ's gift of the Office of the Keys to the Church—"where two or three are gathered" (Matthew 18:20)—Peter asks, "Lord, how often will my brother sin against me, and I forgive him?" (Matthew 18:21). To this question, Jesus responded:

> Therefore the kingdom of heaven may be compared to a king who wished to settle accounts with his servants. When he began to settle, one was brought to him who owed him ten thousand talents. And since he could not pay, his master ordered him to be sold, with his wife and children . . . . So the servant fell on his knees, imploring him, "Have patience with me, and I will pay you everything." And out of pity [mercy!] for him, the master . . . forgave him the debt. But when that same servant went out, he found one of his fellow servants who owed him a hundred denarii, and seizing him, he began to choke him, saying, "Pay what you owe." . . . Then his master summoned him and said to him, "You wicked servant! I forgave you all that debt because you pleaded with me. And should not you have had mercy on your fellow servant, as I had mercy on you?" And in anger his master delivered him to the jailers . . . . So also My heavenly Father will do to every one of you, if you do not forgive your brother from your heart. *Matthew 18:23–28, 32–35*

The Lord's mercy received is mercy lived. The believer lives a merciful life toward others in the home, workplace, congregation, and community.

Growing up, I had never experienced or even contemplated private confession to a clergyman. But during my first years in the parish, I began to comprehend the importance of private confession and absolution. Like every other pastor, I worked with those experiencing trouble in their marriage, broken families, individuals caught in unspeakable sins, those in mourning, and numerous other challenging situations. I was struggling to provide the needed care until I overheard an older pastor say that once he began using private confession and absolution in his pastoral care of married couples, the number of repeat visits diminished markedly. Having the conflict and the sin named, confessed, and forgiven was extremely salutary in distressed lives. It also helped the pastor to apply appropriate portions of God's Word as advice and salve in that situation.

From that moment I began learning how to be a *Seelsorger*, which is a German word for "pastor" that is best translated as "curate of the soul." Many of us never clearly speak forgiveness in our families and in our congregations. But when I began using private confession and absolution for almost every personal, family, or marital difficulty for which my parishioners asked my assistance, what blessings I saw unfold. Like every pastor, after a decade in the parish, I had heard it all. Yet I bear absolutely no burden, because Christ bore everyone's burden on the cross. All is forgiven. Moreover, hearing those saints confess and receive absolution gave me courage to name and confess my own sins. Luther wrote: "Since private Absolution originates in the Office of the Keys, it should not be despised, but greatly and highly esteemed, along with all other offices of the Christian Church."[13]

So Speak!

As much as we Lutherans harp on the importance of forgiveness, it forever amazes me that we can be so inept, so silent, and so unable to speak absolution to one another. We daily live the parable of the unforgiving servant. Our innumerable sins (even those of which we are unaware) are forgiven by Christ. Yet we obsess, we stew, we fret, and we grind our axes over *one* sin committed against us. After *one* untoward word from a brother or sister in Christ or *one* off-the-cuff remark from a family member, we are shouting, "Pay what you owe!"

When problems in the congregation, situations in our families, or ugly things make our lives bitter, we do not need to wallow, wondering about who "means it" or how we feel about it. Absolution heals and makes things new. The Gospel performs miracles! The words hold good because they are God's words. The Lord speaks us free, and He frees us to speak and to be merciful. So, for the sake of Jesus, speak!

I am the same person today as I was on my first day in the parish: intense, impetuous, outspoken, and unsatisfied with the status quo. Such a personality type—like all others—has its strengths and weaknesses. Early in my ministry, I came to loggerheads with an older churchman who was serving with me on a committee. Over the years I would see the man, tensely greet him, then quickly move away—but each meeting caused me to reflect on my actions and thoughts toward him. The Lord put him in front of me on yet one more occasion. My conscience—and the Spirit of Christ at work in me—would not allow this tension to continue. I went up to him and said, "You know, way back when I was a brash, arrogant, young man. I know I made your life bitter, and I want to apologize to you and ask your forgiveness."

Sadly, we usually do not ask forgiveness of one another in the Church! This brother in Christ seemed stunned. He hesitated briefly, then with all the composure and sincerity of Christ, he replied, "Yes, you were those things. But I'm not proud of everything I did then either. I forgive you, and I ask for your forgiveness."

Such transactions are as simple as they are rare. This man was merciful to me. He spoke me free, and I will always respect him. He knew how to live mercifully. But living mercifully in the wake of confession and absolution is not limited to our speaking.

FREED FOR A PURPOSE

God freely gives out His grace, so we also serve Him freely. According to David Yeago, throughout the Lutheran world today *freedom* has come to mean something quite different from what Luther understood it to be. Yeago wrote that "the notion of freedom is essentially negative: release from pressure, the lifting of the burden of an unendurable expectation."[14] However, Luther places a unique emphasis on that fact that freedom in Christ is *toward* something, not only *away from* something. Freedom in Christ has an object, a result. During confirmation instruction, most Lutherans learned these words from Luther's explanation to the Second Article of the Apostles' Creed: "[He] has redeemed me, a lost and condemned person, purchased and won me from all sins, from death, and from the power of the devil." But Luther does not stop there. Instead, he continues: "*That* [the result] I may be His own and live under Him in His kingdom and serve Him in everlasting righteousness, innocence, and blessedness."[15] Luther adapted the long-standing Augustinian tradition of defining the self in terms of love and the "innate directedness toward the good."[16] By contrast, modernity finds the dignity of the self in terms of power and free will, including "the power to impose its will on the world, or to realize its own authentic uniqueness despite the world."[17] The will of God came to be viewed as something fundamentally limiting—and postmodernity concurs with this view. For "we are free insofar as we can do what we want, insofar as our power is unchecked, unhindered by expectations or prohibitions imposed from outside ourselves."[18]

How completely different is our freedom spoken in Christ. It is not a freedom to become an autonomous, atomized, or socially disaffected self. Rather, Lutheran freedom is powerful as well as free. It is a freedom toward community. It is a freedom that pulls one outside of oneself. It is a freedom toward communal purpose, vocation, service, and mercy. It is a freedom toward eternity. Thus Luther offered this advice to those who remained in plague-stricken cities to serve the needy: "Everyone should prepare in time and get ready for death by going to confession and taking the sacrament once every week or fortnight."[19]

The great offense of the unforgiving servant is his utterly selfish misuse of the freedom and mercy that the master so richly and freely bestowed on him. His freedom should have been the greatest source and impetus of mercy and kindness toward his fellow servant. And how his lack of mercy offended the community! Jesus tells us that "when his fellow servants saw what had taken place, they were greatly distressed" (Matthew 18:31). The mercy of Christ effects the community of mercy. While Christ's mercy is always individual, it is born in the context of the Church, and the trajectory of the individual is always toward life with others. Because God shows us mercy, to refuse mercy to our "fellow servant" is a denial of Christ: "Should not you have had mercy on your fellow servant, as I had mercy on you?" (Matthew 18:33).

It is a sobering moment when a parent realizes the need for forgiveness from a child. My son pleaded for mercy. I overreacted. I sinned. He forgave me. That day my son taught me something about being spoken free and living mercifully.

> Forgive our sins, Lord, we implore,
>
> That they may trouble us no more;
>
> We, too, will gladly those forgive
>
> Who hurt us by the way they live.
>
> Help us in our community
>
> To serve each other willingly.
>
> (*Lutheran Service Book* 766:6)

> Christ, the Lamb of God, who takes away the sin of the world,
> have mercy.
>
> (The Litany, *Lutheran Service Book*, p. 289)

NOTES

1   AE 35:17.

2   Eugene F. A. Klug, ed., *Sermons of Martin Luther: The House Postils*, trans. Eugene F. A. Klug et al. (Grand Rapids: Baker, 1996), 1:325. See also John Lenker, ed., *Sermons of Martin Luther*, trans. John Lenker et al. (Grand Rapids: Baker, 1988), 2:152.

3   See Luther's comment (AE 21:29): "Counterfeit sanctity . . . cannot have pity or mercy . . . as soon as there is even a minor flaw, all mercy is gone, and there is nothing but fuming and fury." See also SA III IV (*Concordia*, 278).

4   John Pless, *Handling the Word of Truth: Law and Gospel in the Church Today* (St. Louis: Concordia, 2004), 15.

5   "Absolution: Sermon on John 20:19–31," *Lutheran Standard* XXXI, 26 (July 26, 1873): 855.

6   AC XXVIII 5 (*Concordia*, 58). See also Tr 60 (*Concordia*, 303).

7   C. F. W. Walther, "Sermon on Matthew 16:13–19, for 1870 Synod Convention," *Lutheran Standard* XXIX, 17 (September 1, 1871): 131b.

8   Tr 24; see especially Tr 23–24 (*Concordia*, 297). This is Walther's doctrine of the Office of the Ministry.

9   *Luther's Small Catechism with Explanation*, 29.

10 See Klug, *House Postils*, 3:79–80.

11 SA III IV (*Concordia*, 278).

12 A Brief Exhortation to Confession 13–14 (*Concordia*, 651).

13 SA III VIII 2 (*Concordia*, 280).

14 David Yeago, "The Office of the Keys," in *Marks of the Body of Christ*, ed. Carl E. Braaten and Robert W. Jenson (Grand Rapids: Eerdmans, 1999), 107.

15 *Luther's Small Catechism with Explanation*, 16.

16 Yeago, "Office of the Keys," 110.

17 Yeago, "Office of the Keys," 110.

18 Yeago, "Office of the Keys," 110.

19 AE 43:134.

7

CHRIST'S BODY AND BLOOD

"WITH MIGHT AND MAIN FOR OUR NEIGHBOR"[1]

Because there is one bread, we who are many are one body, for we all partake of the one bread. *1 Corinthians 10:17*

O this is a great sacrament . . . that Christ and the church are one flesh and bone. Again through this same love, we are to be changed and to make the infirmities of all other Christians our own; we are to take upon ourselves their form and their necessity. . . . That is real fellowship, and that is the true significance of this sacrament.[2] *Martin Luther*

"Holy, holy, holy is God the Lord of Sabaoth," chanted the congregation gathered in the fabulous 110-year-old German gothic church at the corner of Hanna and Creighton Streets. Despite the fact that this intersection had long been the demographic bull's-eye of crime, poverty, drugs, gangs, and murder in Fort Wayne, Indiana, the people belted out the Sanctus, led by the massive organ. All in attendance anticipated that joyful moment at the feast of Christ's body and blood when time and eternity are transcended. I was never more honored to serve Christ's Church than at that moment.

I began to chant the Lord's Prayer. As I finished the final petition—"but deliver us from evil"—and the congregation began to sing the conclusion, I noticed a tall, well-built man in disheveled clothes entering the sanctuary. He moved first to the lectern side, then quickly changed course and made his way to the pews directly in front of Zion's magnificently gilded elevated pulpit. The headmaster of our day school, always adroit in such circumstances, quickly moved to help the man find his place in the service. But in a flash, just as I raised my arms and prepared to speak the Words of Institution, the man darted in front of the entire assembly, stretching out his arms in imitation of my posture at the altar. Then the man began blowing kisses with both hands, shouting to the assembly, "I'm gonna die! I'm gonna die!" as he wobbled from side to side, perhaps a symptom of whatever substance he was abusing.

Arms still outstretched, I motioned with an index finger (it must have been a comical sight) to the four ushers who had assembled in the center aisle at the rear and were haltingly inching forward, glancing between the man and me. As they approached the rather large and obviously unstable man, he froze, perhaps caught off guard. The ushers paused, not wanting to make the situation worse, even ugly. The assembly fell silent. At that point—a moment in which I actually felt the Holy Spirit granting me the ability and wisdom to act—I left Zion's magnificent freestanding altar, descended the steps to the man, put my arm around him, and said, "Friend, we are happy to have you here, but I'm going to help you to the rear of the church."

As I put my arm around his shoulder, my green chasuble enveloped both of us, shrouding the man as we walked to the rear of the church in silence. No one gawked or grimaced. Zion knows well that it is a congregation of beggars and that except for the grace of God . . .

I returned to my place at the altar and the liturgy resumed with great joy and deep humility. At some point during that time, the man slipped back into the world of sin, death, and the power of the devil. I never saw him again. I am not sure that he heard those mercy-filled words: "Given and shed for you for the forgiveness of your sins." As I spoke the Pax Domini—"The peace of the Lord be with you always"—holding the consecrated body and blood before the eyes of the saints, I felt no peace. While the parishioners received the Sacrament with great joy and deep humility, I was torn between the mercy I was distributing and the suffering man who so desperately needed this mercy yet had walked out the doors of the church.

Years later, I still have no peace over this man. I deeply regret not asking the ushers to get his name or to find out how to contact him. This incident is typical of the many times poor souls—perhaps baptized but long since fallen away from the Church—would wander into the sanctuary as if drawn by the gaping black hole in their soul. They were looking for a place of peace, a place for rest, a place to have their demons exorcised, a place to meet God. From ministering to such downtrodden people, I knew they wanted to fulfill their deepest need. They hungered to be someone, to be counted, to be recognized as human, to be justified. They coveted a community of love and mercy.

SYNAXIS

The Lord gives His gifts, and He calls us to receive them. He mercifully makes Himself present among us, allowing Himself to be tasted and touched so that we can be sure of His mercy toward us. God extends His love in mercy and delivers the forgiveness obtained by Christ on Calvary's cross. What was accomplished on the cross two thousand years ago must be delivered to us.

> The work of redemption is done and accomplished [John 19:30]. Christ has acquired and gained the treasure for us by His suffering, death, and resurrection, and so on [Colossians 2:3]. . . . So that this treasure might not stay buried, but be received and enjoyed, God has caused the Word to go forth and be proclaimed. In the Word He has the Holy Spirit bring this treasure home and make it our own . . . which we could not get ourselves [1 Peter 3:18]. . . . "But how does He accomplish this . . . ?" . . . "By the Christian Church."³

The Early Church simply called the Lord's Supper *Synaxis*, the "coming together."⁴ The Sacrament of the Altar is the New Testament Holy of Holies, which was the core of the Old Testament tabernacle and temple. Here the blood of the sacrifice was sprinkled on the mercy seat—located between the two golden cherubim atop the ark of the covenant, the chest that held the tablets of the Law (Exodus 25:10–22)—for the forgiveness of the community. Thus the blood of the sacrifice covered the Law. As the writer to the Hebrews noted, "without the shedding of blood there is no forgiveness of sins" (Hebrews 9:22). Although present everywhere, the Lord—Yahweh—was present in His glory *there*, at the mercy seat, with forgiveness of sins (see 1 Kings 8:27–30). Forgiveness is local.

Just as the Israelites located forgiveness and mercy in the mercy seat of the ark of the covenant and in the temple sacrifices, so also St. Paul locates forgiveness and mercy in Jesus and in His body and blood in the Sacrament.

> All have sinned and fall short of the glory of God, and are justified by His grace as a gift, through the redemption that is in Christ Jesus, whom God put forward as a propitiation by His blood, to be received by faith. This was to show God's righteousness, because in His divine forbearance He had passed over former sins. *Romans 3:23–25*

The author to the Hebrews alludes to the Lord's Supper, then ends the Epistle on a strongly communal note:

> Therefore, brothers, since we have confidence to enter the holy places by the blood of Jesus [the Lord's Supper], by the new and living way that He opened for us through the curtain, that is, through His flesh, and since we have a great priest over the house of God, let us draw near with a true heart in full assurance of faith, with our hearts sprinkled clean from an evil conscience and our bodies washed with pure water [Holy Baptism]. Let us hold fast the confession of our hope without wavering, for He who promised is faithful. And let us consider how to stir up one another to love and good works, not neglecting to meet together, as is the habit of some. *Hebrews 10:19–25*

Through Jesus' flesh and blood we have access to God the Father with a clear conscience. In the Sacraments, God dwells among us. Blood, water, forgiveness, faith, and confession all belong together. Where they are, so also is love and good works.

The power of the Supper for creating a community of love is found not in the participants but in the Lord who is "the Donor, the Baker, the Waiter, the Brewer, yes, the Cook, and also the Dish and the Plate that gives us the imperishable food."[5] What makes the Lord's Supper the Lord's Supper? Just as the innate propensity of every human being is to substitute human activity for divine activity, to turn the Gospel into the Law, so also we attempt to change the Lord's Supper, which Luther called "the whole gospel."[6] The Church is not a voluntary association.[7] It is not a fellowship because we share certain human aspirations or social activities, as important as these gifts are in the life of the Church. The Church is a fellowship or communion because we all partake of Christ. The Latin word *communio* can and does mean both things—the Holy Communion of Christ's body and blood, as well as the Body of Christ, the Church—because the Church is manifested by and around the Sacrament.

THE LORD'S BODY AND BLOOD

At the most solemn moment of His life and ministry on this earth

> Our Lord Jesus Christ, on the night when He was betrayed, took bread, and when He had given thanks, He broke it and gave it to the disciples and said: "Take, eat; this is My body, which is given for you. This do in remembrance

of Me." In the same way also He took the cup after supper, and when He had given thanks, He gave it to them, saying: "Drink of it, all of you; this is the new testament in My blood, which is shed for you for the forgiveness of sins. This do, as often as you drink it, in remembrance of Me.[8]

When these words are spoken upon bread and wine among the gathered faithful as Christ instituted and mandated, His "body and blood are truly present, distributed, and received."[9] The Words of Our Lord are "effective and [work] so that in the Supper of the Church His true body and blood are."[10] This is a mystery accepted only by faith in the Lord's promises. When people proclaim that this Sacrament is a mere symbol of Christ's sacrifice, the bread and wine mere symbols of His body and blood, they make a liar out of Jesus. As with Baptism, the New Testament nowhere speaks of the Lord's Supper as a "sign" of something else. Our Lutheran fathers (Luther and Martin Chemnitz[11]) loved to point out that Jesus delivered this Supper "on the night in which He was betrayed," which was the most solemn moment of His earthy ministry. The Supper is Jesus' last will and testament.

Those who claim that the words "this is My body" means "this is not My body but a sign of it" have the burden of explaining why Jesus did not mean what He actually said. As the writers of the Formula of Concord state: "Surely there is no interpreter of Jesus Christ's words as faithful and sure as the Lord Christ Himself."[12] Just as the words of the Lord created in creation, justified in justification, baptized in Baptism, so Jesus' words do what they speak. Luther writes in his Large Catechism: "The chief point is God's Word and ordinance or command. For the Sacrament has not been invented nor introduced by any man. Without anyone's counsel and deliberation it has been instituted by Christ."[13]

The Words of Our Lord that we use in our liturgy are taken from the four biblical accounts of the institution of the Lord's Supper (Matthew 26:26–28; Mark 14:22–24; Luke 22:19–20; 1 Corinthians 11:23–26). According to the Lutheran Confessions, "unanimously and with the same words and syllables [the three evangelists and the apostle Paul] repeat these distinct, clear, firm, and true words of Christ about the consecrated and distributed bread, 'This is My body.' They all repeat these words in one way, without any interpretation, turn of phrase, ‹figure,› and change."[14] How can this be body and blood when it tastes like the earthly elements bread and wine? I have no idea. But just as when someone touched Jesus here on earth and touched both man and God, so we receive bread and wine, body and blood. How can that be? How can the resurrection be? The Scriptures declare it true and we receive it in faith. Luther says, "I am a captive and cannot free myself. The text is too powerfully present, and will not allow itself to be torn from its meaning by mere verbiage."[15] It is not a presence in the sense of seeing food in a grocery store, but somehow, some way, the very body and blood of Christ that hung on the cross is delivered to those who partake of it in, with, and under bread and wine.[16]

While the Words of Institution are the bedrock for this Sacrament, other passages in St. Paul confirm them, for example, 1 Corinthians 10:16: "The cup of blessing that we bless, is it not a participation in the blood of Christ? The bread that we break, is it not a participation in the body of Christ?" *Koinonia*, the Greek word translated as "participation," means "taking part in something" or "partaking of." The Greek word came into Latin as *communio*, from which we get *communion* and *community*. In the Lord's Supper, we are taking part in or partaking of the body and blood of the resurrected Jesus. In the best sense of the word, we are *partaking of* Christ.

Is there a "spiritual" eating in the Sacrament? Absolutely, it is called faith. Faith hears the words "Given and shed for you" and believes them. There is also an oral and sacramental eating in the Lord's Supper. Everyone who receives the elements, the bread and the wine—whether they have faith or not—receives Christ's body and blood. *Faith with* the oral eating receives the blessing: the forgiveness of sins. The presence of Christ's body and blood in the Sacrament does not depend on faith. On the other hand, St. Paul teaches that whoever receives the Sacrament *without* faith or "*without* discerning the body eats and drinks judgment upon himself" (1 Corinthians 11:29). Hence, the Lutheran Confessions state that "it is not our intention to let people come to the Sacrament and administer it to them if they do not know what they seek or why they come."[17] Thus the orthodox Church of all ages practices close(d) Communion, in part because of love.[18]

But there is more to this Sacrament, a lot more. The powerful word of the Lord that brings His body and blood for forgiveness is the same powerful word that uses this body and blood to make us "one, holy, catholic and apostolic" people full of mercy and truth.

"WITH MIGHT AND MAIN FOR OUR NEIGHBOR"

Participation (*koinonia*) in the Lord's body and blood creates a relationship (*koinonia*) among the members of His Body, the Church. This is *exactly* St. Paul's teaching:

> The cup of blessing that we bless, is it not a participation [*koinonia*] in the blood of Christ? The bread that we break, is it not a participation [*koinonia*] in the body of Christ? Because there is one bread, we who are many are one body, for we all partake of one bread. *1 Corinthians 10:16–17*

One bread—one body. Fellowship in the earliest Church meant unity in teaching and unity in love. The Acts of the Apostles records that "they devoted themselves to the apostles' teaching and fellowship [*koinonia*], to the breaking of bread [Lord's Supper] and the prayers" (2:42). *Koinonia* is both vertical—the Lord to me/us—and horizontal, which is the fellowship of unity in faith and charity among the faithful. *Koinonia* was lived out in the Book of Acts as the early Christians shared possessions and demonstrated a unity far beyond the local congregation. St. Paul's amazing collection for the poor Christians in Jerusalem is the theme that unites the Book of Acts. In fact, Paul uses this one word, *koinonia*, for both the Lord's Supper (1 Corinthians 10:16–17) and for the collection for the poor (Romans 15:26)! Thus, for Paul, to extend "the right hand of fellowship" (Galatians 2:9) means concern for needy Christians: After declaring fellowship, James, Peter (Cephas), and John "asked us to remember the poor, the very thing we were most eager to do" (Galatians 2:10).

We laugh aloud at our Lutheran forerunners when we note their enmity for insurance. But the necessity of insurance policies and the reality of the modern welfare state has drastically altered our views of *koinonia* in the Church. As a result, the Church's responsibility and privilege to conduct a corporate, ordered life of mercy has all but dropped from our teaching and even from our preaching. More unfortunate, what was once a strong Lutheran theme in the Lord's

Supper is rarely heard, namely, that this is a sacrament of love.[19]

Beginning in 1519 and continuing until the end of his life, Luther expounded a theme that the Sacrament brings and means a fellowship of love and mercy:

> This fellowship consists in this, that all the spiritual possessions of Christ and his saints are shared with and become the common property of him who receives this sacrament. Again all sufferings and sins also become common property; and thus love engenders love in return and [mutual love] unites. . . . It is like a city where every citizen shares with all the others the city's name, honor, freedom, trade, customs, usages, help, support, protection, and the like, while at the same time he shares all the dangers of fire and flood, enemies and death, losses, taxes, and the like. For he who would share in the profits must also share in the costs, and ever recompense love with love. Here we see that whoever injures one citizen injures an entire city and all its citizens; whoever benefits one [citizen] deserves favor and thanks from all the others. So also in our natural body, as St. Paul says in I Corinthians 12[:25–26], where he gives this sacrament a spiritual explanation, "The members have [the same] care for one another; if one member suffers, all suffer together; if one member is honored, all rejoice together." This is obvious: if anyone's foot hurts him, yes, even the little toe, the eye at once looks at it, the fingers grasp it, the face puckers, the whole body bends over to it, and all are concerned with this small member; again, once it is cared for all the other members are benefited. This comparison must be noted well if one wishes to understand this sacrament, for Scripture uses it for the sake of the unlearned.[20]

For Luther, unity with respect to the Sacrament meant both doctrinal agreement and love. When the prerequisite to church fellowship is defined merely (however important!) in terms of doctrinal fellowship, it can end in a Platonic pursuit of a frigid and rigid mental ideal. Doctrinal unity, true unity in Christ's body and blood, is also a unity of deep love and mercy. If I will not lay down my burden on Christ and the community, or take up the burdens of others who come to the Table, then I should not go to the Sacrament. Close(d) Communion is also a fellowship of love and mercy with my brother and sister in Christ, as Luther taught in the previous citation.

Not long ago I preached in a rural African church. The small mud-and-stick building with its simple wooden benches, simple altar and pulpit, and dirt floor was packed with seventy-five people. I preached, and the congregants nodded in solid Lutheran affirmation as the stern Law and comforting Gospel was translated into their native tongue. What joy it is to travel the world—from Latvia to South Africa, from Central America to Sumatra—and to worship in any language yet be able to follow the service because we have a common liturgy.[21]

Because of the tiny altar and the use of the common cup, Communion took some time. The last to commune, as I approached the presiding minister my mind flashed with the fact that this particular area had one of the highest HIV/AIDS infection rates in the world. No suburban, plastic, hermetically sealed, sterile, individual and individually wrapped communion cups here. For a moment, my fear and sin were before me; I was a wretch worried about himself at this very Sacrament of love. Then I thought of Luther's words: "If one member suffers, all suffer together." The "little toe" in this seemingly forgotten African village is suffering. By faith in the Lord's promise, I drank the blood of my Lord for the forgiveness of sins and will never fail to do so.

It is an honor, privilege, and responsibility to be "one body" with that African community—AIDS or no AIDS. God grant us mercy and strength by His body and blood as we live in His fellowship, the Church. With Luther we can say, "So even though we have sins, the ‹grace of the› Holy Spirit does not allow them to harm us. For we are in the Christian Church, where there is nothing but ‹continuous, uninterrupted› forgiveness of sin. This is because God forgives us and because we forgive, bear with, and help one another [Galatians 6:1–2]."[22]

> May God bestow on us His grace and favor
> That we follow Christ our Savior
> And live together here in love and union
> Nor despise this blessed Communion!
> O Lord, have mercy!
> Let not Thy good Spirit forsake us;
> Grant that heav'nly-minded He make us;
> Give Thy Church, Lord to see
> Days of peace and unity:

O Lord, have mercy!

(*Lutheran Service Book* 617:3)

O Lord, have mercy! Amen.

NOTES

1   AE 36:352.

2   AE 35:58.

3   LC II 38–39, 41–42 (*Concordia*, 403).

4   *Didache* XIX.1 (see Kirsopp Lake, trans., "The Didache," in *The Apostolic Fathers*, 2 vols. [Cambridge: Harvard University Press, 1965]).

5   AE 23:14.

6   AE 36:288.

7   There are only two definitions of church and fellowship, one that is centered on man and one that is centered on Christ. See Werner Elert, *Eucharist and Church Fellowship in the First Four Centuries*, trans. N. E. Nagel (St. Louis: Concordia, 1966), 3ff.

8   *Lutheran Service Book*, p. 162.

9   FC SD VII 75 (*Concordia*, 574).

10   FC SD VII 76 (*Concordia*, 575).

11   FC SD VII 48ff. (*Concordia*, 570–71).

12   FC SD VII 50 (*Concordia*, 571).

13   LC V 5 (*Concordia*, 432).

14   FC SD VII 52 (*Concordia*, 571).

15   AE 40:68; cf. WA 15:394.12ff.

16   See *Luther's Small Catechism with Explanation*, question/answer 291, pp. 234–35.

17   LC V 1–2 (*Concordia*, 431).

18   See *Luther's Small Catechism with Explanation*, 240ff.

19   For Luther's perspective, see AE 35.50ff. For the perspective of C. F. W. Walther, see *Amerikanisch Lutherische Epistel Postille: Predigten* (St. Louis: Concordia, 1882), 182.

20   AE 35:51–52.

21   If non-English speakers cannot do the same among us, then it is perhaps an indication that we have fallen away from the liturgical parameters given in the Book of Concord and the Church catholic.

22   LC II 55 (*Concordia*, 405).

8

CHRIST CARES FOR THE NEEDY, BODY AND SOUL

WE ARE BEGGARS—THIS IS TRUE

As [Jesus] drew near to Jericho, a blind man was sitting by the roadside begging. And hearing a crowd going by . . . he cried out, "Jesus, Son of David, have mercy on me!" . . . And Jesus said to him, "Recover your sight; your faith has made you well." *Luke 18:35–42*

For we are all flesh, whether God makes you a king or a beggar, a wise man or fool.[1] *Martin Luther*

As February 18 passes every year, even Lutherans fail to note its significance. It was on that date in 1546, early in the morning, that Martin Luther died in Eisleben, Germany.[2] He was there because the princes of the little duchy of Mansfeld invited him to help settle some difficulties that had vexed them for some time. Luther preached his last sermon in Wittenberg on January 17, 1546, then the ailing 63-year-old reformer left on the arduous trip.

In a letter to his wife, Katie, Luther compared the ice-swollen Saale River (which he had to cross) to an Anabaptist ready to rebaptize him.[3] Forced to temporarily halt the journey at Halle to await a safe crossing, Luther assisted in the distribution of the Sacrament that Sunday. His hands were unsteady, and he spilled the contents of the cup. The congregation gasped and wept aloud as Luther dropped to his hands and knees to lick up the spill.[4] To us this act may seem bazaar, but it demonstrates how deep was Luther's piety and how high his regard for Christ's body and blood in the Sacrament. On January 28, a group of sixty horsemen sent from Mansfeld was able to get Luther across the Saale River.

Luther was taken to the castle complex at Mansfeld, where the three feuding counts (Albrecht, Philip, and George) and their families resided. How many times Luther must have walked to the wall and looked down on St. George's, the little church where he had served as an altar boy. Viewing the school near the church and his childhood home, perhaps Luther thought of his long-dead parents.

The negotiations at Mansfeld were difficult. During the course of the negotiations, the great reformer preached four times at St. Andrews in Eisleben and received the Lord's Supper twice. Finally, the most difficult problem facing the counts—"a porcupine with more quills than a porcupine"—had "been slaughtered."[5] On Sunday, February 14, Luther ordained two ministers, then preached at St. Andrews the following day. The text was from Matthew 11: "Come unto Me, all ye that labor and are heavy laden, and I will give you rest" (v. 28 KJV). While preaching, Luther was suddenly overcome with fatigue and probably chest pain. He was forced to end the sermon, saying, "This and much more might be said concerning this Gospel, but I am too weak and we shall let it go at that."[6] He descended the pulpit stairs and was assisted to a home across the street.

For two days Luther lay at the portal between time and eternity. The physicians could do little to help him. At 8 p.m. on February 17, he went to the window to say his prayers, as was his custom. He slept on a daybed for a while, but at 10 p.m. Luther asked to retire to his bedchamber in an adjoining room. He prayed Psalm 31:5, a text commonly prayed by the dying: "Into Your hand I commit my spirit; You have redeemed me, O LORD, faithful God." Luther woke at 1 a.m. and cried out, "Oh, Lord God, I'm in so much pain! Oh, dear Doctor Jonas [Luther's close friend], it appears as though I shall remain here."[7] Luther recited John 3:16 and Psalm 68:20 ("Our God is a God of salvation, and to GOD, the Lord, belong deliverances from death") repeatedly. Stirring near 3 a.m., Luther confidently repeated the Nunc Dimittis, the canticle based on Simeon's words upon holding the infant Jesus: "Lord, now You are letting Your servant depart in peace" (Luke 2:29). He repeated Psalm 31:5 three more times, then fell silent. His friend Jonas knew death was imminent, so he asked, "Reverend Father, are you ready to die trusting in your Lord Jesus Christ and to confess the doctrine which you have taught in his name?"[8] *Yes* came the clear response before Luther fell asleep and said nothing more.[9]

But here is what interests us. A scrap of paper was found in Luther's pocket, which turned out to have the last words that he wrote: "Let nobody suppose that he has tasted the Holy Scriptures sufficiently unless he has ruled over the churches with the prophets for a hundred years. . . . We are beggars. That is true."[10]

"We are beggars. That is true." Luther's profound biblical insight clearly depicts us as destitute, sinful, unlovable, unrighteous, and incapable—on our own—of effecting anything positive toward God. In short, we are beggars. Our salvation must be—start to finish—an act of grace. Yet this is precisely how God desires we come before Him. Jesus said, "I came not to call the righteous, but sinners" (Matthew 9:13). Paul writes, "For God has consigned all to disobedience, that He may have mercy on all" (Romans 11:32).

It is interesting to read the Gospels and place ourselves in the people and situations that are recorded: faithless and fearful disciples, hypocritical Pharisees, faithful Mary, brash Peter, etc. Just like us, they are saints and sinners. To refuse to see ourselves in the faithless is to live a lie. As we consider what it means to live mercifully, there is no better mirror than to see ourselves in the destitute, the blind, or the crippled beggars who plead with Christ for mercy. Have you noticed that those who approach Christ crying for mercy always come away with His blessing? (See Matthew 8:1ff.; 8:5ff.; 9:1ff.; 9:18ff.; 9:27f.; 15:21ff.; 17:14ff.; 20:29. Contrast these accounts with that of the rich man in Matthew 19:16–22, who said, "All these [commandments] I have kept," [v. 20].) If you are not a beggar, Christ is not your Savior. Refuse Christ's mercy, and He will not force it on you. You will be left to your own devices to deal with your sin, death, and the devil. But sing out *Kyrie eleison* ("Lord, have mercy!") and Christ is all yours. In fact, He came specifically for beggars and only for beggars. And you *are* a beggar—this is true! How Christ overflows with delight to show mercy to beggars.

ARE WE BEGGING PLATONISTS?

One criticism leveled against Christians is that we are Platonists, trying to give something ideal to real-life beggars. Many a sermon (I include my own in the "many") about the paralyzed man who was healed (Matthew 9:1–8) simply assert that the entire point and purpose of the account is to demonstrate that Jesus is God in the flesh and has the power to forgive sins. However, as central and significant as that fact is, there is much more to Jesus' miracles. While His healing miracles do confirm Jesus as the Messiah, which He Himself preached (Luke 4:16–19), as well as confirm His divinity and ability to forgive sin, if we have preached forgiveness, have we preached the whole text? Have we understood everything these miracles of Jesus mean for the Church today and into eternity? What does it mean that when beggars came to Jesus, He forgave sin *and* healed the body?

Plato was convinced that reality was in the "idea" of things, not in the things themselves (matter). Splitting the idea/spirit from matter is called dualism. According to Plato, what we behold in this world is a copy, an imperfect representation, of the "ideal," which exists in the realm of ideas (man's and God's). The truths of Christianity—which speak of God/devil, heaven/hell, body/spirit, man/woman, body/bread, water/spirit—were and remain tempting targets for the Platonic distortion of dualism.

Platonism wreaked havoc on Christianity's understanding of man as God's good creation, body and soul. In the first centuries and to varying degrees within the Church and among heretical groups, creation was denied, diminished, or rejected in a misguided quest to rid the self of material pollutions and obtain pure "spirituality." Sex, marriage, and even women were disparaged as inherently injurious to the Christian life.[11] This gave rise, for example, to monasticism in the third and fourth centuries. Some heretics held that the physical world is completely disconnected from eternal/spiritual realities; therefore indulgence of the material world had no effect upon one's spiritual state.[12] Thus Platonism mocked the New Testament.

But Platonism's effects upon Christianity went even further. Rejection or even misunderstanding of creation as God's good gift directly affected what was taught concerning Jesus' incarnation. In the early centuries of the Church, various Gnostic sects (so-named because of their conviction that faith is the acquisition of some arcane "knowledge" that is unwritten, unknowable, and unattainable except through their rituals) went through bizarre mental gymnastics to explain Christ. What a challenge to believe in Christ as the God-man when you are convinced that a lesser and evil god is responsible for creation (even of Christ's flesh)! Thus, some heretics alleged, Jesus, a mere man, was conceived, born, and grew up as a normal man. Then at His Baptism, the man Jesus was inhabited by Christ. Just as He was about to be crucified, "Christ" leaped out of the man Jesus, who proceeded to suffer, die, and be buried. But wonder of wonders, "Christ" jumped back into Jesus at the resurrection! The Nicene Creed is the Church's answer to this and many other heretical attempts to explain away the mystery of Christ's incarnation, a mystery that cannot be explained but must be believed and confessed. Jesus Christ is fully God and fully man. He is God in flesh and blood. The apostle John writes: "By this you know the Spirit of God: every spirit that confesses that Jesus Christ has come in the flesh is from God, and every spirit that does not confess Jesus is not from God. This is the spirit of the antichrist, which you heard was coming and now is in the world already" (1 John 4:2–3). By using the word *flesh* repeatedly, John, who was writing late in the first century at a time when Gnosticism was gaining strength, asserts clearly that the flesh (God's creation) is good, though corrupted by sin. Therefore it was redeemed by Christ in the flesh. As he writes in his Gospel account, "the Word became flesh and dwelt among us" (John 1:14).

Where the incarnation of Christ is denied or misunderstood, the sacraments quickly suffer the same fate. For they are eternal, divine, spiritual gifts delivered through common, created, fleshly elements (bread, wine, water). According to Hermann Sasse and Werner Elert, two prominent twentieth-century Lutheran theologians, the word *flesh*[13] in John 6 is a poke in the eye to the Gnostics: "Truly, truly, I say to you, unless you eat the flesh of the Son of Man and drink His blood, you have no life in you. Whoever feeds on My flesh and drinks My blood has eternal life, and I will raise him up on the last day. For My flesh is true food, and My blood is true drink. Whoever feeds on My flesh and drinks My blood abides in Me, and I in him" (vv. 53–56).

From the earliest days of the Reformation, Lutherans have directly asserted this "incarnational" nature of the Christian sacraments. Like Ignatius of Antioch,[14] one of the apostle John's disciples—or Ireneaus, commenting on Justin Martyr[15] after him—Lutherans have not shied away from using concrete, fleshly language to describe the sacraments, particularly the Lord's Supper.

> The Sacrament was instituted to comfort terrified minds. This happens when they believe that Christ's flesh is given as food for the life of the world [John 6:51] and when they believe that, being joined to Christ, they are made alive.[16]

Wherever Platonism lurks, people seek spiritual assurance in places where God has not promised we will find it (that is, they seek it apart from God's Word and Sacraments, and thus apart from the Church). All of us are susceptible to this error. Luther used a delightful but untranslatable German word for this: *Schwarmgeisterei* ("swarming of spirits/ideas"). Early Lutherans also called it "fanaticism" or "enthusiasm" because we are all by nature "fanatics." Luther wrote: "In a word, enthusiasm dwells in Adam and his children from the beginning to the end of the world."[17] Adam and Eve sought to "be like God, knowing good and evil" (Genesis 3:5), which was quite against God's specific mandate and promise. This is precisely why we are so prone to disregard Baptism, Absolution, the Lord's Supper, and preaching of the Gospel—and to disregard the importance of regular reception of these gifts in the Church, distributed by pastors who are called and ordained to deliver them to us.[18]

In his Large Catechism, Luther wrote that "[Christ] leads us first into His holy congregation and places us in the bosom of the Church. Through the Church He preaches to us and brings us to Christ."[19] This directly contradicts a specific platonic and pervasive attitude, namely, that it is not necessary to attend church to be a Christian or to go to heaven. Is it possible to trust in Christ yet not attend church? Yes, it is possible—just think of the thief on the cross (Luke 23:39f.). Is it possible to reject receiving Christ's Word and Sacrament at church and still believe the Gospel and be on the path to heaven? Perhaps it is possible, but by no means is it likely.

Despite teaching that the members of the body can be used for evil (see Romans 7:23) and despite desiring to "depart and be with Christ" (Philippians 1:23), St. Paul asserts that whether he lives or dies "Christ will be honored in my body" (Philippians 1:20). The teachings of Christ and St. Paul are undergirded, framed, and capped by the firm conviction that there will be a resurrection of the body at the Last

Day (see John 11; 1 Corinthians 15). Furthermore, Paul and Christ stress that eternity will be "in the flesh," body and soul. The New Testament knows no diminution or denial of the importance of the body. Baptism is a baptism into Christ and a guarantee of the resurrection of the body (Romans 6:1ff.). The Lord's Supper is, as the ancients called it, "the medicine of immortality" and is likewise a guarantee of resurrection with Christ in the flesh (1 Corinthians 15; Luke 22:16; John 6:51ff.). The body is honored as God's creation and the subject of His redemption. The person—as God's good creation, though fallen in sin—is the subject of redemption. And the Church has always acted accordingly.

This concern for the body extends to conception, the earliest moment of human life. Christ saved us by sinlessly traversing, and thus sanctifying, every stage of human life on His way to the cross. The unborn are human beings, body and soul. The psalmist writes: "Have mercy on me, O God, according to Your steadfast love; according to Your abundant mercy blot out my transgressions. . . . Behold, I was brought forth in iniquity, and in sin did my mother conceive me" (Ps. 51:1, 5). The weak, the ill, and the elderly are, throughout the Bible, the objects of God's admonition to provide care. Christians must not overlook physical needs as if they might be easily separated from spiritual matters. That would be anti-incarnational.

The Church, like Christ Himself and faithful to His mandate, has a ministry to people in need, body and soul. It has a "double sacred duty."[20] Where the Church is missiologically weak, is it perhaps because we have divided body from soul? Can we be faithful to Christ by preaching the Gospel but ignoring the physical needs of people? Christ cared for body and soul. Gospel proclamation is affected when we fail to care for people in need, whether within or outside of the Church.[21] For "if a brother or sister is poorly clothed and lacking in daily food, and one of you says to them, 'Go in peace, be warmed and filled,' without giving them the things needed for the body, what good is that?" (James 2:15–16).[22]

IS MERCY STILL A SIGN OF THE KINGDOM?

It is a common assertion that the Church's care for the needy is a continuation of Jesus' healing ministry. I struggle with this thought and still cannot completely advocate it. There is a qualitative difference between Jesus' miracles and the care we can provide for the needy in our midst. Still, this statement does express a certain truth.

Christ instituted and mandated the preaching of the Gospel, Baptism, Absolution, and the Lord's Supper. They also are eschatological (that is, they are concerned with last things) because they look to eternity. When received in faith, the Word and Sacraments carry recipients through time into eternity with Christ. Instituted by Christ in His earthly ministry, through these means the Church continues Christ's ministry in His stead until the end of this world (1 John 5:6–12).

What about the miracles? Note what Jesus says in response to the question John the Baptist poses through his followers:

> [John's disciples asked,] "Are You the one who is to come, or shall we look for another?" And Jesus answered them, "Go and tell John what you hear and see: the blind receive their sight and the lame walk, lepers are cleansed and the deaf hear, and the dead are raised up, and the poor have good news preached to them." *Matthew 11:3–6*

Christ's miracles were the manifestation of His messianic work. They fulfilled the prophecies concerning the "one who is to come." God does what He desires in the lives of the saints. When miracles take place, they occur for the circumstance and persons concerned. They remain within God's hidden will. Miracles cannot be taken hold of, manipulated, or proclaimed as a mark of the Church. In fact, the New Testament promises the devil will do miracles too! (Matthew 24:24). The miracles that belong to the Church and infallibly testify to Christ and His forgiving Gospel are the Word and Sacraments (1 John 5:6–12).

The ministry of the Church offers a taste of the coming of the kingdom of Christ at the last. When Christ and His Word show up, the kingdom breaks out toward its full revelation at the last. Because of who the Church is and because of the Christian's life in Christ, acts of mercy and love by believers point toward a sinless and suffering-free eternity, as well as to the kingdom of God here and now on earth where sins are forgiven.

Christ's mandate to continue the ministry of the Church can be found in Matthew 28:19–20: "Go therefore . . . baptizing . . . teaching." This is a mandate to both the Church and the Office of the Holy Ministry. The small band of apostles who heard Jesus' words comprised both at the same time. Even as the apostles, after that first Pentecost, shared Christ through Word and Sacrament and merciful care of the needy, so also when we act in mercy, individually or corporately as the Body of Christ, we are Christ to the needy. Thereby we are a "continuation" of the love and care of Christ demonstrated to beggars in Palestine two thousand years ago. We are a continuation of Christ's presence and love shown through myriad saints across the ages in His Church. Just as the sufferings of Christ are perfect, fulfilled, and consummated in His Christians (1 Peter 4:13; Philippians 3:10; 2 Corinthians 1:5; Colossians 1:24), so also Christ's ministry of healing the sick once and for all demonstrated who He is. As the Church continues in mercy and love toward the needy, she does so as Christ's own hands and feet, bearing witness to His love.[23] The apostle Paul writes: "It is no longer I who live, but Christ who lives in me. And the life I now live in the flesh I live by faith in the Son of God" (Galatians 2:20).

In these last days, the love of Christ in the Church is summed up in the following:

1. Baptism and teaching the Gospel: "Go therefore and make disciples of all nations, baptizing them in the name of the Father and of the Son and of the Holy Spirit, teaching them to observe all that I have commanded you. And behold, I am with you always, to the end of the age" (Matthew 28:19–20).

2. The Office of the Keys: "If you forgive the sins of anyone, they are forgiven; if you withhold forgiveness from anyone, it is withheld" (John 20:23; see also Matthew 18:18; 16:19).

3. The Lord's Supper: "The Lord Jesus on the night when He was betrayed took bread, and when He had given thanks, He broke it, and said, 'This is My body which is for you. Do this in remem-

brance of Me.' In the same way also He took the cup, after supper, saying, 'This cup is the new covenant in My blood. Do this, as often as you drink it, in remembrance of Me.' For as often as you eat this bread and drink the cup, you proclaim the Lord's death until He comes" (1 Corinthians 11:23–26).

4. Mercy: "When the Son of Man comes in His glory . . . the King will say . . . 'Come, you who are blessed by My Father, inherit the kingdom prepared for you from the foundation of the world. For I was hungry and you gave Me food, I was thirsty and you give Me drink, I was a stranger and you welcomed Me, I was naked and you clothed Me, I was sick and you visited Me, I was in prison and you came to Me" (Matthew 25:31–36).

Preaching the Gospel, Baptism, the Office of the Keys, and the Lord's Supper are Christ's saving acts of mercy for forgiveness. They are the Church's infallible marks. The fourth item listed above, mercy, is Christ working in and through those who are His Body—the Church—to care for the needy, body and soul. However fallible and weak, Christ's Church will be marked by love for the needy. Where mercy received is not lived, such mercy received is denied. We are beggars—beggars who receive mercy and are merciful.

> Lord of all nations, grant me grace
> To love all people, ev'ry race;
> And in each person may I see
> My kindred, loved, redeemed by Thee.
>
> With Thine own love may I be filled
> And by Thy Holy Spirit willed,
> That all I touch, where'er I be,
> May be divinely touched by Thee.
> (*Lutheran Service Book* 844:1, 5)[24]
>
> *Kyrie eleison.*

NOTES

1   Joel R. Baseley, trans., *Festival Sermons of Martin Luther: The Church Postils, Winter and Summer Selections* (Dearborn, MI: Mark V. Publications, 2005), Summer Section, 25.

2   See Hermann Sasse, "Luther's Legacy to Christianity," in *The Lonely Way*, trans. Matthew C. Harrison et al. (St. Louis: Concordia, 2002), 2:171–77.

3   AE 50:286.

4   Edward Frederick Peters, *The Origin and Meaning of the Axiom: "Nothing Has the Character of a Sacrament outside of the Use," in Sixteenth-Century Lutheran Theology* (Fort Wayne, IN: Concordia Theological Seminary Press, 1993), 192f.

5   AE 50:293–94. See Martin Brecht, *Martin Luther: The Preservation of the Church, 1532–1546* (Minneapolis: Fortress, 1993), 369ff.

6   AE 51:392.

7   Sasse, "Luther's Legacy to Christianity," 2:172.

8   Brecht, *Preservation of the Church,* 376.

9   See Sasse, "Luther's Legacy to Christianity," 2:172; Brecht, *Preservation of the Church,* 376.

10   AE 54:476.

11   Jaroslav Pelikan, *The Christian Tradition* (Chicago: University of Chicago Press, 1971), 1:288.

12   Pelikan, *Christian Tradition,* 1:282.

13   See Hermann Sasse, "Church and Lord's Supper," in *The Lonely Way,* trans. Matthew C. Harrison et al. (St. Louis: Concordia, 2001), 1:413; and Werner Elert, *The Lord's Supper Today,* trans. Martin Bertram (St. Louis: Concordia, 1973), 27–32.

14   Ignatius, "To the Smyrnaeans," 8.1, in *Early Christian Fathers,* ed. and trans. Cyril C. Richardson, Library of Christian Classics 1 (Philadelphia: Westminster Press, 1953), 112ff.

15   Irenaeus, *First Apology of Justin,* LXVI, in *The Ante-Nicene Fathers* (Grand Rapids: Eerdmans, 1979), 1:185.

16   Ap XXII 10 (*Concordia,* 209).

17   SA III VIII 9 (*Concordia,* 281).

18   See LC II 54 (*Concordia,* 405).

19   LC II 37 (*Concordia,* 403).

20   Holger Sonntag, trans., *Löhe on Mercy,* ed. by Adriane Dorr and Philip Hendrickson (St. Louis: LCMS World Relief and Human Care, 2006), 42.

21   James W. Voelz, "Biblical Charity: What Does It Entail and How Does It Relate to the Gospel? A New Testament Perspective," in *A Cup of Cold Water: A Look at Biblical Charity,* ed. Robert Rosin and Charles Arand, Concordia Seminary Monograph Series 3 (St. Louis: Concordia Seminary, 1996), 86.

22   Bo Reicke has pointed out that this passage refers to the dismissal at the end of the Lord's Supper; see Bo Reicke, *Diakonie, Festfreude und Zelos: In Verbindung mit Der Altchristlichen Agapenfeier* (Uppsala: Lundequistska Bokhandeln, 1951), 37.

23   Ap V 71 (*Concordia,* 110).

24   Copyright © 1969 Concordia Publishing House. All rights reserved.

9

THE CHURCH: HOLY AND WHOLE

WE'RE ALL IN THIS TOGETHER

For just as the body is one and has many members, and all the members of the body, though many, are one body, so it is with Christ. *1 Corinthians 12:12*

The Church can never be better governed and preserved than if we all live under one head, Christ . . . diligently joined in unity of doctrine, faith, sacraments, prayer, works of love, and such.[1] *Martin Luther*

"The people want you to stay." I'll never forget how odd those words sounded to me in light of who I was. I was born in the United States in 1962 at the tail end of the baby boom and grew up with a strong sense of individualism. It was the nature of my generation to be individualistic in a community of individuals. Although Boomers drive individualism beyond the breaking point, they were not the first to think of it. The United States is a nation of individuals. Beginning with the Declaration of Independence and our "inalienable rights . . . of life, liberty, and the pursuit of happiness," the United States has been marked by rugged individualism. No caste, no class, no race, not even genetics can restrain the individual bent upon personal achievement.

My immigrant great-grandparents left Europe barely one hundred years ago for a better life in North America. Although distant relatives may still live on ancestral lands in European locales, only the thinnest wisp of rumor has survived in the family regarding those left in the old country. No contacts have endured. Few, if any, ethnic traditions have survived. My forebears struck out to make it on their own in a land of individual opportunities and never looked back. I am sure they often spoke the American mantra, as have I: "I can make it on my own."

For all that is good and right about individualism, it is a rather short trip to narcissism and self-centeredness. Such selfishness is willing to sacrifice honor, vocation, and family so that "I can do this for *me* so *I* can be happy." We look at our individual successes and puff up with pride. Then we see others and expect them to have the fortitude to "pull themselves up by the bootstraps" and grumble when the community is expected to help those who cannot even find their bootstraps, let alone grab them and pull.

The year before I headed to the seminary to study to become a pastor, I learned something about what it means to be part of a community. It forever changed my view of individualism and life together as the Church.

Flying into a remote Canadian Cree Indian village, my stomach fluttered from nervousness in the late October cold. A thousand frozen lakes alternated with dense pine forest below, causing fluctuating air currents to buffet the plane, which added insult to injury. Within minutes of landing on the ice, our packs hit the frozen lake in a muffled thud because of the thick blanket of snow. Soon thereafter, my wife and I stood on the ice as the Cessna decked out with snow skis disappeared from sight. As the sound of the plane faded, our anxiety grew. We did not know a soul in Deer Lake, Ontario, a community of five hundred native Canadians. The two of us brought the grand total of Caucasians to five. But this is where we would be lay missionaries for the year in a great cross-cultural adventure that followed our completion of college at Concordia, Seward, Nebraska. At that moment we had never felt so alone.

But that feeling did not last for long. Several members of the community took me under their wings and taught me how to survive in the Canadian bush. They taught me the Cree language, how to fish, how to make snowshoes from moose hide, and how to read the ice on the lake. I learned to set rabbit snares and to stay alive in forty-below temperatures. I played my banjo and sang English and Cree songs each week with the community singers on their radio station.

The residents of Deer Lake shared everything they had with us. They made us members of their community, and their generosity was abundant. Individuals had all the personal property they wanted or could acquire, but boundaries of "personal possession" were fluid for the Cree. An individual could acquire food, tools, skidoo—but whoever had need of it could use the commodity. The Cree extended this culture of sharing to us. Adian Kakagumik (pronounced Ka-ka-GUM-ik) was born in a bark teepee and spent his entire eighty years in the bush. I came to love the old man, and he treated me like a son. Adian and I would check the nets under the ice and bring the fish to the village. Each of us would take a few fish for the next day or two, and the rest would be left on the frozen ground for whomever took them. No one went hungry. We always had enough.

PRIDE GOETH BEFORE DESTRUCTION

One humorous event reminds me of my propensity toward pride and arrogance. Early in our stay with the Cree, I needed to take my snowmobile and a sled into the bush to find firewood, large quantities of which were needed to heat a small cabin through the Northern Ontario winter. After surveying how the Cree men used small ramshackle sleds to haul a pittance of wood from the bush, I decided to build a "proper" sled to carry large quantities of dry Jack pine (the wood of choice for heating). In the woodworking shop of one of the other Caucasians, I produced a wood sled to drool over. I headed down the frozen lake with a friend, empty sled in tow. I stopped as two Cree friends buzzed up on their machines, their "pathetic" sleds in tow. With classic Cree disinterest, they surveyed my handiwork. I bragged about its capacity, casting an occasional derisive glance toward their sleds. The conversation complete, my friend and I continued on our journey.

I pulled into a small frozen cove and spied a stand of dead Jack pine atop a granite cliff perhaps sixty feet high. I parked my snowmobile and sled, hiked to the top of the cliff, and carefully made my way to the trees. I surveyed the first candidate for cutting and determined the circumstances were perfect. I would topple the large pine, which when felled would rest on the edge of the cliff. Then I would carefully push it over the cliff to the ice-covered lake below (near my snowmobile), where I would saw the log into sections for loading.

I was enjoying the testosterone-filled moment: the noise of a gas engine buzzing at a high revolutions per minute, sawdust flying, exhaust filling the pristine frigid air. Tasting conquest, I stepped back, smiling confidently. I watched as the tree fell toward the edge of the granite cliff. Suddenly, I realized I had made a miscalculation. The tree was considerably taller than I had calculated. Instead of falling to rest on *the edge* of the cliff, it catapulted over the cliff, did a full flip in the air, and came to rest below with a terrific "ccrrraaaaaaaack." Yes, you guessed it, the heavy trunk landed squarely on top of my new sled. My "proper" sled was smashed to smithereens.

Like characters in a Greek tragedy, my two Cree friends drove up at just that moment. They looked at what had been my pride and joy. As I stood above them, mouth gaping, chainsaw in hand, they called out, "Hey, White Man! What happened to your sled?"

I responded, "I was trying to stack the wood from on top of the cliff."

They roared with laughter and sped into the bush.

It was a blessing. Each blunder, each request for advice, only endeared me to the community. I eventually learned that the goal is not for one man to collect a mountain of firewood but enough to survive the day and, as a member of the community, to make sure others survive as well. Jesus said, "Do not be anxious about tomorrow, for tomorrow will be anxious for itself. Sufficient for the day is its own trouble" (Matthew 6:34).

As the final weeks of our unforgettable year began, the Cree sent an official emissary, Cenadius Fiddler, to my wife and me. He sat for a long time in our little cabin before he came to the reason for his visit. "The people want you to stay," he said.

The people . . . As our year with the Cree had progressed, we moved from being simply *Whemph-ta-goozh ee-quay* and *Whemph-ta-goozh-ee—White Woman* and *White Man—*to *Whemph-ta-goozh Matt* and *Whemph-ta-goozh Kathy*. Finally we were simply *Matt* and *Kathy*. But far more important than what we or any of the Cree were as individuals, "the people" opened their community and took us in. Cenadius did not say "The chief wants you to stay" or "The Band Council wants you to stay" or "The old people want you to stay" or "The church elders want you to stay" or even "I want you to stay." He said, "*The people* want you to stay." I was deeply humbled and honored. I learned something about community, about the "we," that year that I had not previously experienced. In fact, as much as it was possible for nonnative Canadians, we became part of the "people."

WHOLE

The New Testament has a great deal to say about "the people" of Christ, the "we." But "we" often overlook what Scripture says because we are thinking "I." Good old American individualism is alive and well in the Church, and it determines how we read the Bible. American religiosity is all about "me." American Protestantism and fundamentalism have, in large measure, adopted the U.S. consumer and marketing perspective; thus all different types of churches are marketing Jesus to particular segments of the community. Individually, we are lords of our lives. No community or family can tell me what my personal faith should be. I can define it myself, then find a church to give me what I think I need.

But we are in this together.[2] Christ gives life, and that life is lived out in a community. The Lord's Supper is a community meal: "You [plural] take drink, this is My blood . . . . Do this as often as you [plural] drink it, in remembrance of Me." The author of the Epistle to the Hebrews writes: "Let us [plural] hold fast the confession . . . . And let us consider how to stir up one another to love and good works, not neglecting to meet together, as is the habit of some" (10:23–25). And Luke records that in the earliest days of the Church "they [plural] devoted themselves to the apostles' teaching and fellowship" (Acts 2:42).

The Church is both whole and holy. As individuals steeped in our culture of individualism, we are very much prone to regard matters of faith and life from the perspective of "me," the pious individual, and my personal experience:

Who am *I*?

What is *my* personal mission?

What is *my* personal relationship with Jesus?

What kind of worship do *I* like?

How do *I* like to take Communion?

What does Jesus mean to *me*?

What do *I* get out of it?

What kind of pastor do *I* like?

Do people at church pay enough attention to *my* ideas?

Do *I* have a personal devotional life?

How much of *my* money do I give?

What kind of congregation do I need to meet *my* needs?

How can I best use *my* gifts to serve the Lord?

What can *I* do at church?

The New Testament, while addressing many of these questions, proceeds from quite a different viewpoint. The apostle Paul writes: "For I decided to know nothing among you except Jesus Christ and Him crucified" (1 Corinthians 2:2). The epicenter of the Christian faith and life is Jesus. I can be sure that if I am the subject doing the verb, then the focus is on me and not Jesus. That means it is probably about something I am doing, not what Jesus has done or is doing. That means it is Law, not forgiving Gospel, which is the life of Christ and His work for me. God's Word sanctifies us (1 Timothy 4:5). His Word sanctifies water for a holy washing in Baptism (Titus 3:5). Jesus' body and blood, actually present in and with the bread and wine, sanctify us and make us the temple of God—together.

Everything Jesus does places people into a community of believers, into the Church. Jesus says, "I have other sheep that are not of this fold. I must bring them also" (John 10:16). The ninety-nine are left so the one can be found and returned to the flock. The plurals are used in Holy Scripture on purpose. Just consider this exchange between Jesus and Peter: " 'But you! Who do *you* say that I am?' And Peter answered for them all, 'But Thou art the Christ, the Son of God' " (Matthew 16:26 RSV); or Jesus' words to the disciples: "And He strictly charged *them* to tell no one" (Mark 8:30, *emphasis added*).

One by one Jesus called individuals into the community of His disciples (Matthew 10:1ff.). He taught them together, sent them out together, criticized them together, praised them together, lamented them together, gave them His Holy Supper together, prayed with them together, gave His promises to them together. Jesus promised the Holy Spirit would be in and among His disciples: "You know Him, for He dwells with you [plural] and will be in you [plural]" (John 14:17).

Jesus told His disciples they would be in paradise together with Him, yet as He died they scattered. After His resurrection, Jesus appeared alive to His disciples as they were gathered together. And the Holy Spirit came upon the community as "they were all together in one place" (Acts 2:1).

Jesus' parables describe the kingdom of heaven as a community event (Matthew 22:1–14, the parable of the wedding feast). Jesus is the singular bridegroom, but the Bride, His Church, is always plural. Greatness in the kingdom is measured by service to others: "But whoever would be great among you must be your [plural] servant" (Matthew 20:26). Christ is the vine with many branches that bear fruit (John 15:1ff.), even as He prayed for all believers "that they may become perfectly one" (John 17:23). Jesus laid down His life for His friends (plural) (John 15:13) and calls His disciples likewise to "love one another" (community, John 13:34).

Yes, the New Testament does often speak of the faith and confession of the individual. Consider Galatians 2:19–20: "For through the law I died to the law, so that I might live to God. I have been crucified with Christ. It is no longer I who live, but Christ who lives in me. And the life I now live in the flesh I live by faith in the Son of God, who loved me and gave Himself for me." However, the individual Christian is never viewed apart from the Church.

No matter the emphasis on individual faith, individual prayer, individual vocation, and so on, whether in the person of Jesus or among believers, the great New Testament sweep of divine action is plural. It is an ingathering ("I will make you [plural] fishers of men," Matthew 4:19). The great events of the New Testament are plural: "they were *all* filled with the Holy Spirit" (Acts 2:4); "and *many* of the Corinthians hearing Paul believed and were baptized" (Acts 18:8); "*many* of them therefore believed" (Acts 17:12); "as *many* of you as were baptized into Christ have put on Christ" (Galatians 3:27); "when *you* [plural] come together" (for the Lord's Supper, 1 Corinthians 11:20). Together "the *entire* Church confesses that eternal life is attained through mercy."[3]

HOLY

Toward the end of the Preface in the liturgy for Holy Communion, the pastor states: "Therefore with angels and archangels and with all the company of heaven we laud and magnify Your glorious name, evermore praising You and saying . . ."[4] Then the congregation belts out the Sanctus: "Holy, holy, holy Lord God of Sabaoth; heav'n and earth are full of Thy glory," quoting Isaiah 6:3 and Revelation 4:8.[5] This earthly community of believers is joined with the heavenly host where earth and heaven meet in the body and blood of Christ. That body and blood makes us evermore Christ's Body, the Church.

The Church is whole and she is holy with the holiness of Christ. In the Third Article of the Apostles' Creed (which addresses sanctification), we confess, "I believe in the Holy Spirit, the holy Christian Church, the communion of saints, the forgiveness of sins, the resurrection of the body, and the life everlasting. Amen." The Holy Spirit brings about "church" and its corporate realities. Our individualistic era is prone to think of this "holiness" only in terms of the Christian individual. Thus sanctification, or the life of forgiveness lived toward God and neighbor, is defined almost exclusively in terms of individual faith, life, and action. But sanctification is also a corporate reality because the whole Church is given the holiness of one Christ. The Apostles' Creed confesses God the Holy Spirit, and immediately the Church, the communion of saints. This is significant for a book about the Church's life of mercy. Too often the mandate for mercy is limited to the individual Christian in his or her individual vocation in the world. But just as the individual has a vocation to mercy, so the whole Church, the body, the plural, the community is holy and called to a corporate lived holiness.

More than a century ago, Theodosius Harnack complained that Lutherans did not view *diakonia*, or the Church's work of mercy, as part and parcel of the doctrine of the Church. Instead, Lutherans considered the work of mercy as something that belonged to parachurch groups and organizations.[6] That describes the theological/practical reality I often see in the LCMS in terms of her related social ministry organizations. The doctrine of sanctification as traditionally explicated in Lutheranism deals only with the individual, which is good and true as far as it goes. But it is difficult to find among us a doctrinal or biblical exposition of the holiness of the Church as it lives out its life as a community. One must dig deep in journals and denominational history to find writers that relate the Lutheran theology to *diakonia*/mercy. Too often, the communal and corporate life of mercy is regarded as something neither commanded nor forbidden (that is, an *adiaphoron*). Mercy is not fundamental to the fabric of a congregation's life. But sanctification is a communal, corporate reality. Luther wrote:

> There is hospitality wherever the church is. For the church, if I may say so, always has a common treasury, inasmuch as it has the command (Matt. 5:42): "Give to him who begs from you." And we must all serve the church and take care of it, not only by teaching but also by showing kindness and giving assistance, so that at the same time both the spirit and the flesh may find refreshment in the church.[7]

THE NEW TESTAMENT

The New Testament drives us toward a corporate view of sanctification. There one finds that the Church is a community that reflects who God is. From the trinitarian shout of "Holy, Holy, Holy" in Isaiah 6 to its repetition in Revelation 4:8, the Bible teaches the corporate communal nature of the Holy Trinity. For example, Jesus calls the Father "holy Father" (John 17:11). The apostle Peter writes, "He who called you is holy" (1 Peter 1:15). The Lord's Prayer calls on the Church to hallow God's name, which can be none other than that one name into which we are baptized—Father, Son, and Holy Spirit (Matthew 28:19). God is Father, Son, and Holy Spirit in communal unity and holiness.

Yahweh showed Himself as "holy" to His Old Testament people (see Leviticus 10:3). His holiness was communicated through His glory, that is, His holy presence for forgiveness. At the time of the exodus and the wilderness wandering, God's glory was manifest in the pillar of cloud by day and the pillar of fire by night. Later, when Solomon had completed the temple as a permanent place of worship, note what happened when the ark of the covenant was brought into the temple: "When the priests came out of the Holy Place, a cloud filled the house of the LORD, so that the priests could not stand to minister because of the cloud, for the glory of the LORD filled the house of the LORD" (1 Kings 8:10–11). We see clearly in Solomon's prayer at the dedication of the temple that though Yahweh fills the earth, and no temple can contain Him, nevertheless Yahweh promised to dwell *there* with His name (1 Kings 8:29). God purposely forgave at that place.

According to the Bible, all forgiveness is local. People gather to receive forgiveness in community. Located glory and holiness without Yahweh's name and forgiveness leave only a dangerous encounter with unmasked divinity. Just as "the glory of the LORD filled the house of the LORD" (1 Kings 8:11), so the New Testament presence of God and His forgiveness is also located in a place. That place is in the person of Jesus, true God and true man.

The apostle John writes that "the Word became flesh and dwelt among us. We have seen His *doxa* ["glory"], the *doxa* of the only begotten of the Father" (John 1:14, *author's translation*). Jesus is the New Testament Holy of Holies. And now after His resurrection, the Holy of Holies is Christ's body and blood in Holy Communion, located in, with, and under earthly bread and wine (Hebrews 10:19–20). Jesus is called the "Holy One" (Mark 1:24; Luke 4:34: John 6:69; Acts 3:14; 1 John 2:20; Revelation 3:7), and He gathers His Church and makes it holy.

Sanctification is also communal. Paul addresses the recipients of his letters, "To the saints [plural]." Whether holiness is imputed to us from outside ourselves (*extra nos*) or is something in which we are made to grow in Christ, it is communal or corporate. In 1 Peter we read, "As obedient children, do not be conformed to the passions of your former ignorance, but as He who called you is holy, you also be holy in all your conduct, since it is written, 'You [plural] shall be holy, for I am holy'" (1 Peter 1:14–16). Communal aspects of holiness mark St. Peter's writings. For example, "Having purified your souls by your obedience to the truth for a sincere brotherly love, love one another earnestly from a pure heart" (1 Peter 1:22). Or, "You yourselves like living stones are being built up as a spiritual house, to be a holy priesthood, to offer spiritual sacrifices acceptable to God through Jesus Christ. . . . You are a chosen race, a royal priesthood, a holy nation" (1 Peter 2:5, 9). Thus Wilhelm Löhe could write, "His whole church is outwardly nothing but a priestly, royal institute of mercy."[8]

Paul's letters also are filled with the corporate nature of sanctification. For example, "Christ Jesus . . . *our* righteousness and sanctification and redemption" (1 Corinthians 1:30, *emphasis added*). Or, "Do you not know that *you* [*yourselves*, plural] are God's temple and that God's Spirit dwells in *you* [or "among *you*," plural]? If anyone destroys God's temple, God will destroy him. For God's temple is holy, and *you* [plural] are that temple" (1 Corinthians 3:16–17). Paul calls the Corinthians "holy" precisely as a unified body. The temple suffering destruction is not the individual, but the Church as a body, torn by disagreement or by individuals going it alone. Sexual immorality defiles not merely the one engaged in such activity (1 Corinthians 6:18ff.), but it is a defilement of Christ's Body, the Church (1 Corinthians 6:15ff.). Each Christian is a temple of the Holy Spirit (1 Corinthians 6:19), and the instant the Holy Spirit dwells in an individual heart, that individual is made a member of Christ's Body, the Church.

An early pastor of the LCMS expressed the practical consequence of all the above:

> Now what Christ says applies to every individual, true faith's fruit and proof—namely love, active, self-sacrificing, self-denying love—also applies to an entire community [*Gemeine*] of Christians. If the preaching of Christ has occurred with power within that community, if it has begun to grow deep roots, it will also be the case within the community as a whole that this love more and more will come into evidence. Works of love will no longer be those of individual members of the community; rather the community as a whole will take part in them.[9]

In Acts 2:42 the Church is described as a community dedicated to the apostles' teaching, to fellowship, to the Lord's Supper, and to common worship. It is a fellowship created by Christ and His Gospel. It is a fellowship of faith, a fellowship of love. In his Small Catechism, Luther writes that "God's kingdom comes when our heavenly Father gives us His Holy Spirit, so that by His grace we believe His holy Word and lead godly lives here in time and there in eternity."[10] Luke records that "all who believed were together and had all things in common" (Acts 2:44) and that "there was not a needy person among them" (Acts 4:34).

We were given a small (one-room) ramshackle frame cabin to be our home that year with the Cree Indians. We had managed to locate only a few odd pieces of furniture when word got out in the village about our predicament. The young chief stopped by and said, "Come by my house. We have a table for you."

I did not want to be a burden, so I tried to decline tactfully. I will never forget his answer; it was so matter-of-fact and so indicative of his culture, which favored such ideas and was supported in that direction by Christianity. He replied, "We have two tables; you have none. Come get it."

God grant us such love in the Church. After all, we are in this together. Where Christ and His Gospel are, there the Church is—whole, holy, and wholly merciful.

> Before our Father's throne
> We pour our ardent prayers;
> Our fears, our hopes, our aims are one,
> Our comforts and our cares.
>
> We share our mutual woes,
> Our mutual burdens bear,
> And often for each other flows
> The sympathizing tear.
> (*Lutheran Service Book* 649:2–3)
>
> We poor sinners implore You
> To hear us, O Lord.
> To rule and govern Your holy Christian Church . . . in the true
> knowledge and understanding of Your wholesome Word and to
> sustain them in holy living . . .
> O Lord, have mercy.
> O Christ, have mercy.
> O Lord, have mercy.
> (The Litany, *Lutheran Service Book*, pp. 288–89)

NOTES

1 SA II IV 9 (*Concordia*, 269).

2 AE 9:148.

3 Ap V 201 (*Concordia*, 132) (*emphasis added*).

4 *Lutheran Service Book: Altar Book*, p. 161.

5 *Lutheran Service Book*, p. 195.

6 Carter Lindberg, "Luther's Concept of Offering," *Dialog* 35, no. 4 (Fall 1996): 252.

7 AE 3:178.

8 Holger Sonntag, trans., *Löhe on Mercy*, ed. by Adriane Dorr and Philip Hendrickson (St. Louis: LCMS World Relief and Human Care, 2006), 22–23.

9 Theodore Julius Brohm, *Mercy and the Lutheran Congregation*, trans. Matthew C. Harrison (St. Louis: LCMS World Relief and Human Care, 2007), 7.

10 *Luther's Small Catechism with Explanation*, p. 20.

10

GOD AGAINST GOD

CROSS, SUFFERING, AND WHAT GOD MAKES OF IT

Though He slay me, I will hope in Him. *Job 13:15*

This God . . . dressed in His promises . . . we can grasp and look at with joy and trust. The absolute God, on the other hand, is like an iron wall, against which we cannot bump without destroying ourselves.[1] *Martin Luther*

Barely a week after the great Asian tsunami, I stood staring at miles of total devastation, a devastation beyond comprehension. Before me were the remains of the Queen of the Sea, a famous Sri Lankan train. The red passenger cars of the wreckage were permeated with the stench of thousands of lost lives. As if in funeral procession, volunteers continued to search for and find the dead. Why did this happen?

I did not know Pastor Ranjith Fernando, but I needed to see for myself the wreckage of the train in which he was traveling when the earthquake-generated waves struck. The first wave had stalled the train, and hundreds made their way to the rooftops of the cars to wait for rescue. Then came a second wave some forty feet high, which hurled the train into the local neighborhood, leaving many of the passenger cars on rooftops. Pastor Fernando, who recently had translated the Book of Concord into Sinhalese, was drowned along with his wife and as many as two thousand other passengers and town residents. Why? I had no answer.

As we were waiting in Paris for the flight to Colombo, Sri Lanka, a group of relief workers from an evangelical Protestant denomination in the United States traded information with me and my traveling companions. One good-natured man pulled me aside and said, "Our people in Sri Lanka tell us they are having great effectiveness in evangelizing." I was interested, and he continued, "They are asking Hindus, Buddhists, and Muslims, 'Where was your god in all this? Was he strong enough to prevent this evil from coming upon you? Jesus Christ can protect you!'"

I thought of the more than two hundred thousand dead. I

thought of Pastor Fernando. I acknowledged the man's comment with a slight smile that belied my internal rage. Inwardly I cringed as if sucker punched. Believe in Jesus and disaster won't strike you? How ironic that I soon found Muslims, Buddhists, and Hindus who were proselytizing with the same questions—albeit inserting their own gods. The evangelicals I met in Paris and the Christ-less religions of the East offered only the crushing anvil of a god of disaster: "God used this tsunami to strike you because you had things wrong religiously."

Lutherans understand suffering as Christ did. We confess with the New Testament and with Martin Luther:

> That person does not deserve to be called a theologian who looks upon the invisible things of God as though they were clearly perceptible in those things which have actually happened [Rom. 1:20]. He deserves to be called a theologian, however, who comprehends the visible and manifest things of God seen through suffering and the cross.[2]

Would a benevolent God cause a massive earthquake that generates massive waves that kill hundreds of thousands? Would an all-powerful God allow this? Is God good? Is God really in control of the world He created? Is there a God? These questions are always heard after death and destruction make such a dramatic mark on human existence. The only answers the Lord gives us are in Christ and His cross. Mark's Gospel bears this out in a remarkable way.

JESUS IS REVEALED IN SUFFERING

At Jesus' Baptism, the Father says from heaven, "You are My beloved Son" (Mark 1:11). Here at the beginning of His earthly ministry, at the beginning of this Gospel account, Jesus is correctly identified as the Son of God. After that, no one in Mark's Gospel (aside from the demons) gets who Jesus is! Jesus healed the paralyzed man only to have the religious officials scoff, "Why does this man speak like that? He is blaspheming!" (Mark 2:7). Then scribes came from Jerusalem and said, "He is possessed by Beelzebul" (Mark 3:22). After Jesus calmed the waves, the disciples asked, "Who then is this, that even wind and sea obey Him?" (Mark 4:41). Jesus casts demons from a man into a herd of pigs only to have the locals plead, "Go away!" (see Mark 5:17). He teaches in his hometown synagogue but the people of

Nazareth are offended, to which Jesus replied, "A prophet is not without honor except in his hometown" (Mark 6:4). For one moment, Peter appeared to get it right: "You are the Christ," he confessed (Mark 8:29). But when Jesus told His disciples that being the Christ meant the cross, Peter "rebuked [Jesus]," to which Jesus replied, "Get behind Me, Satan!" (Mark 8:33). Jesus repeatedly told His followers that He would be killed but would rise on the third day, but "they did not understand" (Mark 9:32). The crowds in Jerusalem sang Jesus' praise as they waved palm fronds, which were symbols of Palestinian liberation, but they got Jesus wrong too (Mark 11:9–10). At Jesus' trial, the high priest could not quite bear to call Jesus who He was when he asked, "Are You the Christ, the Son of the Blessed?" But when Jesus answered, "I am," the priest tore his robe and accused Jesus of blasphemy (Mark 14:61–64). On that first Good Friday, the crowd wanted Jesus' blood. "Crucify Him!" they shouted (Mark 15:13). "Hail, King of the Jews!" the Roman soldiers mocked (Mark 15:18). At Calvary, the passersby taunted Him, calling out, "Save Yourself!" (Mark 15:29–30). Even the criminals crucified with Jesus "reviled Him" (Mark 15:32). And when Jesus called out in agony the words of Psalm 22—"My God, My God, why have You forsaken Me?"—those watching His death got that wrong, too, thinking He was calling for Elijah (Mark 15:35).

Only one man got Jesus right. When our Savior cried out and "breathed His last . . . the centurion, who stood facing Him . . . said, 'Truly this man *was the Son of God*!' " (Mark 15:37, 39). Only when face-to-face with God hanging dead on the cross does someone finally get it right.

Jesus Christ, the Son of God, came to suffer and to die for us. Although risen, He remains the "crucified one" (see 1 Corinthians 2:2). What does that fact mean in the aftermath of a tsunami? I do not know the hidden will of God. However, I do know His revealed will in Holy Scripture. From the cross, God worked His most profound deed—the salvation of all sinners. Jesus' suffering is salvation. His suffering is mercy. God works through and is revealed in suffering. I plunge my feeble and sinful thoughts into Christ's suffering, where I learn that amid trials and crosses, disaster upon disaster, God loves us in Christ. And there, only there, do I find consolation amid the devastation. Faith knows that resurrection follows Good Friday.

The women stood at a distance and watched Jesus die—the situation appeared hopeless (Mark 15:40). This looked to be the end. Perhaps the women thought, "God hates this Jesus and us," or maybe even, "There is no God—or certainly no God who cares about us." Yet right there, on Good Friday, God the Father was doing what He had prepared to do from all eternity for the salvation of the world. The apex of God's love acting in history was veiled and hidden by a bloody, wretched body on the cross.

Where was God in the tsunami? Where He always is—in Christ, in suffering, in the cross. Why did God not prevent the death and destruction? That question merely reveals our selfish desire to be God and demand that He reveal more than what He wills. There is no Elijah or Jeremiah to prophesy to us concerning the reasons. We have a better line of communication: "In these last days He has spoken to us by His Son" (Hebrews 1:2). What I do know I know because God has revealed it to me in Christ and in His Word: "God so loved the world" (John 3:16). Luther writes that "we must take hold of this God, not naked but clothed and revealed in His Word; otherwise certain despair will crush us."[3] The tsunamis of life drive us to confess, "Truly this man was the Son of God!" (Mark 15:39).

GOD AGAINST GOD

We suffer many things in this life. We often suffer because of poor choices. We suffer because of the actions of others. We suffer the ravages of sin and time called "aging." Some of us suffer disease and illness because of genetics. Some suffer illness or death at an inexplicably young age. Some of us die untimely deaths because we are in the wrong place at the wrong time. Christians suffer in the world for being Christians, whether by martyrdom or by ridicule at school or in the workplace. We all die.

The Bible tells us repeatedly that "God is love" (1 John 4:8) and that "in Him we live and move and have our being" (Acts 17:28). All things are within the purview of God's providential control. God is love (1 John 4:7–8) and He is all-powerful. So what do we say when the revealed God of the Bible contradicts the workings of the all-powerful God in our lives or the lives of those around us? If God loves me, why is He doing this to me? The Bible does give some answers.

God threw Abraham into a great contradiction, a true test of faith. God had promised Abraham, "In you all the families of the earth shall be blessed" (Genesis 12:3), and Isaac was the son of the promise. But then God tested Abraham, saying, "Take your son, your only son Isaac, whom you love, and go to the land of Moriah, and offer him there as a burnt offering on one of the mountains of which I shall tell you" (Genesis 22:2). By faith Abraham proceeded to Moriah and bound his son, though God was in apparent contradiction to Himself and His promise. But "faith reconciles opposites,"[4] and Abraham believed that though his son would die, God could raise the dead (see Hebrews 11:17–19). God against God.

Sold into slavery by his brothers, by all appearances, by every "sight" and sense, God had abandoned Joseph. Yet years later, when he revealed his true identity to his brothers, Joseph made a startling confession. The Lord had used the sinful, evil action of his brothers for good. The former slave confessed: "I am your brother, Joseph, whom you sold into Egypt. And now do not be distressed or angry with yourselves because you sold me here, for God sent me before you to preserve life. . . . So it was not you who sent me here, but God. . . . You meant evil against me, but God meant it for good" (Genesis 45:4–8; 50:20). Joseph told his brothers not to be troubled because even their sinful action was co-opted to serve God's will. No, God is not the cause or source of sin. But God does work in afflictions in ways quite contrary to what we would expect. God against God.

Satan was granted the opportunity to "test" Job, who then suffered horribly. At the height of his sufferings, Job's wife bid him "curse God and die" (Job 2:9). By all the evidence, God hated Job and was intent on destroying him. And Job freely granted that he was suffering at the hands of God, saying, "The arrows of the Almighty are in me; my spirit drinks their poison; God's terrors are arrayed against me" (Job 6:4; see also Job 3:23). Like the religious experts in the wake of the tsunami, Job's friends figured the destruction he was suffering was the result of God's desire to destroy him. Amazingly and despite his suffering, Job unwaveringly trusted God. "Though He slay me," said Job, "I will hope in Him" (Job 13:15). God against God.

Three times St. Paul prayed for his "thorn in the flesh" to be taken away (2 Corinthians 12:8). What sort of ailment it was, no one knows. The great mystery is that St. Paul clearly calls the affliction a "messenger of Satan" (2 Corinthians 12:7) and firmly believes that this satanic missive is within God's control.[5] God Himself had afflicted Paul with the thorn, and God Himself could remove it. But Paul writes that in answer to his pleas, God said, "My grace is sufficient for you, for My power is made perfect in weakness" (2 Corinthians 12:9). According to Luther, "when God wants to strengthen a man's faith He acts as if He wants to injure his faith. He puts him in a position where he would not regard God as trustworthy or believe Him. God throws him into all kinds of tragedy, and makes him so weary that he must completely despair."[6]

Only in the cross of Jesus does one grasp the mystery and contradiction of suffering. Reason cannot understand or reconcile this reality.[7] Luther writes, "Reason seeks thus to inquire into God, it does not find him."[8] On one level, the sufferings and death of Christ are the result of cowardly disciples. There also were a traitor, small-minded rulers, an agnostic Roman ("What is truth?" John 18:38), and a crowd of angry first-century Jews. While all these sins remain firmly the fault and result of the humans who perpetrated them, the death of Christ is much more than the result of human sins. It is the action of God in Christ, an action planned from eternity. Jesus explains, "For this reason the Father loves Me, because I lay down My life that I may take it up again. No one takes it from Me, but I lay it down of My own accord. I have authority to lay it down, and I have authority to take it up again" (John 10:17–18). Jesus, the divine and beloved Son of God, suffers at the will of the Father. "Not as I will, but as You will," Jesus prayed in the garden (Matthew 26:39). God the Father wills and effects the suffering of God the Son. God against God.

DOES GOD WILL SUFFERING?

No one can bring us any sorrow unless Christ wants it to happen.[9] *Martin Luther*

Popular religion would have us believe that God does not want us to suffer. But God's Word proclaims this false: "It is for discipline that you have to endure. God is treating you as sons. For what son is there whom his father does not discipline?" (Hebrews 12:7). God willed the suffering of Abraham, Job, the apostle Paul, and, above all, Jesus Christ. Often it is not clear what good may come of suffering, yet Christians are as certain of God's good purposes in suffering as they are in the very cross of Jesus Himself. The Lutheran Confessions state:

> Therefore, troubles are not always punishments or signs of wrath. Indeed, terrified consciences should be taught that there are more important purposes for afflictions [2 Corinthians 12:9], so that they do not think God is rejecting them when they see nothing but God's punishment and anger in troubles. The other more important purposes are to be considered, that is, that God is doing His strange work so that He may be able to do His own work, as Isaiah 28 teaches . . . . Therefore, troubles are not always punishments for certain past deeds, but they are God's works, intended for our benefit, and that God's power might be made more apparent in our weakness.[10]

Suffering and afflictions in the lives of Christians are much like the cross of Jesus. It is the most horrid outpouring of wrath upon sin: "He made Him to be sin who knew no sin . . ." The cross is also, at the same time, the greatest act of the Gospel: "For our sake He made Him to be sin who knew no sin, *so that in Him we might become the righteousness of God*" (2 Corinthians 5:21, *emphasis added*). Luther writes: "[Christ] had to die as an evil man and [sin] had no right to Him. That is how He pays for those sins on your behalf and His flood of mercy gushes out on you."[11] Yet it is quite clear Jesus' followers by no means recognized the Gospel taking place on Calvary. The disciples walking with the resurrected Jesus on the road to Emmaus said, "Our chief priests and rulers . . . crucified Him. But we had hoped that He was the one to redeem Israel" (Luke 24:20–21). What irony. By His crucifixion, Jesus *did* redeem Israel!

Christians find themselves in similar circumstances. They may cry out, "I am being crucified—suffering all sorts of pain, affliction, and difficulty—but I had hoped that God loved me." Yet in God's mysterious way of working, it is precisely in trial and affliction that His loving will is accomplished. By this "strange" or foreign work, God lays hold of us, humbles us, brings about repentance, causes us to think of divine things, and, finally, drives us to the cross and brings us in faith to eternal life. This is how the Lord makes us like our father Abraham, so that it may be said also of us, "In hope he believed against hope" (Romans 4:18). In fact, Luther points out that "he who is not a *crucianus* [a crossbearer], so to speak, is not a *Christianus* [a Christian]: he who does not bear his cross is no Christian, for he is not like his Master, Christ."[12]

MAN VALUES PEACE AND HAPPINESS; GOD VALUES THE CROSS

We value peace, painlessness, happiness, and material comfort. The Lord values the cross and affliction. The psalmist writes, "Precious in the sight of the LORD is the death of His saints" (Psalm 116:15). The Gospel according to John records Jesus' references to His crucifixion as a "glorification": "The hour has come for the Son of Man to be glorified. Truly, truly, I say to you, unless a grain of wheat falls into the earth and dies, it remains alone; but if it dies, it bears much fruit" (John 12:23–24; see also John 13:31–32; 17:1).

In our postmodern world, suffering is increasingly considered meaningless and, therefore, intolerable for any reason. Utilitarian ethics[13] seek to eliminate all hindrances to individual "happiness," especially suffering and even life itself if need be. Like the prodigal of Jesus' parable, we rush away from our father's house (two millennia of ethics informed by the Christian faith) to the pig's trough of captivity to individual choice, which shuns suffering at all costs. But when the going is tough and we shun suffering (none of us should seek it out)—whether by actively ending life or setting aside the holy vocations of spouse, parent, friend, or child—we shun the way God worked on Calvary. We block the way God brings about His goodwill and purposes for us in this life. When we shun suffering by failing to view it in the light of Christ, we shun the cross of Christ. When we shun our suffering neighbor, we shun a "living relic" of the cross. When we put to death those who are suffering instead of caring mercifully, we are putting to death Christ in our neighbor. Luther reminds us, "The poor man in whom God's Word lives is right here."[14] We venerate the cross by caring for our neighbor in need.

I have heard elderly Christians in the final frail days of life say, "Just give me a pill and be done with it!" I have heard them ask, "Why is the Lord continuing to keep me alive in this misery?" The answers are not readily evident, but I do know that the greatest gift elderly Christians can give their family is demonstrating how a Christian dies in the faith, reconciled to God and family in Christ. My mother often asked why my grandmother continued to live well into her nineties, though suffering from dementia. My grandmother suffered exactly what was within the Lord's will for her benefit and perhaps even more so for the benefit of the family. As God told the apostle Paul, "My grace is sufficient for you, for My power is made perfect in weakness" (2 Corinthians 12:9).

The Lutheran Confessions state: "Afflictions are a discipline by which God exercises the saints."[15] The way to divine and eternal happiness is the way of the cross. Suffering poses a myriad of unfathomable and unanswerable questions. What God is doing in a tsunami that takes more than two hundred thousand lives is as complex and varied as each precious life affected, including the millions upon millions (many of whom are Christians) who are left to mourn.[16] As complex as that great question so also is the microcosm of suffering when it comes to our own door. But the Lord has not left us without consolation. Just as the hairs of our head are numbered (see Matthew 10:30), so also the Lord has determined the afflictions and crosses that will be for our good.

> Paul teaches . . . that God in His purpose has ordained before the time of the world by what crosses and sufferings He would conform every one of His elect to the image of His Son. His cross shall and must work together for good for everyone, because they are called according to God's purpose. Therefore, Paul has concluded that it is certain and beyond doubt that neither "tribulation, or distress," neither "death nor life," or other such things, "will be able to separate us from the love of God in Christ Jesus our Lord." (See Romans 8:28, 29, 35, 38, 39.)[17]

A significant reason for the afflictions of Christians is that in being conformed to the image of God's Son, we become merciful people.[18] Thus St. Peter teaches:

> Blessed be the God and Father of our Lord Jesus Christ! According to His great mercy, He has caused us to be born again to a living hope .... In this you rejoice, though now for a little while, if necessary, you have been grieved by various trials .... Having purified your souls by your obedience to the truth for a sincere *brotherly love, love one another* earnestly from a pure heart. *1 Peter 1:3, 6, 22 (emphasis added)*

Likewise, Luther teaches that Christians experience a "happy exchange" with Christ—all the sin that is ours becomes His, and all that is His becomes ours. And in the same way, Christians participate in an "exchange" with their neighbor in need:

> It is God's Son's flesh and blood given and shed for us. That is eating His flesh and blood. From this follows the great true exchange, of which I have often spoken. He remains in us and we in Him. We become one loaf with Him. He, with all of His wealth, becomes mine. I with all my sins and trouble, become His body.... [E]ach must carry the other's burden. That is not easy, but a load which is severe and bows us down. But we must also help others bear their burden whenever they fail .... So this exchange also takes place among us. You take upon yourself the sins, weakness, dishonor and despair of the other person and place upon him your virtue, strength, honor and resources.[19]

But what about suffering we bring on ourselves by our sin? Is that also a cross that we bear and through which God works for good and to conform us to the likeness of His Son? In Christ, absolutely. In fact, one of the most profound examples of this is a Christian I served who committed adultery, which tore apart a small community. His infant child with a second wife (not one of the women involved in the adultery) died in a machinery accident. By the mercy of God, this man gained deep insight and understood the life and penitential psalms of King David like no one I have ever known. His weakness of the flesh and tribulation drove this man to repentance.[20] By God's grace, the tragedies and tribulations worked for his good, now and for eternity. The sins of his flesh—confessed and forgiven—drove him daily to his Baptism, where the cross of Jesus came to him. As Luther wrote, "The Kingdom is not being prepared, but has been prepared, while the sons of the Kingdom are being prepared."[21] The great reformer also writes;

> Not only the passive evils that are inflicted on us result in good, but also the active ones, that is, the evils which we ourselves do. "How can this be?" you say. Because when a godly person is aware of his fall, he becomes ashamed and is perturbed. Thus his fall leads first to humility . . . . Moreover, the evil which remains in our flesh is like a spur which urges us on . . . we are angry with ourselves, condemn ourselves, and cry out with Paul (Rom. 7:24): "Wretched man that I am! Who will deliver me from the body of this sin?"[22]

Living and dying as a Christian is more than a challenging business. It is by affliction and cross that God strengthens our faith and takes us to eternity. How does God move us from what we are to what we shall be, even as His merciful people? Suffering.

> Under burdens of cross-bearing,
>
> Though the weight May be great,
>
> Yet I'm not despairing.
>
> You designed the cross you gave me;
>
> Thus you know All my woe
>
> And how best to save me.
>
> (*Lutheran Worship* 423:2)[23]

> *Kyrie eleison.*
>
> *Christe eleison.*
>
> *Kyrie eleison.*

NOTES
---

1   AE 12:312.

2   AE 31:40.

3   AE 12:312.

4   AE 4:117.

5   See FC SD XI 6 (*Concordia*, 603).

6   Joel R. Baseley, trans., *Festival Sermons of Martin Luther: The Church Postils, Winter and Summer Selections* (Dearborn, MI: Mark V. Publications, 2005), Winter Section, 35.

7   See AE 19:72.

8   Theodore G. Tappert, ed. and trans., *Luther: Letters of Spiritual Counsel*, Library of Christian Classics 18 (Philadelphia and London: Westminster Press and SCM, 1955), 132.

9   Baseley, *Festival Sermons*, Winter Section, 120.

10 Ap XIIB 61–62 (*Concordia*, 181). The Lutheran Confessions say much more than that God "allows" afflictions. God is the actor; He "sends" afflictions (FC Ep X 6; *Concordia*, 497). God brings afflictions (see Ap IV 167; *Concordia*, 108). It is God's "will" that we bear afflictions (Ap IV 170; *Concordia*, 108). In afflictions God is "doing His strange work" (Ap XIIB 61; *Concordia*, 181). Afflictions are "God's works" (Ap XIIB 62; *Concordia*, 181). God imposes "punishments" and "common troubles" (Ap XIIB 156; *Concordia*, 179). God from eternity "has ordained" certain crosses and sufferings for us (FC SD XI 49; *Concordia*, 609).

11 Baseley, *Festival Sermons*, Summer Section, 34.

12 StL 2:467 (*author's translation*).

13 An ethical system that avoids at all costs anything that diminishes personal happiness. See *Dictionary of Philosophy and Psychology* (New York: Peter Smith, 1940), 2:765, s.v. "utilitarianism."

14 Baseley, *Festival Sermons*, Summer Section, 169.

15 Ap XIIB 54 (*Concordia*, 179).

16 See FC SD XI 33 (*Concordia*, 607).

17 FC SD XI 49 (*Concordia*, 609).

18 See AE 17:66.

19 Baseley, *Festival Sermons*, Summer Section, 46–47.

20 See AE 3:334.

21 AE 33:153.

22 AE 3:330–36.

23 Copyright © 1982 Concordia Publishing House. All rights reserved.

11

MERCY, MONEY, AND MISSING THE STEWARDSHIP BOAT

WHERE THE CHURCH IS IN MOTION, THERE IS MISSION, MERCY, AND MONEY

Only, they asked us to remember the poor, the very thing I was eager to do. *Galatians 2:10*

Christ says: "If I suffer hunger or thirst in the person of My apostle or of any Christian, yes, of a Christian child or of any person poor and in want, and you are aware of this situation, you are truly an archmiser if you close your eyes to this. I want you to know that I am the one who is suffering hunger and thirst. . . ." It will profit you nothing to say: "If Christ Himself came, I would hand Him my keys and say: 'Take everything!' "[1] *Martin Luther*

It was a somewhat unlikely event. About a week and a half after Hurricane Katrina hit New Orleans, LCMS World Relief and Human Care asked John Scibilia, then executive director of Lutheran Disaster Response New York (formed to respond to 9/11), to meet in St. Louis, Missouri, to discuss the LCMS response to the hurricane. A former LCMS teacher who left the Synod during the great struggles of the 1970s, John had worked for the ELCA for a time before ending up in New York. Despite the significant theological divide, I highly regard John's pragmatism and no-nonsense New York attitude to getting done what needs to get done. John's first question was, "What are your districts doing?"

To my presentation of the sketchy and emerging information I had from contacts around the Synod, John replied, "I wish after 9/11 we would have gotten out in front and connected specific (ELCA) synods and (LCMS) districts to the various congregations affected. Some districts will do it anyway, and this way your response can be better coordinated and more effective."

John's advice was exactly what the LCMS had to do; however, we had never done it that way before. The LCMS philosophy of disaster relief had been relatively passive since casting its collective lot and funds (capacity) into the now defunct Lutheran Council USA forty years ago. Back then the hope was for one U.S. Lutheran Church—a dream likely dashed for our lifetime as each new declaration of full communion made by the ELCA (with the Presbyterian Church USA, the United Church of Christ, the Reformed Church in America, or the United Methodists), as well as the growing culture within the ELCA of approbation of homosexuality, renders it a more remote (im)possibility. I do not mention these things with relish. I know many dear and committed Christians within the ELCA and call many of them friends. Those who disagree with the LCMS do so out of deep and principled conviction. We can only pray, "Lord, forgive us our (LCMS) sins and grant us all repentance!" It is time, and past time, for the LCMS to develop and reclaim her capacity to act in the realm of human care according to her clear confession of the Gospel. This issue is not about refusing to cooperate; rather, it is about the capacity and ability *to cooperate.* The LCMS has no one to blame but ourselves for our lack of capacity (people, funds, equipment) because we sent our money elsewhere. We took a different route.

MISSOURI'S MOMENT OF MERCY

John and I talked through a few details, then I invited him to accompany me to a meeting with the president of the Missouri Synod. President Gerald Kieschnick had numerous helpful suggestions and raised valid concerns about equity and other issues, which were resolved to his satisfaction. Then we pulled together several LCMS district presidents through a conference call to discuss the plan to pair each of the thirty-five LCMS districts with a suffering congregation and/or school in the Southern District. Michigan District President Bill Hoesman and others, including Southern District President Kurt Schultz, offered advice and hearty approval. Two more conference calls covered the entire Missouri Synod Council of Presidents.

As a result of our discussions, every district sent funding to LCMS World Relief and Human Care *and* to their respective adopted congregations. In addition, teams of volunteers, including clergy with Critical Incident Stress Management and chaplaincy certifications, traveled to assigned congregations to provide help. The people of the Synod were amazing as specific requests for material aid poured into the congregations of the Southern District. As the immediate needs of clergy, teachers, and congregations were addressed, attention quickly moved toward assisting those outside the Synod. We directed thousands of volunteers and hundreds upon hundreds of thousands of dollars in material aid and equipment to cooperative camps (for example, Camp Restore and Lutheran Social Services of the South Disaster Response).

LCMS World Relief and Human Care offered matching funds for dollars the districts raised for their assigned congregations and schools. The dollars flowed far beyond anything in the history of the Missouri Synod. The response to Hurricane Katrina brought the largest collective receipts for a single event in the history of the LCMS. In hindsight there were a lot of things that could have been done better. Surely the disaster heightened existing fissures and differences between clergy or within congregations. But ultimately Katrina and the LCMS response was one of the finest moments in our denomination's history.

Surprisingly and disappointingly, a handful of individuals criticized this congregation-based approach to disaster response as the LCMS "looking out for her own," as though we do not care for nonmembers. This is simply rubbish. Consider this, when a disaster strikes where you have family or close friends, the first thing you do is call to make sure everyone is okay, which is what LCMS World Relief and Human Care did. Then we heard, "I'm okay, but there are thousands upon thousands all around us in terrible need. Help us help them!" As a result of this plea, we can say with St. Paul, "As we have opportunity, let us do good to everyone, and especially to those who are of the household of faith" (Galatians 6:10). With the help of Ray Wilke and Clayton Andrews of Orphan Grain Train (based in Norfolk, Nebraska) and many other unsung heroes, the Missouri Synod responded in love. And as never before in LCMS history, we partnered more broadly with non-Lutherans, with local institutions, and with secular entities.

I am thankful for and proud of the people of the LCMS. In reaching out to care for the needy, they acted and spoke as Christians. They bore witness to Christ in word and deed, with kindness and love. Disasters are not a time for bait and switch or hidden agendas. Disasters are a time to be charitable and considerate. They are opportunities to realize the vulnerability of those affected and to offer love and respect. This does not mean refusing to give "a reason for the hope that is in you" (1 Peter 3:15), but as St. Peter continues, "do it with gentleness and respect, having a good conscience, so that, when you are slandered, those who revile your good behavior in Christ may be put to shame" (1 Peter 3:16). *And there is nothing hidden!* Lutherans are about faith in Christ and deeds that show Christ's love and mercy. We openly confess that word and deed go together, as they did for Jesus Christ (Luke 5:17–26) and His disciples when they assisted those in need (Luke 9:2ff.).

THE APOSTLE PAUL'S COLLECTION FOR JERUSALEM

The Church's life of mercy is not new, as is evidenced by the following: *ministry of care* (2 Corinthians 8:4; 9:1), *service* (2 Corinthians 9:12), *fellowship* (Romans 15:26), *generous giving* (2 Corinthians 9:5), *thanksgiving* (2 Corinthians 9:12), *grace* (2 Corinthians 8:4). These New Testament words are powerfully freighted theological words. Paul uses all of them to refer to his great collection for the saints who were suffering in Jerusalem, which was a revelation for me. Indeed, I despised "stewardship" sermons, principles, and courses while at the seminary. Stewardship Sundays in the parish bothered me. Most of what I heard were principles for living, goals for individual giving, Old Testament regulations about tithing (followed by New Testament principles). Law, Law, Law—everything was Law, individualistic, nothing of the Church, nothing of the Sacrament, nothing of the fellowship of believers, and certainly nothing about the needy. That is what I had been hearing (admittedly, I had not been listening all that carefully!).

Then, as I read St. Paul in context, true stewardship became clear. He uses *grace* to describe the collection in 2 Corinthians 8:6. The most significant word of the New Testament, *grace*, is used for collected money! That was shocking. St. Paul's words began a complete revolution in my thinking about the Church and money or, I should say, the Church, money, *and* mercy.

What is the Book of Acts about? evangelization? mission? Yes, but there is a particular and extraordinary theme that unifies the book: the Great Collection—*mercy*. This collection is a visible and tangible expression of another reality of the Church, namely, fellowship. In fact, St. Paul calls the collection for the poor a *koinonia*, a "fellowship" or "mutual participation." Acts 2:42 famously states: "And they devoted themselves to the apostles' teaching and fellowship, to the breaking of bread and the prayers." The "apostles' teaching" is "the doctrine and its articles"[2] proclaimed. The "breaking of bread" is the Lord's Supper. "The prayers" is shorthand for the life of worship of the early community gathered about these gifts. But what is "fellowship" (*koinonia*)? John's first Epistle shows us that this fellowship is vertical (with the Lord), then horizontal (with fellow believers):

> That which we have seen and heard we proclaim also to you, so that you too may have fellowship [*koinonia*] with us; and indeed our fellowship [*koinonia*] is with the Father and with His Son Jesus Christ. . . . If we say we have fellowship [*koinonia*] with Him while we walk in darkness, we lie and do not practice the truth. But if we walk in the light, as He is in the light, we have fellowship [*koinonia*] with one another, and the blood of Jesus His Son cleanses us from all sin. *1 John 1:3, 6–7*

The apostle John is careful to note these two facets of the *one* fellowship; the vertical is not separated from the horizontal. The fellowship with the Lord is first, and it creates the relationship among the saints. German theologian Werner Elert commented:

> What links those who partake of the Lord's Supper is not that they have something to do with one another, their human relationship with each other, but that which they share together [i.e., Christ in His body and blood]. This fellowship not only embraces still another ingredient besides the human participants but this other ingredient is not even produced by an act of man. It not only antedates efforts of men, but fellowship (*koinonia*) means that this is the very element which unites the multitude.[3]

A relationship with God the Father without a relationship with others in fellowship is impossible. A denial of love to a brother or sister is a denial of fellowship in the Lord (1 John 3:15–17). The Lord creates fellowship by His Gospel of grace (Philippians 1:7). It is a fellowship in the Spirit (Philippians 2:1). It is created by fellowship or participation (*koinonia*) in the body and blood of Christ (1 Corinthians 10:16). As St. Paul writes, "Because there is one bread, we who are many are one body, for we all partake of the one bread" (1 Corinthians 10:17).

The apostles' teaching, fellowship, breaking of the bread, and the prayers describe the Church. The circle of the Church's life of fellowship, whether local or beyond, is exclusive and inclusive. It excludes those who do not believe, but it includes the saints' love for and toward believers and nonbelievers. The Christian loves the unbaptized person and will proclaim the Gospel and point this individual to the sacraments, worship, and fellowship with Christ. Our witness is to the means by which the excluded or faithless can be called by God into the community of the faithful. Fellowship—*koinonia*—brings mercy and compassion.

MERCY AND *KOINONIA* IN PRACTICE

What does *koinonia* mean when members of the fellowship are in need? Luke records in the Acts of the Apostles that "all who believed were together and had all things in common. And they were selling their possessions and belongings and distributing the proceeds to all, as any had need" (2:44–45). Later Luke adds that "there was not a needy person among them" (Acts 4:34). The fellowship of believers acted in Acts 6 to meet the need of the Greek-speaking Jewish widows who were being overlooked in the daily *diakonia*, or distribution, of food. It was the formal beginning to the Church's intentional, ordered life of mercy. It is also the beginning of what is popularly called "stewardship."

According to most church historians, Paul was converted in AD 36, just after the martyrdom of Stephen.[4] By AD 45–46 he was in Syrian Antioch (Acts 11:25–26). An influx of refugees from Jerusalem, escaping the general persecution and martyrdom of Jesus' followers at the hands of the Jewish leaders, kept the believers in Antioch well informed of the situation. In addition to persecution, the Jerusalem

Christians were also affected by a famine (prophesied by Agabus) at a time when Jewish fields were fallow as dictated by the Old Testament rules concerning the Sabbath year. As a result, the Christians in Antioch decided "to send relief [*diakonia*] to the brothers living in Judea" (Acts 11:29). What irony that this gift of love was sent by Paul (formerly Saul, the great persecutor of early Christians) and Barnabas.[5]

The collection must have had a tremendous impact on Paul and on the Jewish Christians in Jerusalem. Gentile Christians had sent a gift that expressed love and fellowship. It is significant that the first account of the proclamation of the Gospel to Gentiles coincides with the first collection for the poor (Acts 11:20), a collection born at the rough edge of the Church's mission to the Gentiles. Mercy and mission go hand in hand. Where Christ is, there is the Church.[6] Wilhelm Löhe said that "mission is nothing but the one church of God in motion."[7] Where the Church is in motion, there is mission, mercy, and money.

The controversy concerning Gentile converts and circumcision grew quickly until AD 49, when the Jerusalem Council determined not to burden Gentile converts with circumcision or the Law of Moses in general (Acts 15:23ff.). However, Gentile Christians were asked to avoid practices that Jewish Christians would find particularly offensive. In Galatians 2:1–10, Paul describes the resolution to the circumcision controversy:

> And when James and Cephas and John, who seemed to be pillars, perceived the grace that was given to me, they gave the right hand of fellowship [*koinonia*] to Barnabas and me, that we should go to the Gentiles and they to the circumcised. Only, they asked us to remember the poor, the very thing I was eager to do. *Galatians 2:9–10*

Paul went to the Gentiles and demonstrated that he was "eager" to remember the poor. For Paul, fellowship means doctrinal agreement with ethical ramifications, which includes a focus on care for the needy. *Koinonia* is vertical and horizontal. In fact, St. Paul took this fellowship (collection) so seriously that it occupied him for more than a decade. From various New Testament references, we know that Paul invited the participation of all his mission churches. Paul's second letter to the Corinthians mentions Macedonia (8:1ff.; 9:2, 4), and he mentions Achaia (along with its major city, Corinth) in Romans 15:26. Acts 20:4 lists the representatives of various churches who traveled with Paul to take the collection to Jerusalem: Sopater of Berea, Aristarchus and Secundus of Thessalonica (Macedonia), Gaius of Derbe and Timothy of Lystra (Galatia), Tychicus and Trophimus of Ephesus (Asia). Commentator Keith Nickle suggests there also may have been delegates traveling with Paul from Troas (Acts 20:5–6), Philippi (Acts 20:6), Tyre (Acts 21:3–4), Ptolemais (Acts 21:7), and Caesarea (Acts 21:16).[8] Imagine the years of hard work it took to pull this together! The collection necessitated Paul's trip to Jerusalem (Romans 15:28), which ultimately put his life on the path to Rome and martyrdom (Acts 24:17ff.).

In chapters 8 and 9 of his second Epistle to the Corinthians, Paul offers his great explanation of the collection.[9] In these chapters, Paul works to convince the wealthy Corinthian Christian community to give generously. From these two chapters are drawn many of the popular "stewardship" texts, such as:

> They gave themselves first to the Lord and then by the will of God to us. (8:5)

> But as you excel in everything—in faith, in speech, in knowledge, in all earnestness, and in our love for you—see that you excel in this act of grace also. (8:7)

> For you know the grace of our Lord Jesus Christ, that though He was rich, yet for your sake He became poor, so that you by His poverty might become rich. (8:9)

> For if the readiness is there, [the gift] is acceptable according to what a person has, not according to what he does not have. (8:12)

> Your abundance at the present time should supply their need, so that their abundance may supply your need. (8:14)

> Whoever sows sparingly will also reap sparingly, and whoever sows bountifully will also reap bountifully. (9:6)

> Each one must give as he has made up his mind, not reluctantly or under compulsion, for God loves a cheerful giver. (9:7)

> He who supplies seed to the sower and bread for food will supply and multiply your seed for sowing and increase the harvest of your righteousness. You will be enriched in every way for all your generosity. (9:10–11)

This list of texts should cause one to pause. The primary reason for giving money in the New Testament is for poor and suffering Christians. The giving begins with Christ, who gave Himself unto death for our sins. Giving is also a demonstration of fellowship. St. Paul spent well more than a decade of his working life organizing, arranging, leading, and bringing to conclusion the great collection for the poor in Jerusalem. Is this what takes place in the Church today?

There are myriad needs in today's Church, as has been the case throughout history. These needs include funding schools, seminaries, church buildings, salaries, programs, mission, and much more. Every one of these needs is vital! But where in this mix—locally, at the district level, nationally, and internationally—is concern for the poor and, more important, for poor Christians who are of the fellowship? Where in our educational system are clergy exposed to the needs of the poor, the orphan, the handicapped, the addicted, and the suffering? (What a blessing the deaconess programs have come to be on our seminary campuses as they raise exactly these issues!) Do church leaders contemplate the administrative structures necessary for an ordered congregational life of *diakonia*? Is there an ordered and intentional life of mercy in the local parish? Above all, the great stewardship promises of the New Testament have to do with generosity to the poor ("He who supplies seed to the sower and bread for food will supply and multiply your seed for sowing and increase the harvest of your righteousness. You will be enriched in every way for all your generosity" *to the poor*, 2 Corinthians 9:10–11). As we care for the needy, doesn't our Lord's promise apply that "all these things will be added to you" (Matthew 6:33)?

The modern welfare state and other pressures have moved the locus of care and concern for the needy—particularly the local needy—out of the realm of the local parish. This shift took place with passive acquiescence—which does not need to continue. When the *koinonia* we have with the Father no longer manifests itself in brotherly love, we risk the denial of that *koinonia*, that fellowship, with the "Father of mercy" (1 John 1:6ff.; 3:10; 3:16–18; 4:11–21). Unity in the faith entails unity in love. The great collection aptly demonstrates that Christian *koinonia*, with all its facets of meaning, transcends geography. Our concern for poor and suffering Christians (with a burden for, but not limited to, Lutherans) is as broad and far-flung as Baptism, Christ's body and blood in the Sacrament, and Christ's Body, the Church.

The great collection demonstrates that the Church at its best is both missionary and merciful. Where Christ is received in faith, there love flows to the neighbor in need. Because Christ's gifts create a body of believers, love and mercy are simultaneously created and flow as collective and intentional acts of the body of Christians. Because the body of Christ transcends space, love flows to the fellowship of believers the world over. Furthermore, the Church also has a mandate to reach beyond the border of "fellowship" (*koinonia*) to those who are in need. Just as the Gospel and the love of Christ reach beyond the boundary of the fellowship, so do the acts of mercy.

Where the Church ceases to be merciful, it misses the stewardship boat. We dare not miss the New Testament's main goal of giving— care for the poor and suffering in our midst. The apostolic promise still holds good, "You will be enriched in every way for your generosity" (2 Corinthians 9:11).

> "You shall not steal or take away
> What others worked for night and day,
> But open up a gen'rous hand
> And help the poor in the land."
> Have mercy, Lord!
> (*Lutheran Service Book* 581:8)
>
> *Lord, have mercy.*
> *Christ, have mercy.*
> *Lord, have mercy.*

NOTES

1   AE 22:520.

2   FC Ep X 7.

3   Werner Elert, *Eucharist and Church Fellowship in the First Four Centuries*, trans. N. E. Nagel (St. Louis: Concordia, 1966), 4–5.

4   For New Testament dating, I am relying on Bo Reicke, *Re-examining Paul's Letters: The History of the Pauline Correspondence* (Harrisburg, PA: Trinity Press International, 2001).

5   Barnabas had been sent to Antioch to deal with the new and challenging situa-
    tion of how to handle pagan converts to Christianity, particularly with respect
    to circumcision (Acts 11:20–26).

6   Ignatius, "To the Smyrnaeans," 8.2, in *Early Christian Fathers*, ed. and trans.
    Cyril C. Richardson, Library of Christian Classics 1 (Philadelphia: Westminster
    Press, 1953).

7   Wilhelm Löhe, *Three Books About the Church* (Fort Wayne, IN: Concordia
    Theological Seminary Press, 1989), 59.

8   Keith F. Nickle, *The Collection: A Study of Paul's Strategy* (Naperville, IL: Alec R.
    Allenson, 1966), esp. 68.

9   Löhe comments that this section is "among the most beautiful passages we can
    possibly read in the apostolic epistles" (Holger Sonntag, trans., *Löhe on Mercy*,
    ed. by Adriane Dorr and Philip Hendrickson [St. Louis: LCMS World Relief and
    Human Care, 2006], 35).

12

MERCY AND THE CHURCH'S CONFESSION

THE CREEDS AND DEEDS

They will glorify God because of your submission flowing from your confession of the gospel of Christ, and the generosity of your contribution for them and for all others. *2 Corinthians 9:13*

There is no doctrine of Christ which can be given up for the sake of charity.[1] *Martin Luther*

A visit to Wittenberg, the German city that gave birth to the Lutheran Reformation, is both exhilarating and depressing. Even a decade and a half after the East German wall came down, the city bears the wounds of fifty years of Communist life in the foreboding gray paint on numerous dilapidated buildings. (Thankfully, a steady rebuilding program has been initiated.) Youth, some leather-clad and spiked, walk the famous *Collegienstrasse* (University Avenue) in the evening between rows of shops where merchandise has been locked away.

Martin Luther walked along this street from his home at the Augustinian Cloister on the east side of the old city to the great Castle Church at the opposite end of town. On October 31, 1517, the reformer's six-minute walk, with the Ninety-five Theses in hand, radically changed the world.

Roughly five hundred years later, as I strolled in the city market in front of the old city council building, I came across crowds of young people near the statues of Luther and his co-worker in the Reformation, Philip Melanchthon. Naively, I thought that it might be a Christian youth rally. But on closer inspection, I realized it was a Communist rally to protest the liberal government of Gerhard Schröder[2] and its forced reduction in social benefits. Most likely these young people were agnostics, if not atheists.

Once the shining light of the Gospel, the city of Wittenberg today is all but dead to Lutheranism as Luther confessed it. The town has nearly fifty thousand inhabitants, but only 18 percent register as

Christians and therefore pay the church tax. Only a fraction of that number will go to church once or twice during the year. And when they do attend church—at St. Mary's, the very church where Luther preached the Reformation to life—they do not attend a Lutheran Church, but a "Protestant" church. How is this so?

Two versions of the Reformation faith vied for the hearts of the German people. "Calvinists" looked to the French reformer John Calvin for guidance, while "Lutherans" looked to Martin Luther. Calvin's spiritual compatriots limited the grace of Christ to the "elect," asserting instead that Christ did not die for all. The Reformed denied that what the pastor holds in his hand at the Lord's Supper is Christ's true body and blood, asserting instead that it is only a symbol. Almost from the beginning of the Reformation, those who claim Luther's name but who lack his bold and unyielding stand in the faith have overlooked such differences for the sake of "unity."

By the time Rationalism dominated church life (ca. 1750), the confidence in the Words of Institution at the Lord's Supper had been further lessened, and the impulse to unify had increased. But such a unity is at the expense of the Lord's own last will and testament. From the beginning, the Reformed (the term we use today for those who follow Calvin) wanted to help Lutherans free themselves of the vestiges of a Roman Catholic past, such as the belief in the bodily presence of Christ in the Sacrament, Confession and Absolution, and much of the liturgy, art, and music. According to the Reformed, such beliefs or practices by the Lutherans meant they were not yet fully "reformed." In 1577, Confessional Lutherans responded to the weakening of biblical and Lutheran doctrines (particularly with respect to the Lord's Supper, the person of Christ, and eternal election) in the Formula of Concord. The Formula drew the line for church fellowship: complete agreement on the Gospel and all its articles.

From the beginning, Luther saw that the Reformed gave too much ground to "the old witch, Lady Reason,"[3] in matters of faith. Calvin's basic philosophical principle was that "the finite is not capable of the infinite."[4] Luther rightly saw in this a Platonic dualism, a separation of the spiritual and physical, a denial that created things could be the bearers of divine realities. Ulrich Zwingli, who spearheaded the Protestant Reformation in Geneva, Switzerland, denied that God could die, therefore he also denied that the Son of God in the flesh could die on the cross. So, too, Zwingli denied that bread and wine could bear Christ's true body and blood, or that Christ's human nature could receive the properties of God (such as omnipresence).[5] Thus the Reformed consider the sacraments to be symbols of spiritual realities, not realities themselves. We say to rationalized and Calvinized Lutherans what Luther once wrote to Melanchthon, "It is your philosophy that is tormenting you, not your theology."[6] I agree with faithful Lutherans who recognize that Reformed Platonism is the seedbed from which grew Rationalism's rejection of Christ's divinity, the Bible as God's Word, sacraments, and the miraculous in general. Influenced by Calvin and Rationalism, many continue to envision one Protestant church with different theological schools within—and this push is evident even within the church body that bears Luther's name. We will sit by the entrance to the tomb of Lutheranism and weep and work until she rises again.

In Luther's day, extraordinary men, convicted by Luther's writings on justification and the Lord's Supper, took a stand for the Gospel and a right interpretation of God's Word. Margrave George of Brandenburg was such a leader. At the Diet of Augsburg in 1530, Charles V, emperor of the Holy Roman Empire, insisted that the Lutheran princes take part in a Corpus Christi procession through the streets of Augsburg. Margrave George responded, "Sire, I would rather kneel down on this spot and have my head chopped off than give up the word of God." That was a real "Augsburg Confession." The Lutherans were adamant against this misuse of the Lord's Supper. They believed that the Lord gave His Supper with the words "Take and eat; this is My body." Therefore, the Sacrament was no Sacrament if the elements were consecrated for the sole purpose of being carried through the streets and "venerated" by the faithful rather than being consumed in the Divine Service. Emperor Charles responded in broken German, "Not head off! Not head off!"[7]

Sadly, George's descendents gravitated to Reformed and rationalistic views of the faith. The great tragedy is that few bishops confessed the faith of the Lutheran Reformation. Thus princes of the various

German states become "emergency" bishops in the Lutheran Church. The princes often saw religion as a means to political ends. Some of these bishop/princes even converted to Roman Catholicism or Reformed Christianity when it was expedient to do so. Such "conversions" produced ridiculous situations. For example, the prince of the German territory of Saxony became Roman Catholic at the beginning of the eighteenth century, which meant that the "head" of the Lutheran Church in Saxony (the very church of Luther!) was not even Lutheran.[8]

Eventually, a series of wars and conflicts brought the portion of Saxony that includes Wittenberg into the Brandenburg kingdom and the German state of Prussia. By 1800, Prussian King Frederick William III was a staunch Reformed Rationalist who wanted one church in Prussia. Completely consonant with his times, he defined religion as a matter of "the heart, feeling and individual conviction."[9] Christian doctrine was defined as "opinion," regarding which there could only be churchly unity if "peace, love and tolerance" prevailed.[10] Already in 1798, now that "better spirits" prevailed, the young prince dedicated himself to moving the "unenlightened" segments of the Prussian church toward such union, which "sectarian spirits" in earlier generations had prevented.[11] Chief among those "sectarians" had been Luther himself. Walter Geppert writes concerning Frederick William III:

> The Lutheran Confessions no longer possessed any real significance. In the king's eyes they were very clearly only documents of religious opinion of earlier centuries. Purity of doctrine, truth in the church's proclamation, unity of the faith, agreement with the fathers, as with the validity of the confessions, only appeared to the king as unbearable coercion. Reason and philosophy were the authorities, which he posed over against the Confessions. . . . It acknowledged no authority outside the religious individual.[12]

With only a couple dozen Reformed congregations and seven thousand Lutheran congregations, King Frederick William, by fiat, effected the Prussian Union, which nullified the Lutheran confession by granting tolerance to the Reformed confession within the Prussian Church. He did so on Reformation Day, October 31, 1817. The

Prussian Union disposed of the Lutheran conviction that in the Lord's Supper the body and blood of Christ are actually present, distributed, and received by all. The *Agenda* (the book that guided the words and actions of the liturgy) of the Prussian Union Church spoke of "the reception of the sign" of the Lord's Supper, not of Christ's body and blood. The words to be spoken by the pastor during the distribution were "Take eat, *Christ says*, 'This is my body.' "[13] Geppert comments:

> The use of this formula for the distribution is nothing other than charac-
> teristic flight from dogma to Bible passages [which are then interpreted
> ambiguously], characteristic of union in every decade. If the Lord's origi-
> nal words were recited, the King believed, the claim of the adherents of the
> Lutheran and the Reformed confessions would be satisfied. In reality this
> formula indicated a flight from the truth claims of the Gospel and a decla-
> ration of neutrality on the basis of the significance of the confession,
> characteristic of his religious views.[14]

This was a far cry from the Bible's uncompromising view of the need to confess the truth and reject every error. It also was a religion quite different from that of Luther, who lived and died by doctrinal assertion. Against Erasmus, the skeptic of his day, Luther confessed:

> Let Skeptics and Academics keep well away from us Christians, but let there
> be among us "assertors" twice as unyielding as the Stoics themselves. How
> often, I ask you, does the apostle Paul demand that *plerophoria* (as he terms
> it)—that most sure and unyielding assertion of conscience? In Romans
> 10[:10] he calls it "confession," saying, "with the mouth confession is made
> unto salvation." And Christ says: "Everyone who confesses me before men,
> I also will confess before my Father" [Matt. 10:32]. Peter bids us give a rea-
> son for the hope that is in us [I Peter 3:15]. What need is there to dwell on
> this? Nothing is better known or more common among Christians than
> assertion. Take away assertions and you take away Christianity.[15]

By 1812 Wittenberg University was still holding tenaciously to the Lutheran Confession, so it was closed. Opened in its place was a Prussian Union seminary, which remains to this day. Frederick William III erected a statue to Luther in Wittenberg's city square to "honor" the spirit of the great reformer, who was now venerated as the great "personality," the great German national hero who threw off man-made dogmas of the pope and freed civilization from autocratic mental and spiritual tyranny. In many minds it was not a great leap, then, for Luther to become the great hero of the atheistic German Democratic Republic: Luther as precursor of the workers' revolution. The Prussian Union Church had been the largest Lutheran church body in the world. Now it became a battering ram for the displacement and disntegration of the Lutheran Confessions.

Since the inception of the Prussian Union, Reformed teachings on the symbolic nature of the Lord's Supper have been granted equal status (not simply tolerance), which means that Luther's former altar now "feeds" both Reformed and Lutherans. Even more tragic, Rationalism and the Enlightenment have muffled and dulled the once-confident clear confession of Christ and His Gospel. For nearly two hundred years, Wittenberg, birthplace of the Reformation, has had no genuine Lutheran congregation. There are Christians in Wittenberg. There are individuals with Lutheran sympathies and convictions. But there is not a Lutheran congregation constituted as a Church of the pure Word and Sacrament.[16] Luther was adamant about confessing the body and blood of Christ in the Supper and that the Sacrament is the Gospel.[17] He broached no compromise nor acknowledged fellowship with those who denied these truths.

> I regard them all as being cut from the same piece of cloth, as indeed they are. For they do not want to believe that the Lord's bread in the Supper is His true, natural body which the godless person or Judas receives orally just as well as St. Peter and all the saints. Whoever (I say) does not want to believe that, let him not trouble me . . . and let him not expect to have fellowship from me. This is final.[18]

The Prussian Union spawned a backlash of Lutheran conviction. C. F. W. Walther, the first president of the LCMS, described this reaction in his evening lectures on Law and Gospel:

> The small remnant of sincere Christians who still believed and confessed with their mouths that the Holy Scriptures are the Word of God, that Jesus Christ is the Son of the living God, that man is justified before God by faith in Christ alone,—these few Christians extended to each other the right hand of brotherly fellowship, like persons saved from a great shipwreck, who, having seen most of their fellow-passengers go down to a watery grave, now embrace each other with tears of joy though they had been perfect strangers before. In that state of affairs the thought had to arise in all hearts that the time had come for putting an end to the abominable church

quarrels (that is what doctrinal controversies were called) and to let down the bars that divided the churches from one another. Especially the confessions, it was held, must be removed, because, like toll-gates along a highway, they hindered progress, and, to sum up, a great universal union of the churches, at least of the Protestant churches, must at last be instituted.

But, lo! what happened? In the year 1817, when this plan was to be executed, Claus Harms, in whom there was still some Lutheran blood flowing, wrote ninety-five theses against Rationalism and the union of churches, which he intended as a counterpart to the Ninety-five Theses of Luther. In these theses he said to the advocates of church union: "You purpose to make the poor handmaid, the Lutheran Church, rich by a marriage. Do not perform the act over Luther's grave. Life will come into his bones, and then—woe to you!" This glorious prediction was fulfilled. When the union of churches was actually put into effect in Prussia, multitudes of Lutherans suddenly awoke from their spiritual sleep, remembered that they belonged to the Lutheran Church, and declared that they would never forsake the faith of their fathers. In fact, they chose to see themselves evicted from their homes, imprisoned, and expatriated rather than consent to a union of truth with error, of the Word of God with man's word, of the true Church with a false Church.

Those were glorious days in the dark period about the middle of the nineteenth century. It is a pity that from the glorious conflict of those trying times there did not emerge the old, pure, genuine Lutheran Church.[19]

Claus Harms (1778–1855), J. G. Scheibel,[20] and others preached and acted valiantly against this rejection of Luther's teaching in the heart of the denomination that took his name. Even as a rebirth of Lutheran conviction arose in many parts of Germany, the revival bypassed Luther's own city.[21] Refusal to join or support the Union Church in Prussia resulted in persecution and even military intervention to force recalcitrant congregations to accept clergy who endorsed unionism.[22] By 1840 numerous faithful Lutheran clergy had been defrocked, even jailed. Some German Lutherans chose to emigrate rather than give up their faith. The Free Lutheran Churches that are now in fellowship with the LCMS were born out of this struggle against unionism. For example, Pastor Johannes Grabau migrated with his flock to Buffalo, New York, and Pastors August Kavel and Gotthard Fritzsche and their flocks left for Australia.

Wilhelm Löhe and his efforts to send clergy to the United States, as well as Walther and the founding of the LCMS, were the result of this great Lutheran reawakening. In the United States, immigrant Lutherans were far more conservative and committed to the Lutheran Confessions than their counterparts in the eastern United States. Congregations in the eastern states had at least one hundred years of history, but it was the new immigrants, who ironically called themselves "Old" Lutherans, who produced the Midwestern synods. And many of these synods eventually merged into the ALC and ultimately the ELCA.

A nemesis of the newly formed LCMS and other German Lutheran churches in the United States was the German Evangelical Synod of the West. This church body was the missionary daughter of the Church of the Prussian Union. Through various mergers this synod ended up in the United Church of Christ, one of the few U.S. denominations to approve officially of both homosexuality and abortion. Seventy years ago the Prussian Union Church became a haven for proponents of Nazism. Hermann Sasse, who grew up in the Prussian Church, never tired of noting that the Nazi "German Christian" movement was strongest in Brandenburg, Prussia, where Lutheran doctrine—in fact, the entire possibility of doctrine—had been displaced. In fact, Ludwig Mueller was installed as *Reich* bishop of the Nazified German Protestant Church in St. Mary's Church in Wittenberg.[23]

Sasse liked to say that Wittenberg reminded him of an empty wine flask, which had the smell of something sweet that once was but is no longer. Since the nineteenth century, the tower of the Castle Church sports a Prussian military helmet. And inside this church where Luther preached and taught are depictions of Luther's greatest Protestant opponents: Zwingli and Calvin. Today Luther's full confession (the Book of Concord) remains absent from St. Mary's and the Castle Church. "Tolerance" has come to dominate virtually all Protestant church life in Germany, though adherence to the spirit and letter of the Lutheran Confessions is not tolerated. Of late the question has become acute whether a "United Evangelical Lutheran Church in Germany" (consisting of the territorial churches that at least nominally retain Lutheran identity) need any longer exist within the Evangelical Church of Germany (the union of Lutheran, Reformed, and Union churches) because all churches are essentially Union churches. According to Elert, "In all this there lives a bit of Lutheranism. But it is heather that has been pulled out. It lasts a long time. But it withers in the end."[24]

MERCY AND CONFESSION

What does confession have to do with mercy? What is necessary for the Church's work of mercy is a clear and solid conviction of who Christ is and what the Gospel is. Absent such conviction (faith), the work of mercy ceases to be the work of the Body of Christ (however valuable and laudable such social work may be in the realm of civil righteousness). The Lutheran Confessions state, "That faith, however, that does not present itself in confession is not firm."[25]

All the pastors and professional church workers of the LCMS bind themselves to the documents included in the Book of Concord. These documents accurately state the teaching of the Bible in all matters of faith that they treat, including and especially the central doctrine of justification by grace for Christ's sake through faith.[26] Like every confessional Lutheran Christian, I confessed this conviction at my confirmation, and as do all confessional Lutheran pastors, I repeated this confession at my ordination. Lutheran pastors pledge to suffer death rather than fall away from that pledge and conviction. This requirement gives a Lutheran congregation assurance regarding what is preached and taught in its midst. And it is the congregation's responsibility and right to see that this confession holds sway.

Christ asked His disciples, "Who do you say that I am?" Despite many options, Peter confessed for them all, "You are the Christ" (Mark 8:29). "Jesus is Lord" became the earliest confession of the faith (Romans 10:9; 1 Corinthians 12:3; Philippians 2:11). "If you confess with your mouth that Jesus is Lord and believe in your heart that God raised Him from the dead, you will be saved" is Paul's great statement in Romans 10:9. And in Romans 10:13, Paul proceeds to quote Joel 2:32: "Everyone who calls upon the name of the Lord will be saved." The Hebrew verse Paul is quoting uses the sacred covenant name for

God: Yahweh. "Jesus is Lord" means "Jesus is Yahweh"—God in the flesh for me! Mercy is built on the confession of who Christ is for me and for the world.

SAYING THE SAME THING

Today when people hear the word *confession*, most think about admitting guilt. Yet the word *confession* is used in three different ways in the New Testament. The word is a combination of two Greek words: *homo* ("the same") and *logein* ("to say"). *To confess* means "to say the same thing." When we confess our sins (1 John 1:9), we "say the same thing" that the Lord says about us as sinners according to His Law. When we make a confession of praise (Matthew 11:25), we say back to God what He has spoken to us about the mighty things that He has done. When we make a confession of faith (Romans 10:9–10), we say the same thing that God has told us about Himself in His Word.[27]

All three are vital for the Church's life of mercy. Without the confession of sin, we cannot apprehend the mercy of Christ. Mercy is only for sinners. Without the strong confession of the content of the faith—of who Christ is and what His Gospel is—we lose the greatest propelling force for mercy. Everything about being a confessional Lutheran finds meaning in mercy, which is "more comprehensive than sin!"[28] Faith that has laid hold of Christ and His cross confesses. It confesses what is true, and it confesses and rejects what is false. One cannot say *yes* to Christ without saying *no* to that which is not Christ. And it does not suffice simply to assert, "I believe what the Bible teaches." The earliest creeds of the Church were formulated against the claims of heretics who firmly and clearly stated they were teaching what the Bible teaches. The Bible is God's Word to us. Confession is our clear response and accounting to God and to the world regarding what His Word says. One cannot confess that Christ's body and blood are in the Sacrament, then fail to reject the teaching that Christ's body and blood are not given in the Sacrament. Henry Hamann, an Australian theologian, has said, "The Church which cannot curse cannot bless either."[29] And the apostle Paul says, "But even if we or an angel from heaven should preach to you a gospel contrary to the one we preached to you, let him be accursed" (Galatians 1:8).[30]

DEEDS NOT CREEDS?

The great plea of pragmatic U.S. Christianity and the twentieth-century concept of "social gospel" remains central today: "Deeds not creeds!" Another version states: "Doctrine divides; service unites." But this view overlooks the fact that "doctrine," or "teaching," is central to the New Testament and is the very source, strength, and motivation for mercy (in Acts 2:42 *koinonia*/mercy and *didache*/teaching are next to each other). Martin Chemnitz, the principal author of the Formula of Concord, defined the Church as "teachers" and "hearers." To the extent Christianity is without teaching, it is not Christianity. John 3:16, the "Gospel in a nutshell," is wholly doctrine or teaching:

> God [doctrine of God, the Trinity] so loved [doctrine of grace] the world [doctrine of sin], that He gave [doctrine of grace] His only Son [doctrine of the incarnation, doctrine of Christ's divinity, doctrine of the atonement], that whoever believes in Him [doctrine of faith] should not perish [doctrine of hell, doctrine of eternal punishment] but have eternal life [doctrine of heaven, of salvation].

The Gospel is teaching, and there is no Gospel without teaching. There is no Church without teaching. Christ is teaching. The Lutheran Confessions advocate creeds *with* deeds. Christ's incarnation, the Gospel and all its articles, bring us salvation and drive us into service and love of our neighbor. In the New Testament, refusal to have mercy is a rejection of apostolic teaching (1 John 3:15–17). Doctrine and love belong together. Luther writes:

> Where doctrine is right, then everything is right: faith, work, love, suffering, good and evil days, eating, drinking, hunger, thirst, sleeping and waking, walking and standing still, etc. Where the doctrine is not right, then it is in vain, all is lost, and everything is completely condemned: work, life, suffering, fasting, prayer, alms.[31]

Much, if not most, of the Lutheran world views the Lutheran Confessions as relics of a significant moment in the history of the Church, but with no real binding authority today. The question of authority is a vexing problem in all of Lutheranism and has been throughout its history, but especially since the Enlightenment.

Lutherans do not believe in an infallible and inspired magisterium (a pope). Nor do we believe in an infallible written confession. Lutherans came together around "confessions," and specifically the Formula of Concord and the 1580 *Book of Concord*. We make these confessions our own because we are convinced that they confess the faith of the Bible. While these confessions set a limit on church fellowship, they clearly and charitably assert that there is salvation outside the Lutheran Church (see the Preface to the Book of Concord).

Outside of the LCMS, the WELS, and their partner churches, the binding authority of the Book of Concord has been set aside in most of the Lutheran church bodies of the world, a continuing legacy of the Prussian Union. The Lutheran World Federation actively and aggressively promotes this nullification of the binding authority of the Lutheran Confessions in its dealings with church bodies (in part by promoting church fellowship with Reformed and other denominations). Instead of this vision, we must provide a "faithful, patient, fearless witness [which is] used by the Lord to bring about real union. He does unite—there is no doubt about it—and he does it by means of truth, on the basis of truth."[32]

One's view of the Lutheran Confessions hinges on the question, "Do I believe that they get the Bible right?" In the Lutheran world today, the answer to that question depends in large measure on what one thinks the Bible is. Is the Bible what Christ says it is, namely, the written Word of God?[33] Or is the Bible fundamentally or partially the ruminations of ancient individuals and their communities about what God might be like? When the Gospels provide us with Jesus' words and deeds, is it possible to be a faithful Lutheran and deny that all, any, or some of those words and deeds were spoken or done by Jesus? May we hold that they are the invention of the early community of believers? If one cannot be certain that the Words of Institution were spoken by Jesus on the night in which He was betrayed, then the entire doctrinal content of the Lutheran Confessions (including Luther's Small Catechism) simply cannot be confessed and, in fact, ceases to be confession. This is precisely what has happened in broad stretches of the Lutheran Church since the Enlightenment.

Contrast the following treatment of the Words of Institution from a contemporary text on doctrine:

> However the institution narratives may have come into being, and whatever relation to the events of Jesus' Last Supper they may have, it is as rubrics and interpretation of the church's Supper that we have them. Within the narrative structure of the accounts, it is decisive for the meaning of the sayings that they appear in the mouth of Jesus.[34]

with the following two quotations from the Book of Concord:

> The word or work of any man does not produce the true presence of Christ's body and blood in the Supper. This is true whether we consider merit or recitation of the minister or the eating, drinking, or faith of the communicants. Christ's presence should be credited only to Almighty God's power and our Lord Jesus Christ's word, institution, and ordination. Jesus Christ's true and almighty words, which He spoke at the first institution, were effective not only at the first Supper. They endure, are valid, operate, and are still effective. So in all places where the Supper is celebrated according to Christ's institution and His words are used, Christ's body and blood are truly present, distributed, and received, because of the power and effectiveness of the words that Christ spoke at the first Supper.[35]

> For the Sacrament has not been invented nor introduced by any man. Without anyone's counsel and deliberation it has been instituted by Christ.[36]

According to the Lutheran Confessions, the Scriptures are the norm, judge, and rule of all teaching in the Church. If the individual Christian scholar or historian must judge the "judge," then one replaces divine wisdom with human wisdom. Faith receives what the Lord gives. The Lord has given us His "divine Scriptures"[37] as the "pure, clear fountain of Israel."[38] To refuse to receive that gift is to refuse the Lord Himself. Is Jesus' use of "Father" determinative for how we call on God, Father, Son, and Holy Spirit (Matthew 28:19)? Or is "Father" as God's name culturally defined and limited so we are free to find new and "meaningful" names for God for our time (for example, "Mother")? Is the central issue of the Christian faith today that of "justice" for the poor or downtrodden in the same way that the doctrine of justification was once central to the Reformation? Is the Gospel ultimately liberation from poverty or injustice (both important issues!) instead of the forgiveness of sins? Is there salvation outside of faith in Christ's cross?

Following Luther and the Lutheran Confessions, we cannot accept such approaches to the Bible. We stand in the great tradition of the apostolic and orthodox Church of all ages and will gladly suffer any and all ridicule for this confession. With Löhe we can say, "If the Scriptures cannot be the uniting force in the church, then there is nothing to unite it since everything else without the backing of the Scriptures is empty and vain."[39]

Subscription to the Lutheran Confessions is widely viewed as confessional legalism, Formula of Concord fundamentalism, unscholarly obscurantism, and so on.[40] For those of us who willingly submit to the divine authority of the written Word of God and the relative authority of a human confession that accords completely with Christ and His Word, the Lutheran Confessions are ultimately freeing. We speak to God what He has first spoken to us about Himself. And because what we say is what He has said about Himself, it is completely sure and firm.

As a confessional Lutheran I am freed from my individualistic and wrong interpretation of the faith. Within the doctrinal bounds of the Book of Concord, I stand within the great sweep of the Church's doctrinal life. Within the bounds of that confession (that is, within the limits placed by the "We condemn" formulas), I am free to think, to roam through the Scriptures, and to solve theological problems creatively. Within the limits of the confession, I am freed by the blessed and clear Gospel of Christ. Within the confession, I claim all of its rich promises, all of its consolation in the Gospel, and all of its ultimate concern for the pastoral care of souls. Within the confession, I am pulled outside of the limits and weaknesses of my era and firmly placed within the Church catholic of all times and places. I am free to say *yes* where I find other Christians and church bodies saying what is true!

The Confessions of the Lutheran Church provide all the motivation, cause, limits for, and freedom she needs to practice mercy. While faith justifies, the Lutheran Confessions assert:

> We do not love unless our hearts are firmly convinced that forgiveness of sins has been granted to us.[41]

> We also say that love ought to follow faith.[42]

> Love necessarily follows [faith].[43]

The Confessions also assert that the highest worship of Christ is to receive mercy.[44] High praise of Christ is to show love and mercy to the neighbor.[45]

The Formula of Concord quotes Luther when it defines faith as a "living, active, daring thing," ready to act at the Church's "rough edge of mercy":

> Faith, however, is a divine work in us that changes us and makes us to be born anew of God, John 1[:12–13]. It kills the old Adam and makes us altogether different men, in heart and spirit, and mind and powers; it brings with it the Holy Spirit. O, it is a living, busy, active, mighty thing, this faith. It is impossible for it not to be doing good works incessantly. It does not ask whether good works are to be done, but before the question is asked, it has already done them, and is constantly doing them. . . . Faith is a living, daring confidence in God's grace, so sure and certain that the believer would stake his life on it a thousand times. This knowledge and confidence in God's grace makes men glad and bold and happy in dealing with God and all creatures. And this is the work that the Holy Spirit performs in faith. Because of it, without compulsion, a person is ready and glad to suffer everything, out of love and praise to God, who has shown him this grace. Thus it is impossible to separate works from faith, quite as impossible as to separate heat and light from fire.[46]

That is the kind of faith we need so we may be bold in stepping out on the Church's rough edge of mercy! The Confessions provide clear ethical boundaries.[47] The Confessions hold out the promise of forgiveness where we fail to live up to the Law: "God is pleased if anything is done. This is not because we satisfy the Law, but because we are in Christ."[48] The Confessions assert that the Church has a corporate life of mercy and that the Church is unified by "doctrine, faith, sacraments [and] works of love."[49] The bishops are to carry out the work of "alms" in behalf of the Church.[50] Charity is "the outward administration of Christ's kingdom among people."[51] The Confessions cajole us not to disregard the plight of the poor[52] nor allow the "public alms of the Church" to be squandered.[53] The Confessions call works of charity a way in which we praise God.[54] The Confessions promise a rich reward for the assistance of the needy.[55] The Confessions call Christians to social responsibility.[56] The Confessions call on us to "let harm come to no one, but show him all good and love. As we have said, this commandment is especially directed toward those who are our enemies."[57]

Far from being the enemy of mercy, the Lutheran Confessions are the greatest aid, directive, motivation, guide, and source for the Church's life of mercy. Confession and mercy belong together. The Confessions unequivocally maintain the full truth of the God who was incarnate in human flesh. Just as God in Christ threw Himself wholly into human flesh to redeem us, we throw ourselves fully into the flesh and blood of our neighbor in love. May the Church ever hold fast her confession, precisely for the sake of mercy.

> To demean such works (the confession of doctrine, sufferings, works of love, suppression of the flesh) would be to demean the outward rule of Christ's kingdom among people.[58]

> Thy strong Word bespeaks us righteous;
> Bright with Thine own holiness,
> Glorious now, we press toward glory,
> And our lives our hopes confess.
> Alleluia, alleluia!
> Praise to Thee who light dost send!
> Alleluia, alleluia!
> Alleluia without end!
> (*Lutheran Service Book* 578:3)[59]

> We poor sinners implore You to hear us, O Lord. . . .
> To put an end to all schisms and causes of offense; to bring into the way of truth all who have erred and are deceived; . . .
> To send faithful laborers into Your harvest . . . .
> We implore You to hear us, good Lord. . . .
> Christ, the Lamb of God, who takes away the sin of the world, have mercy.
> (The Litany, *Lutheran Service Book*, pp. 288–89)

Notes

1 WA 20/2:447.8 (*author's translation*).

2 Chancellor of Germany from October 1998 to November 2005.

3 Luther, as quoted in FC SD VIII 41 (*Concordia*, 588), writing against Ulrich Zwingli's denial of the death of God in Christ.

4 Werner Elert, *The Christian Ethos*, trans. Carl J. Schindler (Philadelphia: Muhlenberg, 1957), 228.

5 FC SD VIII 56ff. (*Concordia*, 590).

6 Theodore G. Tappert, ed. and trans., *Luther: Letters of Spiritual Counsel*, Library of Christian Classics 18 (Philadelphia and London: Westminster Press and SCM, 1955), 146.

7 The full account is found in German in StL 2:16:736ff.

8 See Hermann Sasse, "Church and Lord's Supper," in *The Lonely Way*, trans. Matthew C. Harrison et al. (St. Louis: Concordia, 2001), 1:369–429; and Werner Elert, *The Structure of Lutheranism*, trans. Walter A. Hansen (St. Louis: Concordia, 1962), 465. Elert, *Structure of Lutheranism*, 513 n. 6: "The three electoral families to which the most important parts of the German Lutheran Church entrusted themselves went over to other churches one after another."

9 Walter Geppert, *Das Wesen der preussischen Union [The Nature of the Prussian Union]* (Berlin: Furch, 1939), 41. All translations from this volume made by the author.

10 Geppert, *Das Wesen der preussischen Union*, 43.

11 Geppert, *Das Wesen der preussischen Union*, 44–45.

12 Geppert, *Das Wesen der preussischen Union*, 41.

13 Geppert, *Das Wesen der preussischen Union*, 143.

14 Geppert, *Das Wesen der preussischen Union*, 143.

15 AE 33:20.

16 As of the time of the writing of this book, the "Old Gymnasium" (or the school for boys) next to St. Mary's in Wittenberg has been purchased for a mission start for the Independent Evangelical Lutheran Church in Germany (SELK), the German partner church body of the LCMS.

17 See AE 36:289.

18 FC SD VII 33 (*Concordia*, 568).

19 C. F. W. Walther, *The Proper Distinction Between Law and Gospel*, trans. W. H. T. Dau (St. Louis: Concordia, 1929), 332–33.

20 While in Breslau, Germany, Johann Gottfried Scheibel (1783–1843) deeply influenced Martin Stephan, who would have a profound impact on the Saxon fathers of the LCMS.

21 Helmar Junghans, *Wittenburg als Lutherstadt* (Göttingen: Vandenhoeck & Ruprecht, 1979), 176.

22 See Hermann Sasse, "The Century of the Prussian Church," in *The Lonely Way*,

trans. Matthew C. Harrison et al. (St. Louis: Concordia, 2001), 1:159ff.

23 See Hermann Sasse, "Union and Confession," in *The Lonely Way*, trans. Matthew C. Harrison et al. (St. Louis: Concordia, 2001), 1:265–305.

24 Elert, *Structure of Lutheranism*, 464.

25 Ap V 264 (*Concordia*, 141).

26 See AC IV (*Concordia*, 33).

27 See Hermann Sasse, "The Confession of the Church," in *The Lonely Way*, trans. Matthew C. Harrison et al. (St. Louis: Concordia, 2001), 1:103.

28 Ap V 28 (*Concordia*, 106).

29 The now sainted Hamann was principal of Luther Seminary, Adelaide, South Australia. He made this memorable statement in a sermon in the chapel of Concordia Theological Seminary, Fort Wayne, Indiana, during the in 1986–87 academic year.

30 See FC SD Rule and Norm 8–10.

31 AE 43:281.

32 Wilhelm Löhe, *Three Books About the Church* (Fort Wayne, IN: Concordia Theological Seminary Press, 1989), 160.

33 Two classic defenses of the traditional view of Holy Scripture are J. A. O. Preus, *It Is Written* (St. Louis: Concordia, 1971); and David P. Scaer, *The Apostolic Scriptures* (St. Louis: Concordia, 1971). See also Ralph A. Bohlmann, *Principles of Biblical Interpretation in the Lutheran Confessions* (St. Louis: Concordia, 1983).

34 Robert W. Jenson, "The Supper," in *Christian Dogmatics*, ed. Carl E. Braaten and Robert W. Jenson (Philadelphia: Fortress, 1984), 347.

35 FC SD VII 74–75 (*Concordia*, 574).

36 LC V 4 (*Concordia*, 432).

37 FC SD Rule and Norm 17 (*Concordia*, 510). See also AC XXVIII 43 (*Concordia*, 60) and Preface to the Book of Concord 3 (*Concordia*, 3).

38 FC SD Rule and Norm 3 (*Concordia*, 508).

39 Löhe, *Three Books About the Church*, 65.

40 And it has always been so. See Walther, *Proper Distinction Between Law and Gospel*, 347–48.

41 Ap IV 110 (*Concordia*, 100).

42 Ap IV 111 (*Concordia*, 100).

43 Ap IV 114 (*Concordia*, 100).

44 Ap V 33 (*Concordia*, 106); see also FC SD IV 14.

45 Ap V 4 (*Concordia*, 102).

46 FC IV 10–12 (*Concordia*, 548).

47 FC SD IV 7 (*Concordia*, 547).

48 Ap V 19 (*Concordia*, 105).

49 SA II IV 9 (*Concordia*, 269).

50 Tr 80–81 (*Concordia*, 305).

51 Ap V 72 (*Concordia*, 112).

52 LC I 297 (*Concordia*, 393).

53 Ap XXVII 5.

54 See Ap V 71–72 (*Concordia*, 110–12).

55 LC I 252 (*Concordia*, 387).

56 LC I 240 (*Concordia*, 386).

57 LC I 193–94 (*Concordia*, 381).

58 Ap V (*Concordia*, 11-12)

59 Copyright © 1969 Concordia Publishing House.All rights reserved

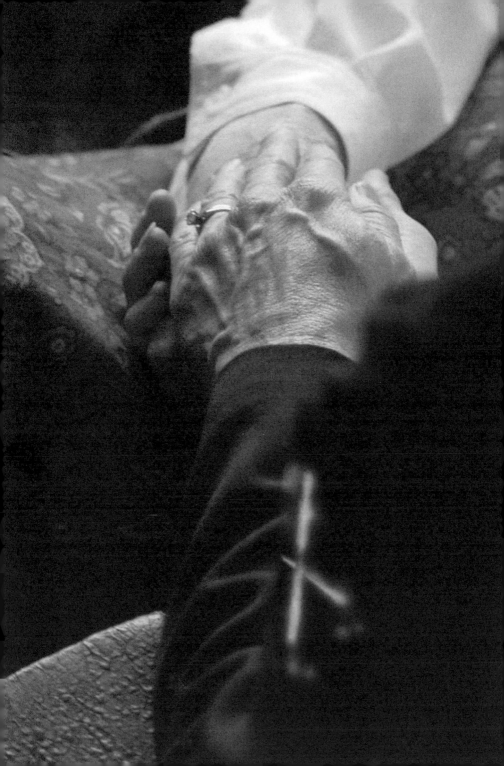

13

MERCY AND OFFICE

ADMINISTERING THE MARKS AND MARKING THE CHURCH WITH MERCY

Having gifts that differ according to the grace given to us, let us use them: . . . the one who does acts of mercy, with cheerfulness. *Romans 12:6, 8*

I just said that the task of the spiritual office is to wait on people in spiritual matters. But they must also see to it that no one suffers bodily need because of poverty.[1] *Martin Luther*

My first congregation was in a rural community of about two hundred in Iowa. The parish had a membership of some 440 souls. I served that congregation with great joy and fidelity by the mercy of Christ, but as I went around the community, something nagged at me. People were hurting in physical and psychological ways, and I did not have the tools to address their need. The community and congregation were buffeted by drug use, alcoholism, depression, unemployment, and other social ills. I gave them Law and Gospel. I preached Christ crucified. I absolved them of their sins when they confessed, baptized them, and gave them the Sacrament of the Altar. I gave them everything. But I felt as though I were the person described in James 2:16 who says after the Lord's Supper, "Go in peace, be warmed and filled." I felt powerless to help the unchurched and inactive members who were suffering amid life's travails. Moreover, I had no idea nor direction that such issues should be the concern of the Office of the Holy Ministry or even of the Church.

MARTIN LUTHER AND MERCY IN THE CHURCH

In earlier chapters I have laid out the biblical texts that mandate a corporate life of mercy in the Church. There also are a few significant writings by Lutheran fathers that speak directly to the Office of the Holy Ministry and its diaconal responsibilities. These writings also speak about the offices of deacon and deaconess.

On St. Stephen's Day, December 26, 1523, Martin Luther

preached on Acts 6–7, a section of Scripture well known to the fathers of the LCMS:

> In the first part [of the text] you have here [Acts 6], you see how a Christian church should be formed and a correct picture of a spiritual government. The apostles proceed to care for souls. They go around preaching and praying, and they see to it that also the body is cared for by setting up certain men who distribute goods. Thus the Church's governance [regiment] is concerned with body and soul and that no one suffers need. As Luke says [in Acts 4:32ff.] all are richly fed with respect to the soul and well cared for in the body. That is a correct picture. It would be very good . . . if we had the people to do it, that a city such as this one [i.e., Wittenberg] be divided into four or five sections. Each section would be given a preacher and a deacon to distribute goods and care for people who are ill and see to those who have need. But we do not have the people to carry this out. Therefore I trust we will not see this happen until our Lord God makes Christians. Currently we make deacons [mere] readers of the Epistle and the Gospel . . . . Thus deacons are not chosen for the office that they had at the time of the apostles. Instead, they stand by the altar and teach the Epistle and Gospel. What belongs to preaching and praying has been called the mass. What belongs to the office of caring for the people has been turned into the "Epistler and Gospeler." The head of the hospital, the head nun, and the person who has the guardianship of the poor, all have a part or form of the deaconate. And when you establish a common chest, you thus distinguish what the bishop and deacons are. *Bishop* means an official of God, who should have ministers [*dieners*]. He should distribute the divine goods, namely, the Gospel. The deacons, however, that is the ministers [*diener*], shall have the registry of the poor so they can be cared for.[2]

Here Luther asserts that the "spiritual government" (that is, the system of governance of the Church per se) is to be concerned with "body and soul," as is evidenced in Acts 6 at the time of the apostles. The apostles preach and care for the soul, but they see to it that the body is cared for as well. The bishops or pastors dole out the spiritual goods; the deacons, as servants to the bishops and the Church, provide the poor with what is needed for physical well being. As Norman Nagel has pointed out, the deacons of the Church can fail to be what they can and ought to be in one of two ways: They can become mere liturgical functionaries (in this sermon Luther complains about the "Epistler and Gospeler"), or they can become detached from the Church's life of worship and become totally consumed with care for the physical needs of people without reference to altar, font, and pulpit![3] For Luther, the Office of the Holy Ministry has concern for the needy. Deacons serve as an extension of the office for the specific purpose of caring for the needy.[4]

MARTIN CHEMNITZ AND MERCY IN THE CHURCH

Following Luther and preceding Johann Gerhard, Martin Chemnitz (1522–1586) is the second of the three great Lutheran fathers. As the author of the Formula of Concord (which established broad consensus out of the discord that followed Luther's death), what does this "second Martin" have to say about the Office of the Holy Ministry and care for the needy? Chemnitz wrote in his famous *Examination of the Council of Trent*:

> This ministry does indeed have power, divinely bestowed (2 Cor. 10:4–6; 13:2–4), but circumscribed with certain duties and limitations, namely, to preach the Word of God, teach the erring, reprove those who sin, admonish the dilatory, comfort the troubled, strengthen the weak, resist those who speak against the truth, reproach and condemn false teaching, censure evil customs, dispense the divinely instituted sacraments, remit and retain sins, be an example to the flock, pray for the church privately and lead the church in public prayers, be in charge of care for the poor [*pauperum curam agere*], publicly excommunicate the stubborn and again receive those who repent and reconcile them with the church, appoint pastors to the church according to the instruction of Paul, with consent of the church institute rites that serve the ministry and do not militate against the Word of God nor burden consciences but serve good order, dignity, decorum, tranquillity, edification, etc.[5]

JOHANN GERHARD AND MERCY IN THE CHURCH

And what of Johann Gerhard (1582–1637), who wrote the greatest doctrinal work in the history of Lutheranism (*Loci Theologici*)? Gerhard lists the seven "duties of the office of the ministry":

> The most important duty of ministers of the church is to preach the Word. . . . The second duty of ministers is to administer the Sacraments. . . . The third duty of ministers is diligently praying for the flock entrusted to them. . . . Their fourth duty, then, is the honest control of their life and behavior. . . . The fifth duty of ministers is to administer church discipline. . . . The sixth duty of ministers is to preserve the rituals of the church. Finally,

because among the hearers are orphans, widows, the poor, the homeless, the ill—duties of charity are especially owed to alleviate their poverty and affliction. Therefore, the seventh duty of the ministry is the care of the poor and the visitation of the sick. He should collect and spend faithfully the money destined for use for the poor. If this duty is entrusted to those in charge of the church treasury, he should exhort members diligently to demonstrate their generosity toward the poor. He also should see to it that dispensing the goods is done lawfully and correctly (1 Cor. 16:2; 2 Cor. 9:1).[6]

Gerhard writes that the "ministers of the church should not think that anything related to caring for the poor is foreign to them."[7] Why? Christ Himself diligently cared for the poor as evidenced by the money He and the disciples kept for their aid (John 13:29). Paul carried out the collection for the poor saints in Jerusalem (1 Corinthians 16:1; Galatians 2:10). The love feasts of the ancient Church were instituted to assist the poor. In the New Testament Church, care for the poor was appointed to the diaconate (Acts 6:5). Gerhard writes that "to emulate them, today we have church treasurers who are responsible for collecting and distributing the goods of the church."[8] Finally, Gerhard encourages pastors to exhort their hearers to be generous, and by their own example they are to encourage generosity, hospitality, and mindfulness of the church treasury and the needs of the poor.

C. F. W. WALTHER AND MERCY IN THE CHURCH

C. F. W. Walther (1811–1887), the greatest U.S. Lutheran of the nineteenth century, was the major architect and founder of the LCMS. He revered Luther as the German prophet and reformer and also highly regard Chemnitz and Gerhard. But did Walther share their views that the Church has a corporate life of mercy and that the pastoral office has a responsibility to see that the needs of the poor are addressed? Consider Walther's comments in *The Pastor's Responsibility to Care for the Physical Needs of Members of His Congregation*:

> Although a preacher above all has concern for the spiritual needs of the members of his congregation, concern for the physical well-being, particularly the needs of the poor, the sick, widows, orphans, the infirm, the destitute, the aged, etc., are within the scope of the duties of his office. Gal. 2:9–10; Acts 6:1ff., 11:30, 12:25, 24:17; Rom. 12:8,13; James 1:27; I Tim. 5:10; I Thess. 4:11–12.[9]

Indeed, Walther notes the texts cited in Luther's St. Stephen's Day sermon, as well as those from Gerhard on the duties of the Office of the Holy Ministry.[10] Walther urges that "the pastor is more responsible than all others to express fatherly care for the suffering persons."[11] The pastor should diligently care for the souls of the poor and afflicted, urge generosity on the part of all for the congregation's poor chest, and "diligently investigate which among those of his flock are suffering, and who deserve to be mercifully cared for."[12] The pastor is to maintain a list of the poor and oversee the distribution of funds to the needy. Particularly if the pastor serves a large congregation, he is to ensure that a proper administration of the funds for the poor is established along the lines of Acts 6. In *Proper Form of a Christian Congregation*, Walther states that "the congregation shall also provide food, clothing, habitation, and all other necessities for the poor, widows, orphans, aged, and invalids, which these themselves cannot procure and [for which] they have no relatives who first of all owe them these things."[13]

When the Lutheran Confessions define the Office of the Holy Ministry, they do so with precise brevity: "So that we may obtain this faith, the ministry of teaching the Gospel and administering the Sacraments was instituted."[14] Likewise, Walther lays out the nature of the Church and its ministry with dogmatic precision in his magisterial *Church and Ministry*.[15] But like Luther, Chemnitz, and Gerhard before him, Walther's description of the nature of pastoral practice and his explication of the duties of the office include the ordering and practice of *diakonia*, which is care for the needy in the congregation.

I recently discovered and translated an extraordinary sermon by Walther on the Office of the Holy Ministry. He explains that Romans 12:6–12 has to do explicitly with the duties of the pastoral office! Walther says:

> Now concerning the range of this task, that is given by the apostle in the following words: "the one who teaches, in his teaching; the one who exhorts, in his exhortation; the one who contributes, in generosity; the one who leads, with zeal; the one who does acts of mercy, with cheerfulness." All of these things, I repeat, are not descriptions of general Christian work. They are rather a brief register of the duties of the public preaching office. There are five parts here which belong to this office: The first and most

important is teaching; the second is admonition; the third is giving or the office's concern for the poor; the fourth is governing or the administration of discipline and order; and finally the fifth is the exercise of mercy or the concern of the office for the sick, the weak, and the dying.

> Behold how great, how broad, how all encompassing the task of a preacher is! He is to teach. . . . He is to admonish. . . . When they suffer earthly need, he shall assist them in their need. . . . Where consolation and help are needed, he shall be the Good Samaritan of the congregation, ready with mercy. Thus the great task of his office is to see to it that no one in his entire congregation is abandoned and suffers need without assistance, be it in external or inner matters, in bodily matters or spiritual matters. He sees to it that everyone who belongs to the holy brotherhood of Christ is well cared for. He shall receive the whole as much as the individual. . . . All this shall be the concern of his heart. And this shall be his concern at opportune or inopportune times, in evil or good days, in times of rich earthly blessing as much as in times of hunger and pestilence, in war and in peace, publicly and privately.[16]

It is time once again to hear Walther, a consummate theologian, on the Office of the Holy Ministry. He has said what must be said; I can add nothing. "It is always a sign of a deep spiritual sickness when a church forgets its fathers."[17]

OFFICE AND OFFICES: THE DEACONESS

Lutheranism is unique among church bodies because it sees no "order by which the Lord mandates his church be governed."[18] As German theologian Hermann Sasse noted repeatedly, everyone from Congregationalists to the Eastern Orthodox read out of the Scriptures a specific form of church governance or order.[19] For Rome and the Eastern Orthodox there must be the deacon, priest, and bishop. Calvinism finds a presbyterate. Congregationalists find a lay vote. As Walther and other Lutherans have noted, there is no one biblical form of church order. Lutherans may have bishops or choose not to have them. A synod may choose an episcopal polity or a more congrega-tional/synodical form of governance. The matter is free. The New Testament bears witness to more than one type of governance—from Paul's appointing of clergy in various mission congregations to what is essentially "voting" (Acts 6:5 and elsewhere). There is, however, one divinely mandated office in the Church: the Office of the Holy Ministry. Its chief tasks are the preaching of the Word and the administration of the Sacraments.[20] Without these tasks the Church cannot exist.

The New Testament is also flexible with regard to the establishment of other offices that complement or assist the Office of the Holy Ministry in the life of the Church. Both Walther and Wilhelm Löhe believed that the "almoners" (as Walther calls them) in Acts 6 not only cared for the physical needs of the widows but also received an apostolic mandate to carry out this work. The money bag was evidence of the apostolic office's concern for the needy.[21] The Church always and everywhere must preach the Word and distribute the Sacraments. The particular physical and or diaconal needs of the Church will change from time to time, so special offices and tasks may freely be established to accomplish such needed work.

The office of deaconess is such a special office. Through its diaconal work, the Church cares for body and soul. Thus Löhe can write that "the office of holy deacony became a spiritual office, an office of double mercy."[22] The question is often asked, "What does a deaconess do?" The answer can be found in "The True Deaconess Spirit," a poem written by Löhe: "What is my want? I want to serve. Whom do I want to serve? The Lord in his wretched ones and his poor."[23] Early in the life of the Church, perhaps yet during New Testament times (consider Phoebe, as mentioned in Romans 16:1–2), women were given a particular vocation/office in service to the Church. By the early second century, particularly in the Eastern Church, deaconesses were consecrated "by the laying on of hands."[24] As monasticism came to dominate the Church's life in the early Middle Ages, the office of deaconess slipped from history until it was reestablished and invigorated, most notably in nineteenth-century German Lutheranism.

The deaconess office is a *Geist*, a spirit, a conviction, an attitude of service. Christ Himself is the great *diakonos* of the New Testament, who "came not to be served but to serve, and to give His life as a ransom for many" (Matthew 20:28). And Jesus bids His followers go the same way of humble service to others (Luke 22:25–27). So what does a deaconess do? A deaconess serves as the Church needs her, so far as the service is appropriate to the vocation of woman. What may she do? A deaconess may do anything but carry out the functions of the Office of the Holy Ministry. That is, she may freely be asked by the Church to do virtually anything except those tasks specific to the Office of the Holy Ministry. What should deaconesses do in the Church today? They may participate in even more vocations and tasks than those already being accomplished with zeal and fidelity: teaching, social work, care for the elderly, human care outreach in the congregation and into the community, administrative duties, running the Church's institutions of mercy. The Church needs many more women to serve and in many more ways, as Löhe noted in the nineteenth-century: "The field of mercy had already been great, now it is altogether overwhelming."[25]

The Church, in its congregations and schools and in its multiplicity of diaconal agencies and synodical functions, makes use of literally hundreds of individual vocations. The deaconess brings to any of these vocations a commitment to Lutheran theology, a determined resolve to be of service to the Office of the Holy Ministry while respecting that office, and a deep appreciation of the importance of the Church as it gathers around the Lord and His gifts in the Divine Service. Service to the needy flows from Christ's service to the needy (us!) in Word and Sacrament.

It is time and past time for consecrated women—deaconesses—to be serving as leaders at every level and in every capacity in the Church's diaconal institutions. It is time for deaconesses to form and be assisted in forming diaconal organizations that are connected with congregations. It is time for an international organization of confessional Lutheran deaconesses who are engaged in mercy ministries, hospitals, clinics, family care, care for women and children, and so on. Indeed, though the catholic and apostolic Church must say *no* to women in one office (the Office of the Holy Ministry), the Church can and must say *yes* to her service in a thousand other offices. The moment of the Lutheran deaconess is now.

Called workers, and particularly pastors, have enormously challenging vocations. These vocations carry with them great opportunities to lead God's people in showing mercy to the needy. In an article published by Walther in 1861 in *Der Lutheraner*, Theodore Julius Brohm told the story of Pastor Hess of Breslau:

> A very intriguing history was recounted for us of the first establishment of the care of the poor in Breslau. Johan Hess, the first Lutheran preacher in Breslau (d. 1547) could no longer accept how beggars, crippled, and mentally ill people lay on the streets and in front of all the churches in Breslau. He began to publicly admonish the governing authorities from the pulpit. But from it came no establishment of means to care for the poor in the community. Then Hess quit preaching. This had a significant effect upon the magistrate and the congregation, because he very much enjoyed preaching and they knew it. Finally they resolved to ask him why he stopped preaching. The answer was this: "My Lord Jesus lay in His members at the doors of all the churches. I cannot simply step over Him. If He is not cared for, neither will I preach." These words had a very significant influence. Places to care for the poor were prepared. Illegitimate beggars were dismissed and in one day 500 persons were brought to newly established hospitals. Thus there arose gradually in all the cities and villages of Lutheran Germany a well-ordered and equipped way of caring for the poor and the sick, as we now see it everywhere.[26]

In many places around the world today, the poor, the blind, the lame still wait beside the doors of churches and cathedrals. As Jesus said, "You always have the poor with you" (Matthew 26:11). But because this is so, so also Matthew 25:40 remains in effect, "Truly, I say to you, as you did it to one of the least of these My brothers, you did it to Me." In our U.S. churches the poor, the needy, and the hurting may be less readily visible, but they are there—in our pews, in our congregations, in our communities. May our called pastors take up the office of Christ and, like our orthodox Lutheran fathers, be heralds of the mercy and love of Christ, for the sake of His Gospel and His needy ones. With Löhe, may they understand that "the whole apostolic order of office and church is . . . nothing but an instruction for a shepherd to show merciful love."[27]

> Forth in Thy name, O Lord, I go,
> My daily labor to pursue,
> Thee, only Thee, resolved to know
> In all I think or speak or do.
>
> The task Thy wisdom has assigned,
> O let me cheerfully fulfill;

In all my works Thy presence find,

And prove Thy good and perfect will.

(*Lutheran Service Book* 854:1–2)

We poor sinners implore You to hear us, good Lord.

To rule and govern Your holy Christian Church; to preserve all pastors and ministers of Your Church in the true knowledge and understanding of Your wholesome Word and to sustain them in holy living . . . .

O Christ, hear us.

O Lord, have mercy.

O Christ, have mercy.

(The Litany, *Lutheran Service Book*, pp. 288–89)

NOTES

1 AE 52:222.

2 WA 12:476 (*author's translation*).

3 Norman Nagel, *The Twelve and the Seven in Acts 6 and the Needy* (St. Louis: LCMS World Relief and Human Care, 2005).

4 AE 46:167–68: "If I were emperor, king, or prince and were in a campaign against the Turk, I would exhort my bishops and priests to stay at home and attend to the duties of their office, praying, fasting, saying mass, preaching, and caring for the poor, as not only Holy Scripture, but their own canon law teaches and requires."

5 Martin Chemnitz, *Examination of the Council of Trent*, trans. Fred Kramer (St. Louis: Concordia, 1978), 2:678–79.

6 Johann Gerhard, *On the Duties of Ministers of the Church*, trans. Richard Dinda (St. Louis: LCMS World Relief and Human Care, 2005), 5–7.

7 Gerhard, *On the Duties of Ministers of the Church*, 59–60.

8 Gerhard, *On the Duties of Ministers of the Church*, 60.

9 Matthew C. Harrison and J. T. Mueller, trans., *Walther on Mercy* (St. Louis: LCMS World Relief and Human Care, 2006), 5.

10 Harrison and Mueller, *Walther on Mercy*, 6–7.

11 Harrison and Mueller, *Walther on Mercy*, 8.

12 Harrison and Mueller, *Walther on Mercy*, 9.

13 Harrison and Mueller, *Walther on Mercy*, 19.

14 AC V 1 (*Concordia*, 33).

15 C. F. W. Walther, *Church and Ministry*, trans. J. T. Mueller (St. Louis: Concordia, 1987).

16 C. F. W. Walther, *Lutherische Brosamen, Predigten und Reden . . . von C. F. W.*

Walther (St. Louis, 1876), 59–68 (*author's translation*).

17 Hermann Sasse, "Fathers of the Church," in *The Lonely Way*, trans. Matthew C. Harrison et al. (St. Louis: Concordia, 2002), 2:229.

18 Gallican Confession XXIX.

19 Hermann Sasse, "The Lutheran Doctrine of the Office of the Ministry," in *The Lonely Way*, trans. Matthew C. Harrison et al. (St. Louis: Concordia, 2002), 2:121.

20 AC V and AC XIV (*Concordia*, 33, 39).

21 See Holger Sonntag, trans., *Löhe on Mercy*, ed. by Adriane Dorr and Philip Hendrickson (St. Louis: LCMS World Relief and Human Care, 2006), 29: ". . . the communal breaking of bread and the office of the care of the poor, which first grew out of the apostolic office."

22 Sonntag, *Löhe on Mercy*, 24.

23 http://www.lcms.org/pages/internal.asp?NavID=9094 (accessed October 17, 2007).

24 *Apostolic Constitutions* VIII.19.

25 Sonntag, *Löhe on Mercy*, 41.

26 Theodore Julius Brohm, *Mercy and the Lutheran Congregation*, trans. Matthew C. Harrison (St. Louis: LCMS World Relief and Human Care, 2006), 13.

27 Sonntag, *Löhe on Mercy*, 23.

14

WHAT IS LUTHERAN LEADERSHIP?

REASON SERVING THE GOSPEL TO GET IT DONE

Having gifts that differ according to the grace given to us, let us use them:
. . . the one who leads, with zeal.[1] *Romans 12:6, 8*

The sectarians rise up and at bottom seek nothing else except to gain great
honor among the people, so that people will say of them: There's the right
man; he'll do it! And with this praise they also want to strut and tickle their
own vanity: This you have done, this is your work, you are the first-rate
man, the real master. But that isn't even worth throwing to the dogs. For
right preachers should diligently and faithfully teach only the Word of God
and seek only his honor and praise.[2] *Martin Luther*

On a recent trip to Madagascar, I visited the south central town of
Antisrabe. The serene countryside and racial melting pot that is
Madagascar belies the deep challenges the Church faces in caring for
the needy. Heading from the hotel to the vehicle, I was confronted by
an elderly man, calling, "Merci, merci, monsieur?"[3]

As a general rule when I travel, I do not give to professional beggars and I try never to intentionally support addiction, though I
usually make small offerings to the crippled or incapacitated elderly
who seem to be everywhere. Looking at this man, obvious ill health
betrayed a life of addiction and life on the street. His ancient hat in
hand, brown with dirt and tattered like every stitch he wore, he was
speaking my language, "Merci."

As I declined the man's request for cash, I noticed his ankle was
swollen and the flesh was raw and oozing. I could have mercy on him
without feeding his addiction, so I asked Pastor David, my host for the
trip, to translate for us.

"Are you sick?" I asked

"Yes, sir," the man replied.

"It looks like there is something wrong with your ankle. Why
don't you take my card and present it at the Lutheran Hospital. Tell
them I will pay for any treatment you need," I said as I handed the
man a business card.

Pastor David and I sped off for a long day of visiting vibrant and enormous Malagasy Lutheran churches and institutions of mercy. Returning to the hotel, I stepped out of the car to find that same man standing only inches away, smiling and chattering, quite obviously delighted. Again, Pastor David translated his Malagasy.

"Did you go to the hospital?" I asked.

"Yes! They helped me and even gave me this medicine," was the man's excited reply.

"What did the doctor say about your foot?" I asked.

The response took me back: "Leprosy."

Less than twenty-four hours earlier, I had visited a great health facility, something rare in the developing world. Dr. Harison Rasamimanana, the administrator, is a Lutheran layman and medical doctor. He and his wife, Damoina, have been key in an HIV/AIDS education effort in Madagascar funded by LCMS World Relief and Human Care. After frequent e-mail correspondence with this extraordinary couple, I finally had the pleasure to meet them face-to-face as they took us around the hospital that is their life's passion. As we walked through the entire facility, we met patient after patient who was suffering from some illness or injury that, while often easily treatable, was devastating if not addressed.

We visited a young Lutheran girl gasping for breath, unconscious, fighting cerebral malaria. She had failed to take her medication, and the disease quickly intensified before her father could bring her to a hospital where they could afford treatment. She was near death. I laid my hands on her head as we prayed.

Another young woman lay in recovery. That morning her baby had been taken by Cesarean section; it was stillborn. Other hospitals would not take this woman because she had no money. By the time she found Dr. Harison's hospital, it was too late. The baby was lost, but her life was spared.

We walked the halls of the facility, hearing story after story, and Dr. Harison repeatedly turned to me and said in his Malagasy French accent, "How can we turn them away? Jesus would have us take them. We can't say *no*. How can we say *no*?"

This hospital operates for the entire year on about $50,000—with seven doctors on staff! Dr. Harison makes around $100 a month. Although he could make five or ten times more money at a state-owned hospital, Dr. Harison chose to accept a position where his Lutheran faith, his deep passion for those in need, and his brilliant administrative skills could bring about something extraordinary to benefit the most needy in the name of Jesus. It is amazing and inspiring to observe passion, skill, and enough funding to get the job done meet at the nexus of mercy.

Dr. Harison and Damoina are real leaders. That hospital board got "the right people on the bus," to borrow a phrase from author Jim Collins.[4] There is a great deal written about leadership. Much of the literature is not written from a theological perspective, which is fine. Leadership is not so much a product of God's Word as it is of reason. As a fruit of reason, Lutherans submit leadership principles to the Word of God. Where they do not contradict God's Word, the freedom of the Gospel allows us to make wise use of such principles.

The study of leadership and the application of what is learned to serve the Gospel is a legitimate use of the social sciences. Study can give us insight into why (from a human standpoint) some individuals and institutions are able to succeed in their vocational endeavors. Lutherans recognize that reason and skills for leadership are good First Article (creation) gifts. When we reject or ignore the blessings of God's First Article gifts, we not only deny God's good creation, but we also may end up being ineffective leaders of the Church or her work of mercy, even placing obstacles in the way of the Gospel. There is a tendency among those who take the Church seriously to eschew or even shun the disciplines of leadership and administration. St. Paul did not do so.[5] Instead, because these disciplines lay within the realm of God's good created gifts, they can and should be studied and used for churchly endeavors.

Lutheran leadership makes full use of God's good gifts of reason and science as they are under and in service to our commitments to Scripture and the Lutheran Confessions. Francis Pieper, the premiere doctrinal theologian of the second generation of the LCMS, offers helpful guidance when he distinguishes between the "ministerial" and "magisterial" use of reason. Reason and its disciplines must be used to serve the Gospel and may not be allowed to contradict clear teachings of the Bible. The Bible and the Confessions are the limit for reason. Pieper asserts that reason per se (in this case sociology, psychology, and the study of leadership) is not a threat to the truth of Christ, but "a contradiction arises only when reason, gone mad, presumes to judge things that transcend its sphere. . . . If reason leaves its boundaries, all mysteries of faith, as the Trinity, the Incarnation, etc., conflict with it."[6] If reason has "gone mad" with leadership principles so that the Gospel and the Church's primary task to proclaim it suffers, the Church has gone wrong. The Church can and should make use of the study of leadership and administration, for the Gospel "allows us to use medicine or the art of building, or food, drink, and air."[7]

Our temptation as confessional Lutherans is to think that if we simply have the right faith and confession, then all other matters in the Church will go smoothly. We can become inverted First Article fanatics, guilty of First Article fanaticism (*Schwarmgeisterei*), which by Lutheran definition looks for God to reveal Himself, His name, His Gospel for forgiveness and certainty where He has not promised to do so (that is, outside His Word and Sacraments[8]). First Article fanaticism denies God's good use of First Article gifts, especially that He has given us our reason and even the social disciplines. Such fanaticism holds that God has nothing to teach us in His created realm of good old human reason. While creation does not preach the Gospel to us, it does bear witness to God's gift of reason. And we can learn much from reason that can and must assist in the Church's work of mercy.

GREATNESS IN THE SOCIAL SECTOR

Although there are numerous helpful books on leadership, two books by Jim Collins stand out and have been particularly helpful for me. In 2001 Collins published *Good to Great: Why Some Companies Make the Leap—and Others Don't,*[9] which released the findings of a study of approximately a dozen companies that had outperformed competitors by enormous margins. *Good to Great and the Social Sectors,* a shorter companion volume, was published in 2005.[10] This volume applies to the nonprofit world what was learned in the first study.

According to Collins, nonprofits in many ways have greater challenges on the path to excellence and effectiveness than do for-profit businesses. Applying Collins's insights, if you are thinking of doing something great to serve the needy, it will take disciplined leadership, people, and thinking. The old adage "not many, but much" applies.

Collins writes that "we must reject the idea—well-intentioned, but dead wrong—that the primary path to greatness in the social sectors is to become 'more like a business.'"[11] Collins explains that this is incorrect thinking because most businesses "fall somewhere between mediocre and good. . . . So, then, why would we want to import the practices of mediocrity into the social sectors?"[12] According to Collins, the social sector does not need business practices but discipline in planning, people, organization, and distribution of resources. These are not business principles per se, but principles of greatness. So, says Collins, what is needed is not the language of the business world, but the language that inspires individuals to reach for what is great.[13]

LEADING IN THE MINISTRY OF MERCY

The following are a few suggestions for a disciplined start toward a great ministry of mercy. The list comes from personal experience coupled with insights from Collins's book.

STEP 1: GET THE RIGHT PEOPLE INVOLVED
AND ALLOW THEM SPACE TO BE CREATIVE.

We all have heard the old bromide, "He has all the qualities of leadership . . . except followers." Such "one-man shows" may produce interesting, even spectacular, results, but over time they will fail because it takes a community to sustain the Church's work of mercy. Mercy takes people. According to Collins's extensive and credible studies of for-profit and nonprofit leadership, great leaders get the right people in the right positions and the bad apples out of the picture. Great leaders ask, "First who, then what."[14]

The place to begin an emphasis on mercy in your congregation may not be a social ministry committee—if, as is sometimes the case, the committe has been filled with well-meaning individuals simply to occupy positions and not to provide critical reflection on the congregation's life of mercy. It would be better to pull together a handful of the most capable and concerned individuals in the congregation, such as doctors, nurses, other health care professionals, those with particular organizational skills, those willing to donate time or money, creative individuals with a proven track record of garnering consensus in the congregation. Designate this group as a think tank on the congregation's life of care and mercy for those in need. Encourage the group to study *Theology for Mercy*,[15] this book, and *Good to Great and the Social Sectors*. Let them think about possibilities and be creative. The LCMS is full of creative, faithful, and talented laypeople who are ready for a challenge.

STEP 2: IDENTIFY CRITICAL ISSUES.

What are the issues within your congregation? What are the issues in your surrounding community? Before a congregation can decide its diaconal direction, it must have a realistic picture of its context. This takes honesty. If your congregation simply has no evident active care for the needy, admit it. Collins heartily recommends such confrontation.[16]

Many congregations provide a food pantry for the needy or referrals for the same. While such ministries of mercy can be appropriate, they rarely address the more serious issues behind indigence or poverty. Moreover, acts of mercy that fail to incorporate recipients into the community of the congregation often have little positive effect on the lives of the recipients of such charity. There is often little opportunity to share Christ meaningfully. Setting up a food pantry might be a quick and easy way to salve our consciences, but it will probably have little enduring effect on lives.

This was a hard lesson for me to learn as an inner-city pastor. Neither the congregation nor I had the capacity to assist the large numbers of street people in our area, often because these individuals were long-term addicts, homeless, and typically mentally ill. They needed a lot of help. Other individuals were habitual transients who would panhandle from congregation to congregation. The welfare system, despite its absolute necessity for the most chronically needy, can perpetuate indigence and addiction.

Look internally and externally. Does your congregation know its own demographics? What are the needs of the elderly in your congregation? Is mental health an issue? Is addiction a significant issue? Is family counseling a necessity? What about marriage issues? Does your congregation have a logical tool to assess internal needs? What are the needs within the broader community? Is affordable housing a problem? What about elder care? What is your community's demographic makeup? Are there significant immigrant populations, and if so, what needs do they have?[17]

The people of the community. Friend and colleague the Rev. Carlos Hernandez introduced me to an effective way to learn what your community is thinking. He developed a simple method for a congregation to assess its community and its most critical needs, which he calls "planting Gospel seeds while serving human needs." The assessment process asks neighbors of the church to self-identify the most critical issues facing the immediate neighborhood of the congregation.

Rev. Hernandez's method trains congregation members to canvass the homes and institutions in the neighborhood, asking the simple leading question, "What do you think are the most critical issues facing our neighborhood?" The person asking the question is not doing so as a "religious expert," ready to impart knowledge, but as a person truly concerned about the community and its needs and challenges. And people respond; they invite the canvassers into their homes, saying, "Let me tell you" or "I do know one thing that is really a concern to this community." The method works in any type of community—inner city, suburban, rural. It results in genuine contacts and real information. In such a context of honesty and real concern, Christ is shared. Information gleaned from the community is of great importance as the congregation works toward defining the precise purpose of its mercy ministry.

The institutions of the community. Pastor and people also can visit police and fire departments, hospitals, schools, and community institutions. Ask about the types of calls the police make. What are the principal issues in the schools? Who is the hospital treating or unable to treat? City hall and public school offices can provide a wealth of information about the community. From this legwork may emerge a vision for how your congregation might address need in the name of Christ, both within the congregation and in terms of the broader community.

Should your congregation focus its efforts internally or externally? St. Paul gives us a clear and simple answer: "So then, as we have opportunity, let us do good to everyone, and especially to those who are of the household of faith" (Galatians 6:10). Many Lutheran congregations need serious "in reach." In the wake of the post-World War II growth of the welfare society, the Church retreated from one realm of care for the needy after another. Hospital and social ministry institutions that once cared for needy Lutherans rightly branched out to care for others in the community, but in so doing, these institutions accepted necessary government funding, which in turn has moved the focus of their mission to the needy non-Lutheran community. Care for the needy by and within congregations has often fallen by the wayside. However, I have seen that congregations who care for the needy internally are the very congregations who also look outside themselves to the needy in their communities. The goal is to be intentional. A congregation can intentionally become a community that reflects the mercy of Christ that is so richly delivered every Sunday morning.

STEP 3: ASSESS THE POTENTIAL FOR PARTNERSHIPS TO INCREASE CAPACITY.

What is capacity? Capacity is the people, the funds, and the expertise to get a job done. A congregation or a pastor may have a deep desire and commitment to care for the needy, but the congregation and pastor may have no ability, no funding, or no expertise to do so.

It is *crucial* in the work of mercy to act in ways that treat those assisted with dignity, to call for accountability, and to enable those in need to retain and gain as much control over their own lives as possible. It is easy to give a hand out, but it is complex to give a hand up. It is also crucial for the long-term well-being of the work that resources are used well and with full transparency and accountability to those who generously provide them.

Are there possibilities for partnership? Is there a Lutheran institution that may be interested in partnering in some fashion? Lutheran institutions of mercy are often eager to develop partnerships with congregations to meet specific needs. These institutions realize that the more connected they are to Lutheran congregations, the healthier they are as institutions. These agencies often can bring tremendous capacity, know-how, familiarity with the community, professional and even financial expertise to the table. Do other organizations serve the mentally ill, handicapped, addicted, or those suffering with other afflictions? Is there a nonprofit housing organization in the community? Many such organizations partner with congregations and are eager to find leaders to serve the community from the basis of an established and respected parish within the community. What of the medical community? City and county governments are deeply involved in social services and often provide such services in cooperation with local congregations and other nonprofit organizations. Are there other Christian congregations that could provide an opportunity for "cooperation in externals" or shared work that does not involve joint worship or compromise convictions of the faith?

In all these situations the congregation needs to be brutally honest with itself, faithful to confessional commitments, and clearly and charitably communicative with her partners. In terms of LCMS World Relief and Human Care, I follow this motto: "The LCMS is a people of deep conviction. We respect others who have deep convictions, even where we may disagree." Hermann Sasse, veteran of the Faith and Order Movement, often said, "There is more true unity of the Spirit where Christians of differing confession are honest about their differences, than where they ignore those differences as though they did not matter."[18]

Step 4: Look for best practices.

As your congregation's social ministry task force hones in on one or, at the most, two diaconal specifics, it is time to look at how others might be doing the same or similar work and communicate in person. Some years ago I heard of a Baptist church in Chicago that revolutionized its care for the indigent through its soup kitchen. At most soup kitchens food is distributed, but there is little effort to create "community." The addicts and the poor, the homeless, and the mentally ill come out of the shadows of the night, their humanity perceptible for but a moment. They eat and quietly disappear into the chaos of the city—their world of cardboard, shopping carts, and indigence. But this Baptist congregation discovered that when recipients of charity can participate in the charitable activity, they gain dignity. Thus a community of care is created. So where the people once emerged from the shadows only to receive and leave, now each individual is interviewed and given an opportunity to help themselves and others. It is as simple as asking: "What are you good at? Would you like to cook? to clean? to serve? to set the table? Can you paint or draw?" The individual task is unimportant, but the contribution of the individual to the community is essential.

Once this practice was put in place, the kitchen changed. It became a real community of people with specific vocations, people caring for one another, people with names, people who could be spoken to and who could speak to others, people who were appreciated, often for the first time in their lives. It seems like such a simple change, but one with profound results as the Gospel is shared in the context of a community. Luther understood this well and refused assistance to otherwise able vagabonds who refused to help themselves.[19]

Somewhere, a congregation has done what you are contemplating or something similar. Go. See. Get ideas. Evaluate. Use everything that works.

STEP 5: GO WITH WHAT YOU CAN BE GOOD AT.

In *Good to Great*, Jim Collins brought to light what he called the "Hedgehog Concept." Unlike the fox (which survives by a multitude of cunning activities), the hedgehog protects itself by doing one thing well: it curls up in a ball when endangered. Collins studied the Hedgehog Concept of successful for-profit companies. He writes:

> The essence of a Hedgehog Concept is to attain piercing clarity about how to produce the best long-term results, and then exercising the relentless discipline to say, "No thank you" to opportunities that fail the hedgehog test. When we examined the Hedgehog Concepts of the good-to-great compa-

nies, we found they reflected deep understanding of three intersecting circles: 1) what you are deeply passionate about, 2) what you can be the best
in the world at, and 3) what best drives your economic engine.[20]

In his later monograph for the social sector, Collins asserted that
this Hedgehog Concept is even more critical for the success of the
nonprofit. The for-profit can simply measure success by the bottom
line. Nonprofit measurements of success are more challenging
because their goal is *meeting human needs*. Nonprofit organizations
often have funding structures that are more varied and complex. Thus

> the inherent complexity requires deeper, more penetrating insight and rig-
> orous clarity than in your average business entity. You begin with passion,
> then you refine passion with a rigorous assessment of what you can best
> contribute to the communities you touch. Then you create a way to tie your
> resource engine directly to the other two circles.[21]

You cannot be the best at, or even good at, what you cannot fund.
Let me repeat that because it is so important: *you cannot be the best at,
or even good at, what you cannot fund*. In many cases, and certainly in
the case of the average Lutheran congregation, that means the intentional work of mercy will begin and may well remain something that
is modestly funded and largely volunteer driven.

Finances are key in determining your congregation's diaconal
direction. The stewardship chapter in this book offered a few thoughts
on this topic. Your task force will need to analyze the sources of poten-
tial funding in the congregation and community, including charitable
organizations, local foundations, individuals, and so on. It may be
advisable for your nascent ministry of mercy to employ a grant writer
or even a fund developer.

Putting together a mercy mission that will reach its goals requires
passion of purpose, a clearly defined mission, and funding. Your congregational leaders will need the passion to act even as the mercy of
Christ burns and sears His passion into individual hearts and souls.
Great leadership will work to identify a clear mercy mission that is
appropriate to your context. Great leadership will define results that
are measurable and tasks the congregation can do well. Great leadership will look for a specific mission that can attract requisite funding
and will work to enliven a passion among people for charitable ends

in Christ's name. Finally, great leadership will act, for "what is love and mercy without works?"[22]

God grant His Church leaders that have passion, clear purpose, and resources to get done what needs to be done for those in the most need.

> Jesus, lead Thou on
>
> Till our rest is won;
>
> Heav'nly leader still direct us,
>
> Still support, console, protect us,
>
> Till we safely stand
>
> In our fatherland.
>
> (*Lutheran Service Book* 718:4)
>
> *Christe eleison.*

NOTES

1   The Greek word *spoude* is translated generally as "zeal," as well as, more specifically, the aggressiveness and efficiency needed to get things done. See Hans Dieter Betz, *2 Corinthians 8 and 9: A Commentary on Two Administrative Letters of the Apostle Paul* (Philadelphia: Fortress, 1985), 57–58.

2   From Luther's last sermon, AE 51:388.

3   Literally, the French means, "Thank you, thank you, sir!" But those who speak French use the word as we would use the word *please*. In this context, it amounts to begging with anticipation.

4   Jim Collins, *Good to Great: Why Some Companies Make the Leap—and Others Don't* (New York: HarperBusiness, 2001), 41.

5   Hans Dieter Betz notes on nearly every page of his commentary on 2 Corinthians 8–9 that Paul makes constant use of contemporary legal and administrative language for his great collection for the poor in Jerusalem. See Betz, *2 Corinthians 8 and 9*, passim.

6   Francis Pieper, *Christian Dogmatics*, trans. J. T. Mueller (St. Louis: Concordia, 1950), 1:199.

7   Ap XVI 54 (*Concordia*, 195).

8   See SA III VIII 2–3 (*Concordia*, 280).

9   See n. 4.

10   Jim Collins, *Good to Great and the Social Sectors: Why Business Thinking Is Not the Answer, A Monograph to Accompany* Good to Great (Boulder, CO: Collins, 2005). Hereafter *GGSS*. This monograph and the original book are worth a library. Buy them.

11   *GGSS*, 1.

12   *GGSS*, 1.

13 *GGSS*, 1.

14 Collins, *Good to Great*, 13.

15 *Theology for Mercy* (St. Louis: LCMS World Relief and Human Care, 2004).

16 Collins, *Good to Great*, 13.

17 Tools for assessing and measuring these issues are available from the Department of Districts and Congregations of LCMS World Relief and Human Care. Ask for *Planting Gospel Seeds while Serving Human Needs: A Practical Non-threatening Way to Discover and Address the Needs of the Neighbors Outside Your Church Door*.

18 Hermann Sasse, "Confessional Churches in the Ecumenical Movement," *Lutheran Theological Journal* (August–December 1968): 61ff.

19 See AE 45:186.

20 *GGSS*, 17.

21 *GGSS*, 20.

22 Holger Sonntag, trans., *Löhe on Mercy*, ed. by Adriane Dorr and Philip Hendrickson (St. Louis: LCMS World Relief and Human Care, 2006), 28.

15

Mercy in the City

A CASE FOR TWO-KINGDOM THEOLOGY
AND COOPERATION IN EXTERNALS

Desolation is left in the city; the gates are battered into ruins. *Isaiah 24:12*

But stay in the city until you are clothed with power from on high. *Luke 24:49*

All those who hold secular offices . . . are obliged to remain [in the city]. . . . It would be a great sin for somebody who has been commanded to take care of a whole community to leave it without head and government in time of danger (such as fire, murder, rebellion, and other calamities which the devil might prepare) because there is no order there.[1] *Martin Luther*

The problem of housing in the decaying inner cities of the United States is a deeply spiritual one. The depth of this problem is not easy to grasp without firsthand experience. This problem begs to be addressed by the local congregation. I hope that what follows challenges you to reconsider the role of the Church in the life of the inner city. The Scriptures and the Lutheran Confessions propel the Church headlong into the chaotic exigencies of city life precisely for the sake of the Gospel, and thus to give the devil the boot.

What follows describes my experience of the Church's involvement in neighborhood renewal, which I will attempt to place within a theological framework. Although I refer to these experiences and impressions in the first person, many other dedicated people were involved in this effort. Without them, the project would not have existed, succeeded, nor would it have continued to succeed as it has.

There was no particular moment early in my pastorate at Zion Lutheran Church, Fort Wayne, Indiana, when I decided that the congregation must attempt to make a positive impact on its physical neighborhood. I do recall early on becoming aware that the issues of housing, of livability, of functioning community and neighborhood had deep spiritual significance. The Gospel does not prosper in chaos, while the devil loves chaos. The first creative act of the triune God was to create order and beauty out of what had been a formless void and to bring material existence into being. In this context, the collects of the Church's liturgy, which plead for peace and order in the world that the Gospel might prosper, become particularly meaningful.

When I arrived at Zion in 1995, the neighborhood surrounding the church building had been part of the poorest census tract in the state of Indiana. There were some forty dilapidated, vacant homes and commercial buildings within a two-block radius of the church. That material decay represented much more than mere economic or physical malaise. Those buildings represented lives without plans, people who were living moment to moment, owners who were not investing in community or in continuity, renters who were burdened and buffeted by aimlessness, people who were struggling to survive, whose lives were in the grip of chaos.

I vividly recall requesting permission from Zion's church council to begin purchasing properties. "We have no money to do this, but I would like permission from this body to begin buying properties in this neighborhood," I said. As I unveiled a plan to approach donors outside the congregation for assistance, quizzical expressions gave way to humorous resignation. What's to lose? seemed the general response.

I worked out an agreement with a local Neighbor Works Corporation (a nonprofit housing entity) to hold title to the properties, which later would be disbursed and traded to the best ends among Neighbor Works, Zion, and St. Peter's Catholic Church, which became the third partner in our triumvirate of neighborhood hoodlums "razing hell." And it really was a matter of "razing hell" (not *raising* or *elevating*, but *razing*, which means "demolishing" or "destroying"). I hope you are not too offended by that expression. Amid inner-city chaos, that double entendre became quite meaningful.

WHERE SIN IS ALL IN ALL

Over the next few years, Father John Delaney; his successor, Father Phil Widmann; and I managed to crawl over the entire neighborhood and, in my case, through every single building to assess its value. Once a working-class German neighborhood, over time owners, invariably from outside the neighborhood, acquired the properties; hacked larger homes into three, four, and five apartments; and extracted rental dollars from the community while allowing the homes to disintegrate. Once a roof failed to be repaired, financial usefulness was soon over. Tax dereliction and abandonment followed. As we surveyed the houses, we worked hard to find owners (or to purchase properties, if possible) and to convince the city to condemn or demolish.

The first demolition was a notorious crack house across the street from St. Peter's Catholic Church. Addicts had cut out the copper piping to be sold to support their habit, though others had scavenged (not infrequently by "reputable" sellers of antique accoutrements) the property and left it open to the wind and rain. In addition to the crack addicts, it had been occupied intermittently by vagrants—many of whom were mentally ill—and prostitutes.

One particularly poignant yet far from uncommon scene from a second-floor room has stayed in my mind: a few old couch cushions with a baseball bat lying on the floor nearby. In another home where a mentally ill squatter had lived, all the rooms were filled as much as four or five feet deep with objects from charities for the poor. Used toys, mounds of clothing, kitchen utensils, blankets, Bibles, literature from the Jehovah's Witnesses, pornography, drug paraphernalia, and human excrement combined with the rotting building to make what became for me a most familiar stench. Oh yes—and rats.

With great difficulty, we acquired the last of several homes to be demolished on the block north of Zion. As they went down one by one and basements were filled, the rats made their way through the sewer system to the half-vacant Catholic school building across the street. The janitor recounted that when he opened a door to a section of the school's subbasement, "The rats parted like a herd of buffalo!" The next day the exterminators arrived, and the rodents were carried out in five-gallon buckets. Despite chasing these vermin from Lutheran territory and sending them off to Rome, we were never accused of a lack of ecumenical spirit. *Cooperatio in exter-*MIN-*is!*[2]

SEEING IS BELIEVING?

Luther tells us in the Smalcald Articles that "hereditary sin is such a deep corruption of nature that no reason can understand it. Rather, it must be believed from the revelation of Scripture."[3] But these experiences were the closest I had come to seeing what must be believed. No socialist, no liberal ideology, no mere "systemic" evil, no hyperindividualist conservative pundit could explain the reality and totality of sin's effects on a community. Sin was in all and through all. The addict suffered mental illness and addiction because of the horrendous sinfulness of a hopeless family situation, which produced the ultimate individual "turned in upon himself" (*curvatus in se*). Luther wrote: "Scripture . . . describes man as so turned in on himself that he uses not only physical but even spiritual goods for his own purposes and in all things seeks only himself."[4] The myopia of the beggar who would one moment spout Bible verse after Bible verse and profess Jesus with apparently complete conviction, only to steal any merchandise left unguarded, bore witness to individual sin run amok. There were always two-bit, would-be inner-city land "tycoons" who would refuse to sell a vacant, horrendously dilapidated property merely because someone wanted to buy it. There were suburbanites who would shun any involvement with "that church," "those people," or "that neighborhood." There were African Americans in the neighborhood who would have nothing to do with a white pastor trying to bring good things. City bureaucrats genuinely wanted renewal, yet they always wanted much more than what was reasonable for the penny-ante commitments made.

The system allowed African American neighborhoods to go to Hades (literally) as dilapidation, dereliction, and atrocity persisted year after maddening year. Yet if the same "abuse" occurred in suburban neighborhoods, it would be dealt with in a matter of days or even hours. One difficult property remained vacant throughout my five-year pastorate at Zion. It was my "thorn in the flesh." Its shattered windows and doors caused me to believe such a reality was insane and ultimately forced me to do something about it. I had heard suburbanites and others who lacked understanding of the complexities of the situation—and often harboring deep-seated resentment or racist views—say, "You're crazy, Pastor. Those people will destroy anything they get." But as I stood on the sidewalk in front of that house, I nearly shouted, "I'm *not* crazy! *That* is crazy!"

I called code enforcement to complain about the building. "Are the windows broken out on the ground level or only on the upper level?" asked the voice on the other end of the line. "If they are open only on the upper level, we can't do anything about it."

"That's crazy!" I shouted at the poor woman on the phone. And it was crazy—not me! Such insanity produced residents unwilling to commit, residents numbed into civic inaction by years of neighborhood neglect, who saw racism behind every bush and who drove well-meaning white city officials, initially intent on bringing initiatives for improvement, running for the safety of the suburban hills. In short, sin brings sin and chaos. Chaos feeds on and perpetuates sin on all sides.

But then there is Christ. And where Christ is, there is the Church (*Ubi Christus, ibi ecclesia*)![5] Where Christ and His Church are, there is mercy, life, light, love, and determination. (Shortly after I accepted the call to LCMS World Relief and Human Care and moved to St. Louis, Missouri, the difficult home was demolished.)

Mere *Pragma*?

There is a pragmatic argument for the Church involving itself in neighborhood renewal. I will not spend much time on it because we know well that pragmatism is in the air Americans breathe and often becomes the enemy of New Testament truth. Pragmatism finds a willing bedfellow in a theology of glory. That is not to say that a congregation involved in housing must not be pragmatic—quite the opposite! However, the pragmatic argument cannot carry the day in the attempt to provide a theological rationale for a congregation's participation in neighborhood renewal.

As a result of Zion's participation in its neighborhood, numerous positive developments occurred and continue to occur. Forty dilapidated buildings were brought down. Some twenty-five new homes (from 1,200 to 2,400 square feet) were constructed—all for home ownership, not for rent. The Allen County Public Library built a new African American emphasis library branch across the street from Zion. Next door the Urban League built a multimillion-dollar headquarters, which boasts marvelous facilities for youth education, job training, and the elderly. Both facilities occupy property acquired on behalf of Zion (the rat property mentioned above!). One firm acquired the once rat-infested Catholic school and invested $9 million to turn the property into an apartment complex for seniors. Meanwhile, Zion built a $2 million congregational hall to replace a small administration building. The new structure matches the graceful lines of the magnificent old German Gothic church.

In June 2007 I returned to Fort Wayne to participate in a groundbreaking for a city initiative bringing $70 million in new housing to the neighborhood around Zion and St. Peter's. Fort Wayne is one of the few cities in the country to devote virtually all of its HUD funding to a neighborhood project that is faith-based. I am shocked and humbled by what has continued to take place in this community.

All this activity, and everything that led up to it, made Zion the most frequently referenced LCMS congregation in Fort Wayne media. The project made Zion the most ecumenically involved LCMS congregation in the region. The project made Zion the most popular, well-known, and respected LCMS congregation within the African American community. The neighborhood work and all the positives have given Zion's members a profoundly positive view of their congregation as a catalyst for good in the community, which in turn has improved the overall health of the parish.

But none of this alone, or in total, can justify a confessional Lutheran congregation's involvement in neighborhood renewal. Confessional Lutherans need solid theological rationale for such activity. Ultimately, any other secular or nonsecular institution in similar circumstances, doing something "positive" in the city, might have accomplished all these results. But thanks be to God, Zion did not sell her soul to get this done. She remains a confessional Lutheran congregation in the city.

A LUTHERAN CONGREGATION WITH
SOUL SO THAT SOULS DO NOT PERISH

What will it profit a Lutheran congregation if it gains the whole neighborhood but loses its soul? The soul of the Lutheran congregation is Christ. The presence of Christ in a congregation's life is outwardly evident in what the Lutheran Confessions repeatedly describe as "marks" of the Church: "Word, profession, and Sacraments."[6] While the "who" of the Church on the subjective side is hidden (membership in the Church is a matter of faith in Christ, which is an unseen reality), the "where" is evident and knowable. There is an altar, pulpit, and font at Hanna and Creighton Streets in Fort Wayne that, for many years, was the demographic bull's eye of crime, drugs, murder, and poverty in that city. Faith is engendered by and gathered around Christ, that is, in "the pure doctrine of the Gospel and the administration of the Sacraments in accordance with the Gospel of Christ."[7]

Helpful in recognizing the priorities of a Lutheran congregation's life and mission is the order of the Augsburg Confession: (1) God, (2) sin (man's dilemma), (3) Christ (God's solution for man's dilemma), (4) justification by grace through faith, (5) the Office of the Holy Ministry (as delivery of Gospel and Sacraments, that is, the application of justification), and (6) good works. Thus the perennial priority of the Lutheran congregation remains the application of the divine remedy for sin—preaching the Gospel and rightly dispensing the Sacraments through the office given to deliver these gifts. The Lutheran Confessions state: "Since we know that our Confession is true, godly, and catholic . . . we know that the Church is among those who teach God's Word rightly and administer the Sacraments rightly."[8] It is precisely for the sake of the Gospel surety that the Lutheran Confessions limit the public administration of the Gospel and Sacraments to those men legitimately called and ordained,[9] who act in Christ's stead at the behest of the Church. The Apology of the Augsburg Confession states: "Because of the call of the Church, the unworthy still represent the person of Christ and do not represent their own persons, as Christ testifies, 'The one who hears you hears Me' (Luke 10:16)."[10]

All this clearly sets the emphasis for the Office of the Holy Ministry as well. The chief and essential functions of that office dare not be set aside while the pastor becomes a junior housing developer. There is general New Testament and confessional Lutheran freedom in structuring the tasks—in addition to preaching the Word and administering the Sacraments—performed by those who occupy the Office of the Holy Ministry. For as strong as the Lutheran Confessions are in emphasizing the "marks" as the central reality of the Church's life—and the Office of the Holy Ministry's responsibility for the administration of these marks—they do bear witness to churchly tasks beyond such administration. The Church's role in diaconal tasks is precisely in view here.

ALMS FOR THE POOR—THE CHURCH'S CORPORATE LIFE OF MERCY

At first glance it may seem as though the Lutheran Confessions do not acknowledge a corporate life of mercy for the Church. Nearly all the fodder of theological dialogue regarding works, alms, and so on is directed at the individual Christian (for example, see Article VI of the Augsburg Confession, which is titled "New Obedience," and Article XX of the Augsburg Confession, which is titled "Good Works"). Article VII of the Augsburg Confession finds the unity of the Church precisely in the Gospel and Sacraments and nothing else.[11] There is no "gospel reductionism" here nor is the Gospel reduced to any "nut-shell." The Formula of Concord states that Lutherans "believe, teach, and confess that if the term *Gospel* is understood to mean Christ's entire teaching that He proposed in His ministry, as His apostles did also, then it is correctly said and written that the Gospel is a preaching of repentance and of the forgiveness of sins."[12]

It is common (since the 1817 Prussian Union) to describe Lutheranism as a "confessing movement" within the Church catholic, but as it is often used, this description gets confessional Lutheranism wrong. First, such a definition suffers the affliction of a theology of glory. It overlooks doctrinal truth to *see* the Church's unity rather than to *believe* its unity. Division and error always hide the Church on earth. Public separation (that is, not practicing church fellowship where there is not doctrinal unity) is required precisely for the preservation of the "full" and sacramental Gospel.[13]

Second, it overlooks the fact that the Lutheran Confessions view the Church of the Lutheran confession as "Church." Moreover, the Confessions themselves are the best expression of the Church catholic,[14] while at the same time freely and liberally recognizing that the Church is found wherever the Gospel and Sacraments are found.[15] Confessional Lutheranism is to find its expression in Lutheran congregations that confess the faith as Church, not in movements. Self-definition has been and continues to be promoted by moderating Lutherans who have ceased to insist on the clear dogmatic definitions and church-dividing boundaries of the Formula of Concord or of the Augsburg Confession.

At several points the Lutheran Confessions bear witness to the fact that confessional Lutheranism continued and should continue the Church's corporate life of mercy. From the following texts it is clear that the Lutheran Confessions recognize the corporate churchly responsibility of addressing diaconal need.

> The Church can never be better governed and preserved than if we all live under one head, Christ. All the bishops should be equal in office (although they may be unequal in gifts). They should be diligently joined in unity of doctrine, faith, sacraments, prayer, works of love [*operum caritatis; Werken der Liebe*], and such.[16]

> We think this way also about every good work in the humblest callings and in private affairs. Through these works Christ celebrates His victory over the devil, just as the distribution of alms by the Corinthians (1 Corinthians 16:1) was a holy work [and also a corporate work of mercy in 2 Corinthians!], a sacrifice and battle of Christ against the devil, who labors so that nothing may be done to praise God. To demean such works (the confession of doctrine, sufferings, works of love [*officia caritatis; offices of charity*], suppression of the flesh) would be to demean the outward rule of Christ's kingdom among people.[17]

> Monasteries were schools for Christian instruction; now they have deteriorated, as though from a golden to an iron age (or as Plato says, the cube deteriorates into bad harmonies bringing destruction). All the most wealthy monasteries support only a lazy crowd, which gorges itself upon the public alms of the Church.[18]

[The bishops who are devoted to the pope] should remember that riches have been given to bishops as alms for the administration and advantage of the churches. As the rule says, "The benefit is given because of the office." Therefore, they cannot with a good conscience possess these alms and defraud the Church. The church has need of this money to support ministers, aid education, care for the poor, and establish courts, especially for marriage.[19]

These texts clearly recognize and assume that the Church's life of mercy ("public alms") is a normal, corporate reality. In the context of the sixteenth-century Church, the Confessions speak negatively of poverty and the system long established to provide for the impoverished because it is wrapped up with the vow of the medieval monk (poverty, chastity, obedience).[20] According to medieval Roman Catholic theology, self-assumed poverty would help the one who assumed such a "self-chosen" work merit salvation. Furthermore, Roman Catholic theology taught that the one who provided alms also would reap merit toward salvation.[21]

The Reformation decidedly rejected the medieval preferential option for the poor. In no uncertain terms, Luther condemned self-chosen poverty as an affront to the Gospel of Christ.[22] As he treated the topic at length, Luther asserted that poverty in and of itself made no one more or less holy. The poverty desired by Christ was a spiritual poverty, that is, repentance. Luther's point is quickly evident to anyone who has worked on the street in the inner cities of the United States. In fact Luther viewed the maladies common to today's inner cities as the rule of the devil's kingdom:

But there is included in this petition [But deliver us from evil] whatever evil may happen to us under the devil's kingdom: poverty, shame, death, and, in short, all the agonizing misery and heartache of which there is such an unnumbered multitude on earth. Since the devil is not only a liar, but also a murderer [John 8:44], he constantly seeks our life. He wreaks his vengeance whenever he can afflict our bodies with misfortune and harm. Therefore, it happens that he often breaks men's necks or drives them to insanity, drowns some, and moves many to commit suicide and to many other dreadful disasters [e.g., Mark 9:17–22]. So there is nothing for us to do upon earth but to pray against this archenemy without stopping. For unless God preserved us, we would not be safe from this enemy even for an hour.[23]

Thus the Lutheran Confessions do recognize and even suppose the Church's corporate life of diaconal mercy, though the details of that *diakonia* are not expounded at length. For the Christians at Leisnig, Luther dealt at length with the tradition of the "common chest" administered by the Church.[24] This tradition persisted, as is evidenced by the church orders of the Reformation and post-Reformation periods.[25] These expressions of diaconal mercy are completely in accord with the Lutheran Confessions.

HOUSING AS *DIAKONIA* IN THE U.S. INNER CITY

At the end of the Treatise on the Power and Primacy of the Pope, Philip Melanchthon acknowledges and accepts the Church's corporate role of mercy. This text also clearly indicates something of the situational diversity of *diakonia*. While the preaching of the Word and the administration of the Sacraments forever remain the Church's heart and soul, its chief gift and task, the Church also remains diaconally engaged in love in a way that coincides with its ever-changing contemporary context.

Many years ago, German theologian Hermann Sasse described this churchly, diaconal flexibility as something not of the essence of the Church but as something essential to its life:

> There are indeed essential functions which remain those of the church, namely, the proclamation of the Word and the administration of the Sacraments. But the church also exercises accidental functions. Among these are the fulfillment of organizational tasks in the area of the formation of laws and the domestic side of ecclesiastical life (diaconate and the maintenance of the ecclesiastical organization) of which we have spoken. The church would also remain church if it finally did not exercise these functions, although their continuing neglect would finally destroy the church because it is at once a spiritual-corporal organization. . . .

> There have been times when the church took care of the entire educational system and when the ecclesiastical diaconate helped preserve society. There were times when the church retreated from these spheres or when state and church encountered each other and therefore a legal regulation of the relationship was necessary.[26]

It is here that the realm of neighborhood renewal and housing fits in confessional Lutheran theology. The Church has a corporate life of mercy.[27] This life of mercy is not a constituting reality of its life; rather, it is a constituent reality of its life. The marks of the Church (Christ's Word and Sacraments) guarantee the Church's presence and life. What Luther stated about the individual can well be applied to the Church as a whole: "Faith and good works well agree and fit together; but it is faith alone, without works, that lays hold of the blessing." The Formula of Concord follows Luther's statement with this concluding thought: "Yet [faith] is never, ever, alone."[28] Luther speaks in corporate terms, touching on concern for the needs of people as a natural consequence of the Gospel:

> Our churches are now, through God's grace, enlightened and equipped with the pure Word and right use of the Sacraments, with knowledge of the various callings and right works. So, on our part, we ask for no council. On such points, we have nothing better to hope or expect from a council. But we see throughout the bishops' jurisdictions so many parishes vacant and desolate that it breaks our heart. Still, neither the bishops nor the Church officials care how the poor people live or die. Christ has died for them.[29]

ISN'T HOUSING A CIVIL ISSUE?

Two institutions remained in the Hanna/Creighton neighborhood as it went downhill: a liquor store and the churches. Everything else—grocery stores, pharmacies, furniture stores, hardware stores, and so on—left. It was in chaos. The devil is not happy until he has successfully destroyed all institutions and all order and replaced them with chaos. Meanwhile, institutions of chaos thrive in the stench the devil leaves behind. I defend with full Lutheran gusto the freedom of the Christian to make sanctified use of alcohol. However, the liquor store, which long remained in the neighborhood, was of duplicitous ethical value. Its clientele were primarily addicts. When government checks were delivered on the first of the month, business boomed. The local "bootleg" house (which sold alcohol illegally and on the weekends) was a constant source of drugs, and I witnessed cocaine sold openly at the site. Sadly, it was the hangout for the most severely mentally ill and addicted. I regularly met and "conversed" with individuals who could do little more than ramble in disconnected syllables of gibberish. The house was also a focal point of crime, theft, sexual misconduct, and so on, as most crime in the neighborhood occurred en route to or from the "burn barrel" constantly alight in the rear of the house. When the house was finally condemned and demolished, the liquor store also took a financial hit.

I spent nearly six years trying to get rid of this building and its negative activity. The owner did not live at the address yet was making money from the nefarious activity. As a result of the elimination of vagrancy laws coupled with the closure of state mental health institutions, the police had little recourse in dealing with illicit operations like the bootleg house. When I informed the police (stationed only a few blocks away) of the illegal nature of the weekend business conducted out of this building, I was directed to the Indiana State Excise Police because the Fort Wayne Vice Squad did not maintain weekend hours. Although the State Excise Police had jurisdiction over illegal alcohol matters, their office was in Indianapolis and the documentation and prosecution of the case would require an African American agent to work overtime in an undercover operation. It was a bureaucratic dead end.

Even as I pursued legal options, I was stopping by the barrel at regular intervals, offering assistance to anyone who might be ready to take a different direction in life. I regularly told those gathered around their little altar, "When you want to get serious about your alcoholism and take a different direction, you come up the hill to that church and see me. I'll help you. Jesus has something better in store for your life than this." My invitation was often met with angry derision.

Finally, one of my conversations with Gary at the Fort Wayne City Code Enforcement Office worked.[30] After six years of constant negative activity, the bootleg house with its burn barrel was condemned and demolished. The residence that was my theological cross—"a thorn ... given me in the flesh ... to keep me from being too elated" (2 Corinthians 12:7)—was gone.

Imagine the effect that derelict residence and liquor store within a block or two had on neighboring property values, as well as the less tangible impact on neighborhood morale, confidence, quality, and so on. Imagine the harm to all those lives, to those children who grew up in its proximity. Did Zion have a responsibility to take on any role in dealing with that particular problem or, for that matter, the broader ills of the neighborhood? Yes. But how does this fit with Lutheran theology?

DEMANDING ACCOUNTABILITY IS TO "HOLD THE CIVIL REALM IN HONOR"

Confessional Lutheranism asserts a doctrine of "two kingdoms," that is, that there is a civil and a spiritual realm, church and society.[31] Each kingdom has its unique sphere of concern. In the community around Zion, the state was derelict and had abandoned its God-given responsibilities toward the community. There were numerous and complex reasons for this dereliction of both neighborhood and duty, including race, racism, economics, and other sociocultural factors. Many pastors and congregations throughout the inner cities of the United States have had the same experience. It was proper for Zion Lutheran Church (often through its senior pastor) to step out into the civil realm for both civil *and* religious ends.

The Lutheran Confessions, while acknowledging the reality that God established these two distinct realms in which we all operate, are primarily concerned that the two kingdoms are not mixed. Just as the Christian individual lives in two kingdoms simultaneously, so does a Lutheran congregation. As the strongest, or perhaps the only, positive corporate "citizen" left in an inner city, the confessional Lutheran congregation has a particular burden to lead in good citizenship. That does not in the least imply a mixing of the kingdoms, any more than a Lutheran grade school is a mixing of the kingdoms. A congregation, as also an individual Christian, bears witness to Christ in the course of professional vocation. The Augsburg Confession states:

> Therefore, the Church's authority and the State's authority must not be confused. The Church's authority has its own commission to teach the Gospel and to administer the Sacraments [Matthew 28:19–20]. Let it not break into the office of another. Let it not transfer the kingdoms of this world to itself. Let it not abolish the laws of civil rulers. Let it not abolish lawful obedience. Let it not interfere with judgments about civil ordinances or contracts. Let it not dictate laws to civil authorities about the form of society. . . . This is how our teachers distinguish between the duties of these

two authorities. They command that both be honored and acknowledged as God's gifts and blessings.[32]

By participating in neighborhood renewal, a confessional Lutheran congregation is not confusing the kingdoms, any more than a citizen who attends the Divine Service on Sunday or a Christian who votes. The Lutheran Confessions assert repeatedly that God ordains the civil realm and that participation by Christians in the civil realm is God-pleasing. However, it would be confusing the kingdoms if a Lutheran congregation asserted that all who wanted to be good Christians must purchase or sell property, or participate in the assembly of a "Christian" kingdom in the inner city that is subject to the Bible and not civil government. While the Church, through the Office of the Holy Ministry,[33] preaches the Gospel and administers the Sacraments, it also participates corporately in the civil realm. Thus it is quite literally a corporate citizen of its community. For example, the legal name of Zion Lutheran Church is Zion Evangelical Lutheran Church of the Unaltered Augsburg Confession, *Inc.*—that is, *Incorporated*, or a legal "person" according to state law.

By participating in neighborhood renewal, a Lutheran congregation is merely serving God in the kingdom of the left.[34] In reality, this is little different from a congregation that keeps proper legal records; files tax and wage reports with the government; adheres to property laws, fire and building codes, tax and civil rights laws; and so on. The Apology of the Augsburg Confession states: "It is lawful, however, for Christians to use civil ordinances, just as they use the air, the light, food, and drink."[35]

Where government is derelict in its duties, it is the sacred and God-given right, privilege, and task of a Lutheran congregation to raise the issue with the government and to begin to require, even demand, accountability. In fact, denial of a Lutheran congregation's right and responsibility to participate to the full extent possible in neighborhood renewal is to fundamentally deny the Lutheran doctrine of the two kingdoms. As the Confessions say, "It is lawful for a Christian to make use of public ordinances and laws. This rule protects consciences. It teaches that contracts are lawful before God just to the extent that the public officials or laws approve them."[36] Insisting that the local government provides for the legally appropriate services required for a decent, safe, and peaceable life is to honor God's work in the kingdom of the left. Where the law is not being followed in a community of which a congregation is a part, it is the God-given responsibility of the congregation as a citizen of its community to insist on compliance. In such communities, the congregation takes up a role of "chief citizen."

The Church has the right and responsibility to insist on the protection of the rights of citizens, equal treatment under the law, and so on. In short, love compels a congregation to step up to its responsibilities of citizenship. Much is required of those to whom much is given. In the case of derelict neighborhoods, the congregation remains one of the only citizens capable of major influence of public and private entities beyond the immediate community.

The action of a congregation to become a leading citizen in neighborhood renewal, to work for a decent existence in the civil realm, to advocate for the increase of civil righteousness is a diaconal task. The Lutheran congregation ties her diaconal work as closely as possible with the Church's worship life and with the proclamation of the Gospel. Often the destitute, the immigrant, and the elderly do not have access to human services. The congregation can offer assistance to such people, including connecting individuals with available, legal, and helpful government-funded social services, especially when these services are aimed at self-sufficiency and self-reliance. This is one way to love our neighbors, and it does not confuse the two kingdoms.

TWO-KINGDOM THEOLOGY IS NOT THE SEPARATION OF CHURCH AND STATE

The modern understanding of church and state are heavily affected by secularizing twentieth-century court decisions. The courts should not make decisions based on the Bible, nor should Congress pass "biblical" laws. The courts and Congress should not interpret the Bible for Lutherans or for anyone else! Such an outcome would be a mistake in the opposite direction of the Church entering the secular realm. However, the United States was founded by people who were deeply convinced that there is a Creator and there is an eternally valid and applicable natural law. The state rules not by revelation but by reason.

"We hold these truths to be self-evident, that all men are created equal." This simple statement of the Declaration of Independence asserts a God, a Creator, and self-evident truth. In our postmodern context, many people no longer accept any such eternal constants. Thus some two thousand years of agreed upon Western law and ethics have been severely truncated or rejected altogether. It is no longer "self-evident" that marriage should be between a man and a woman, for instance. While this is arguably the most self-evident reality in all of history, it does make sense that the attack on natural law should be most intense over God's crowning creative act, that of creating mankind as male and female. The postmodern individual will not tolerate limits to personal freedom. Therefore, any natural law or knowledge of God must go. Indeed, God must go! And any reference to a divine rationale or cause, carefully based on clear reason, is decried as a breach of the alleged wall of separation between church and state. Yet a society that rejects divinely created order (reason!) is in chaos.

The great period of cultural engagement that was the 1960s unfortunately was a period of great secularization of both government and church institutions. Some theologians even redefined the Gospel in political terms. Even in LCMS circles it became popular to assert that serving the poor or building houses is the Gospel. This view of social work (which confuses Law and Gospel) caused a significant portion of the LCMS to recoil against social concern and the Church's life of mercy. This was in part out of a deep desire to be faithful to Scripture and the Confessions. Thus many pastors and others abandoned the social ministry playing field altogether. This understandable mistake was made in an effort not to lose the focus of Christ and justification, but it was a mistake nonetheless.

Lutherans confess that there is a divinely ordered relationship between the two kingdoms. The civil realm needs and counts on the Church to bring order and a sense of divine accountability to the community. Government officials need Christians to stand up for right and wrong. Lutherans call this sense of morality "civil righteousness." The Church, however, confesses the need and necessity of an orderly and moral civil realm so it can preach Law and Gospel. Without community order, the proclamation of the Gospel suffers.

In summary, two-kingdom theology honors reason as that which orders the civil realm, yet it teaches that only Christians know the one true God as He has revealed Himself in Holy Scripture as the Trinity. Two-kingdom theology teaches that the two realms are interdependent. The two kingdoms must not be artificially separated in practice such that the Christian or the Church as corporate citizen has no civil cause to love the neighbor or to serve the community. We are called to love our neighbor, and not just our Lutheran neighbors. Confessing its life in both kingdoms, the Church participates in God's "left-hand kingdom" (the civil realm) not by making laws or enforcing them, but by cajoling the state to take up its God-ordained role. Doing so, the Church serves a role in the community, especially in the inner-city chaos, as "chief citizen" of the community.

THE ECUMENICAL CHALLENGE IN THE WORK OF MERCY

One memorable day I was chatting about the progress of our neighborhood project with my ecclesiastical neighbor, Father John Delaney, the priest at St. Peter's. The conversation with my good friend went like this:

"My, your predecessor was conservative. He wouldn't even do a joint wedding with me," commented John.

I smiled. "Well, John, you know that's basically LCMS canon law." I wasn't disparaging the LCMS practice of not having joint worship, but I was trying to put the matter in terms he could understand. Knowing that as a faithful priest, John confesses that ordinations without the alleged apostolic confession are invalid, I asked, "John, you don't really think I'm a 'priest,' do you?"

"Well, no," he said.

"You don't really believe that when I absolve my people, that it is a real priestly absolution, do you?" *No* came the answer, and I continued, "When I consecrate the elements on the altar of Zion Lutheran, you don't really believe that I distribute Christ's body and blood to my people, do you?"[37]

"Well, no, Matt," he replied again, "but I believe Christ is spiritually present among you."

I responded, "John, you deny everything from which I and my people live. How can I possibly stand before my people and conduct a service with you?"

I had made my point. Our friendship and our working arrangement flourished. It was a wonderful relationship, and from a Lutheran perspective it was how two-kingdom theology works in the reality of daily life. Two-kingdom theology allows us to maintain Lutheran integrity while respecting other people's theological perspectives, even when we sincerely disagree.

And that is not easy. As a young pastor fresh from the seminary, I was insecure about many things as I began my work in Iowa. Who wouldn't be? Such insecurity can result in one of two unfortunate choices: A new pastor may become exceedingly rigid as he attempts to cope with challenging circumstances. Or he may compromise the faith beyond the bounds of clear Lutheran confession, usually for the sake of wanting to be loved. Thankfully, I had the ready advice of an older and trusted circuit counselor. I also developed a habit of translating the writings of Hermann Sasse every morning for an hour or so those first years in the parish.

Sasse was a confessional Lutheran who was absolutely committed to the doctrine and practice of orthodox Lutheranism. He reflected Scripture's teaching that there should be no jointly led worship where there is no agreement on the Gospel and all its articles. Yet Sasse was thoroughly engaged in ecumenical contact and discussion.[38] Thus I decided early on to begin to get to know the clergy in my area. I would stop at a neighboring church, find the clergy-"person," and sit down for a chat. I quickly discovered that coming through the LCMS seminary system had provided me with an education far superior to most of those with whom I had contact.

That early experience was important for what came next. Because of the neighborhood project, I was asked by then Indiana District President Timothy Simms to represent him on the Lutheran/Catholic Dialogue with the Fort Wayne/South Bend Indiana Diocese of the

Roman Catholic Church. Because of my participation, I grew in surprising ways. Although I clearly recognized the many doctrinal problems of Rome, especially the synergism and lack of clarity on Law and Gospel, I also rejoiced when I heard the Gospel clearly enunciated as pure gift. I was thankful when I did hear it, though I did not hear it as often as I would have preferred. I rejoiced that in Rome the text of the Holy Scriptures was read, that Baptism claimed children for Christ, and that the body and blood of Jesus were distributed to sinners.

Like Wilhelm Löhe, I spoke a clear, tactful, respectful *no* to what was not true. However, I also spoke a clear, resounding *yes* to everything that was true, no matter who said it.[39] I grew as a confessional Lutheran. Being in ecumenical dialogue forced me to understand who I was and answer why. I was invited by the bishop to speak to local Lutheran and Catholic clergy about the nature of ecumenical dialogue. After I finished my presentation, Roman Catholic Bishop D'Arcy leaned over to me and said, "That is exactly my view on these matters. Would you write something up for our diocese newspaper?"

The ecumenical dialogue opened other interesting doors. In 1998 the chief ecumenical officer of Pope John Paul II, Cardinal Cassidy, was to visit Fort Wayne. As it was the Missouri Synod's first opportunity to host a Lutheran/Catholic Dialogue meeting, an interesting and important question needed to be considered. In keeping with the Roman Catholic practice, a worship service was usually scheduled as part of the event. While both the Roman Catholic Church and the LCMS believe and practice close(d) Communion, the LCMS does not jointly lead worship with other denominations. The committee representing the LCMS, ELCA, and Rome knew full well the LCMS confession on joint worship and respected it, so the suggestion was made to switch venues away from the LCMS to accommodate us. However, I suggested that we make the most of this ecumenical encounter and hold the meeting at Concordia Theological Seminary. We could have a full dialogue on issues between Lutherans and Roman Catholics, invite the area clergy of the three communions (Rome, LCMS, ELCA), and end with Vespers in the seminary chapel. I checked with both my district president and the LCMS president before proceeding. Thus according to LCMS doctrine and practice, Zion Lutheran (my congregation) hosted the service, and I was the sole liturgist. We prayed for unity and humility in truth. Talking with both Bishop D'Arcy and Cardinal Cassidy revealed that they were happy to accommodate us because they did not want us to act against conviction. Their response was as I expected, for I had read the papal encyclicals of John Paul II on ecumenism and dialogue.[40] While these documents contain much with which Lutherans will disagree, there also is a great deal said about truth and doctrine that is true.

When we worked at neighborhood renewal, it was necessary to bring as many players to the table as possible. Having the Catholics involved was tremendously beneficial because there are many faithful Catholics in all areas of the private and public spheres of city life. When this type of "cooperation in externals" (working together in areas other than Word and Sacrament) begins, it is necessary to be clear and kind about expectations. It is also necessary for confessional Lutherans to be true to their public commitments to Scripture, the Confessions, and one another. For if we lose our fidelity and integrity, if we sacrifice the clear teaching of Holy Scripture, our efforts in the community may well have no lasting or eternal significance. I enjoyed working with Rome. They allowed me to be Lutheran, and I allowed them to be Rome. I was honest with them and they with me. What a wonderful experience to learn how people of integrity respect people of integrity. Thanks be to God.

THE CROSS OF CHRIST IS OUR CROWN
(*CRUCE CHRISTI NOSTRA CORONA EST*)

Being part of an effort to bring about significant change in a small and otherwise insignificant part the world was invigorating and maddening. I learned a great lesson and will use a metaphor to summarize pastoral work in the city: "Serve in the inner city and you will soon have the 'glory' beat out of you!" The issue of housing is enormously complex. It touches on all aspects of sociocultural reality. As one attempts to make a difference, there are many failures and disappointments, which drive you repeatedly to the cross. I am thankful and proud of Zion's work and accomplishments in the urban setting. By faith, Zion and I confess it was all God's grace. God placed us in the right place at the right time. The congregation was ready. The neighborhood was ready. The partners were ready. It was something only our Lord could pull together in His hidden will. Amid all the challenges, I found the greatest solace and consolation in the very gifts I had been called to distribute from Zion's altar, font, and pulpit. Far greater than anything that occurred in that limited neighborhood project was the reality of sinners—regardless of financial and social status or race—receiving Christ's forgiveness Sunday after Sunday.

I pray that the Lord will use my experiences with such work along with His Word to help and bless others who desire to make a difference in their community. The Lord has taught me many hard lessons through community work, and I continue to learn more every day. He uses my vocation to teach me about the process of organizing larger housing efforts, community organizations, federal funding, and so much more.

Serving Christ's people at the altar, font, and pulpit of Zion Lutheran Church was the highest honor and privilege. What a gift to proceed from that altar and the presence of those dear saints into the community as a representative of Zion and confessional Lutheranism! As He always does, God works through means. He used my gifts and vocations as one piece of the puzzle to make a difference in one community, to bring light to the darkness and order to chaos, so that the Gospel might flourish.

> Kyrie! God, Father in heav'n above,
> You abound in gracious love,
> Of all things the maker and preserver. Eleison! Eleison!
>
> Kyrie! O Christ, our king,
> Salvation for all You came to bring.
> O Lord Jesus, God's own Son,
> Our mediator at the heav'nly throne;
> Hear our cry and grant our supplication. Eleison! Eleison!
>
> Kyrie! O God the Holy Ghost,
> Guard our faith, the gift we need the most,
> And bless our life's last hour,

That we leave this sinful world with gladness. Eleison! Eleison!

(*Lutheran Service Book* 942)[41]

Notes

1 Theodore G. Tappert, ed. and trans., *Luther: Letters of Spiritual Counsel*, Library of Christian Classics 18 (Philadelphia and London: Westminster Press and SCM, 1955), 232. This comes from Luther's admonition to leaders in Breslau to remain in the city during a time of plague in 1527.

2 Clergy and Latin scholars will recognize this play on words. The technical theological term for cooperating in externals is *cooperatio in externis*, which means to cooperate to good ends with people who do not share the same confession of faith.

3 SA III I 3 (*Concordia*, 270).

4 AE 25:345.

5 Ignatius, "To the Smyrnaeans," 8.56, in *Early Christian Fathers*, ed. and trans. Cyril C. Richardson, Library of Christian Classics 1 (Philadelphia: Westminster Press, 1953).

6 Ap VII–VIII 3 (*Concordia*, 144).

7 Ap VII–VIII 5 (*Concordia*, 144).

8 Ap XIV 26–27 (*Concordia*, 187).

9 AC XIV and Ap XIV 24 (*Concordia*, 39, 187).

10 Ap VII–VIII 28 (*Concordia*, 148).

11 See *Concordia*, 34.

12 FC Ep V 6 (*Concordia*, 485).

13 FC SD VII 33 (*Concordia*, 568).

14 Ap II 51; Ap VII–VIII 10; Ap XIV 27 (*Concordia*, 89, 144, 187).

15 See the Preface to the Book of Concord 20 (*Concordia*, 9) and C. F. W. Walther, *The Proper Distinction Between Law and Gospel*, trans. W. H. T. Dau (St. Louis: Concordia, 1929), 337.

16 SA II IV 9 (*Concordia*, 269).

17 Ap IV 192–93 (*Concordia*, 110–12).

18 Ap XXVII 5 (*Concordia*, 237).

19 Tr 80–81 (*Concordia*, 305).

20 See Ap XXVII (*Concordia*, 237–47).

21 Carter Lindberg, *Beyond Charity: Reformation Initiatives for the Poor* (Minneapolis: Fortress, 1993).

22 See Ap XXVII 46 (*Concordia*, 244).

23 LC III 115–16 (*Concordia*, 422).

24 See AE 45:169–94.

25 See Lindberg, *Beyond Charity*, 128.

26 See Hermann Sasse, "Church Government and Secular Authority according to Lutheran Doctrine," in *The Lonely Way*, trans. Matthew C. Harrison et al. (St. Louis: Concordia, 2001), 1:226–27.

27 See Matthew Harrison, "The Church's Role of Mercy in the Community," *Lutheran Forum* (Winter 2002): 12ff.

28 FC SD III 41 (*Concordia*, 543).

29 SA Preface 10–11 (*Concordia*, 261).

30 By the time I left the congregation, I knew Gary very well. A midlevel, nonpolitical city bureaucrat, Gary genuinely wanted to help. He could get things done on a shoestring, even while being yanked around by the politicos. He would say, "Pastor, just tell me what buildings you want down, and I'll do my best to get them on the next bid package." Then he would hire contractors to take down five or ten or twenty derelict homes at a time.

31 See David L. Adams and Ken Schurb, eds., *The Anonymous God: The Church Confronts Civil Religion and American Society* (St. Louis: Concordia, 2004). The appendix of this book clearly explicates two-kingdom theology and will help clarify how two-kingdom theology is put into practice.

32 AC XXVIII 12–18 (*Concordia*, 58–59).

33 See AC XIV.

34 AE 40:284: "The preachers, accordingly, should faithfully remind the authorities to maintain peace, justice, and security for their subjects, to defend the poor, the widow, and the orphan, and not to look on them as chattel, as God commanded Jeremiah, in Jer. 7[:2ff.], to preach to all the people of Judah and proclaim his promise to dwell with them."

35 Ap VIII 50 (*Concordia*, 152).

36 Ap XVI 64 (*Concordia*, 196).

37 "Ecclesial communities derived from the Reformation and separated from the Catholic Church, have not preserved the proper reality of the Eucharistic mystery in its fullness, especially because of the absence of the sacrament of orders" (*Catechism of the Catholic Church* [Vatican City: Libreria Editrice Vaticana, 1997], 353).

38 See Ronald Feuerhahn, "Hermann Sasse as an Ecumenical Churchman" (doctoral dissertation, University of Cambridge, September 1991).

39 Wilhelm Löhe, *Three Books About the Church* (Fort Wayne, IN: Concordia Theological Seminary Press, 1989), introduction.

40 See, for example, *Ut Unum Sint* [*That They May Be One*], in *The Encyclicals of John Paul II* (Huntington: Our Sunday Visitor, 1996), 895ff.

41 Copyright © 1941 Concordia Publishing House. All rights reserved.

16

REPENTANCE, WORD, VOCATION, AND THE COURAGE TO BE LUTHERAN AND MERCIFUL

COURAGE IS FEAR THAT HAS BEEN BAPTIZED

Be watchful, stand firm in the faith, act like men, be strong. Let all that you do be done in love. *1 Corinthians 16:13–14*

Christ says, "Come to me, all who labor and are heavy-laden" [Matt. 11:28], and it is as though he were saying: Just stick to me, hold on to my Word and let everything else go. . . . That is to say: If things go badly, I will give you the courage even to laugh about it; and if even though you walk on fiery coals, the torment shall nevertheless not be so severe and the devil shall nevertheless not be so bad, and you will rather feel that you are walking on roses. . . . Only come to me . . . . For when you suffer for my sake, it is my yoke . . . I myself am helping you to carry it and giving you power and strength to do so.[1] *Martin Luther*

It has been said that courage is simply fear that has said its prayers. I prefer to say that courage is fear that has been baptized (by water and tribulation!). Now is the moment of the Lutheran Church. Now is a time for mercy. More than anything else, we need the courage to make "the best use of the time" (Colossians 4:5).

In 1932, Hermann Sasse was thirty-seven years old and serving as "social pastor" in a Berlin parish of ten thousand members. His duties were to attend to the pastoral needs of the down and out. Adolf Hitler and the National Socialist Party had taken over nearly all the political institutions of Germany and were beginning to act on the party platform. Shockingly, there was broad support for Hitler within Lutheran territorial churches, as well as those church bodies that had been Lutheran (but were now Union churches in which Rationalism dominated), especially Sasse's own church body, the Church of the Old Prussian Union. Sasse was the first among the very few to publicly reject Article 24 of the Nazi Party platform, which stated:

We insist upon freedom for all religious confessions in the state, providing they do not endanger its existence or offend the German race's sense of decency and morality. The Party as such stands for a positive Christianity, without binding itself denominationally to a particular confession. It fights against the Jewish-materialistic spirit at home and abroad and believes that any lasting recovery of our people must be based on the spiritual principle: the welfare of the community comes before that of the individual.[2]

At the time, Sasse was editor of the *Church Year Book* for all Protestant Germany, and he provided a public response to the Nazi Party in the 1932 edition. His response has gone down in history as one of the most courageous and earliest rejections of Nazism during the Hitler period. Directed against the force that would murder millions and sacrifice millions more for its vain cause, Sasse wrote:

> One can perhaps forgive National Socialism all its theological sins, but this article 24 excludes any possibility of a dialogue with the church. . . . About this article, however, no discussion at all is possible . . . for the Protestant church would have to begin such a discussion with a frank admission that its doctrine constitutes a deliberate, permanent insult to "the German race's sense of decency and morality", and hence that she can have no expectation of tolerance in the Third Reich. . . . According to the Protestant doctrine of original sin, the newborn infant of the noblest Germanic descent, endowed in body and mind with the optimal racial characteristics, is as much subject to eternal damnation as the genetically gravely compromised half-caste from two decadent races. And we must go on to confess that the doctrine of justification of the sinner *sola gratia, sola fide*, is the end of Germanic morality just as it is the end of all human morality. . . . We are not much interested in whether the Party gives its support to Christianity, but we would like to know whether the church is to be permitted to preach the Gospel in the Third Reich without let or hindrance, whether, that is, we will be able to continue undisturbed with our insults to the Germanic or Germanistic moral sense, as with God's help we intend to do.[3]

Knowing the context in which it was written, Sasse's statement raises the hair on the back of my neck every time I read it. The Gospel gives courage. This man, diminutive in stature (barely five-feet, four-inches tall), was a giant confessor. How he survived the Hitler years is a mystery and a miracle. Sasse recognized, as few others did, that the racist dogma of Nazism struck at the very heart of Christianity—repentance and justification by grace alone through faith. The Gospel of Christ gave him the courage to act in the face of perhaps the most powerful demonic political/philosophical force in history. The Reich's satanic theology of glory precluded the preaching of repentance and the Law's damning rejection of all human "morality," including the most damnable Nazi "Germanistic moral sense." Where the Law cannot be preached to condemn, there is no repentance. Where there is no repentance, there is no possibility of forgiveness, of grace, of faith, of renewal. Sasse had the divinely wrought courage to confess for the sake of the Gospel what is stated in the Apology of the Augsburg Confession: "Paul says [in Romans 10:9–10] that confession saves in order to show what sort of faith receives eternal life, namely, that which is firm and active. That faith, however, that does not present itself in confession is not firm."[4]

Where can we find the courage to make such a confession in word and deed today? The Lutheran Church stands at a moment of opportunity unlike anything in the past, but do we have the courage of conviction to act? The forces we face today are no less diabolical than those of Nazi Germany. As Lutheran Christians, as a Lutheran Church, we are uniquely poised for the challenge we face. Ours is the Church of courage.

Martin Luther found the greatest personal consolation and courage in three things: repentance, the Word of God, and vocation. These keys unlock courage and boldness for us today, so we can bear witness to Christ for the sake of His mercy.

THE LUTHERAN CHURCH IS THE CHURCH OF COURAGE BECAUSE IT IS THE CHURCH OF REPENTANCE

When they saw the boldness of Peter and John, and perceived that they were uneducated, common men, they were astonished. And they recognized that they had been with Jesus. *Acts 4:13 NIV*

A good conscience fills a man's heart with courage and boldness.[5] *Martin Luther*

Repentance is the path to forgiveness; a good conscience before God is a gift of His mercy. The Lutheran Confessions state: "Sin terrifies consciences. This happens through the Law, which shows God's wrath against sin. But we gain the victory through Christ. How? Through faith, when we comfort ourselves by confidence in the mercy promised for Christ's sake."[6]

Repentance acknowledges that our lives are in God's hands and we live from His mercy. John the Baptist's first recorded words are, "Repent, for the kingdom of God is at hand" (Matthew 3:2). And the first recorded words of Jesus' preaching are, "Repent, for the kingdom of God is at hand" (Matthew 4:17). After Jesus' ascension, Peter preached to the crowd in Jerusalem, "Repent and be baptized every one of you in the name of Jesus Christ for the forgiveness of your sins, and you will receive the gift of the Holy Spirit" (Acts 2:38).

COURAGE TO "DO GREAT THINGS"

In the first of the Ninety-five Theses, Luther states: "When our Lord and Master Jesus Christ said, 'Repent' [Matt. 4:17], he willed the entire life of believers to be one of repentance."[7] In the Smalcald Articles, Luther wrote of God's Law: "This is God's thunderbolt. By the Law He strikes down both obvious sinners and false saints. He declares no one to be in the right."[8]

At the time of the Prussian Union (1817), Claus Harms preached repentance, saying: "When our Lord and Master Jesus Christ says, 'Repent,' He wants men to conform themselves to His teaching; He does not conform His teaching to men, as is now the custom in accord with the changed spirit of the time. 2 Tim. 4:3."[9] C. F. W. Walther was a preacher of repentance: "A preacher must proclaim the Law in such a manner that there remains in it nothing pleasant to lost and condemned sinners. Every sweet ingredient injected into the Law is poison; it renders this heavenly medicine ineffective, neutralizes its operation."[10] Repentance is the path to faith and brings courage to "do great things."

Why is this so? Repentance and faith free us from doubt about eternity so we can live confidently and courageously. Luther writes that Adam "is called to account that he might acknowledge his sin and, after he is thoroughly frightened by his sin, be given courage through the promise of the remission of sins."[11] And the humblest vocations take courage! The Law damns all my thoughts, words, and deeds. The best of my deeds are as "filthy rags" (Isaiah 64:6 NIV), yet in Christ my sins are forgiven, and those thoughts, words, and deeds that are tainted with sin are cleansed by the blood of Christ. It is as though they were performed by the very Son of God Himself!

As laypeople, church workers, congregations, and as a church body, life throws moments of crisis and decision in our path. But indecision does not need to paralyze us, no matter how weighty the matter. We cannot and need not attempt to uncover the hidden will of God in a matter clearly not decided by the Word of God. But we can act boldly, knowing that in repentance and faith God will bless and work all things for good.

Perhaps your congregation is considering starting a mission or beginning a ministry of mercy. But if you release one hundred members, it will jeopardize your ability to support the ministry of the mother congregation. The school could suffer to the breaking point. But if the new parish or ministry of mercy is started, it will bring untold blessings to an area of the community that is growing and is largely unchurched. Some members want to start the new parish to get out from under the "thumb" of the old guard. Others are excited about mission and the opportunity to bring a faithful Lutheran congregation to a new area. What to do? Repent, knowing that all our thoughts, words, and deeds are shot through with sin and wrong motivations. Study. Consult. And act—with courage! The Lord will bless, for as St. Paul says, "All things work together for good" (Romans 8:28). So be bold! Luther points out that "God does not abandon even him who is weak in faith. Indeed, the apostles themselves and the prophets were not strong in faith, especially when they were about to do great things through faith."[12]

The greatest and strongest missiologic periods in the life of the Church have been eras of the preaching of repentance, the preaching of total guilt under the unwavering and damning Law of God. At these times, sinners are directed to the pure, holy, soothing, comforting, forgiving Gospel of Christ, who says, "I came not to call the righteous, but sinners" (Matthew 9:13). The Gospel is for sinners and only for sinners. And because the precious blood of God in the flesh flowed down the cross of Calvary, we are forgiven. Our sins are wiped out. I and all the world are reconciled to God (2 Corinthians 5:19). By faith in Jesus and His actions on the cross, I am reconciled with God. In fact, the sins of the world are canceled. Now is the time to preach repentance and faith in Christ and His cross within, without, and to a Church desperately in need of courage for the task at hand of mercy and mission. Our sins are covered. Eternity is ours. We can dare "to do great things" for Christ!

This courage is not a personal "heroic strength." The literature of the Lutheran Church is replete with depictions of Luther or Paul as conquering heroes. But another story must be told. Both Paul and Luther were bold in weakness (2 Corinthians 11–12) because their consciences had become captive to the Word of God. Luther suffered depression, doubt, illness, anxiety, struggles with dear friends and enemies, weakness, serious mistakes of judgment, frustration, anger, financial struggles, and other grave weaknesses throughout his life. At one point toward the end of his life, Luther was so angry with the faithlessness of his Wittenbergers that he had resolved to leave the city for good.[13] All these weaknesses drove the great reformer to his knees in repentance. Yet amid all this, Luther could quote Vergil to a friend in need of courage, "Yield not to ills; press on the bolder."[14]

PRESS ON THE BOLDER!

These weaknesses made Paul and Luther tremendous blessings to the Church. The greatest gift the LCMS can give the world on the eve of the five-hundredth anniversary of the Reformation (October 31, 2017) is repentance for its own many and grave sins and weaknesses, as well as the consequent unequivocal humble confession of the truth of the Gospel. With Walther we can say, "Let us acknowledge that the greater the knowledge of the Gospel which God has given us, the greater must be the recognition of our guilt. For unto whom much is given, of him shall much be required."[15] Jesus says, "Take heart . . . your sins are forgiven" (Matthew 9:2), so *Press on the bolder!* Lord, have mercy.

THE LUTHERAN CHURCH IS THE CHURCH OF COURAGE BECAUSE IT IS THE CHURCH OF THE WORD OF GOD

> For whatever was written in former days was written for our instruction, that through endurance and through the encouragement of the Scriptures we might have hope. *Romans 15:4*

> I am bound by the Scriptures I have quoted and my conscience is captive to the Word of God. I cannot and I will not retract anything, since it is neither safe nor right to go against conscience. I cannot do otherwise, here I stand, may God help me, Amen.[16] *Martin Luther*

In every era of vitality in the Church's life, the message of repentance for sin is accompanied by a cry to return to the Word of God. In the Old Testament, the prophet Isaiah cried out, "To the teaching and to the testimony!" (Isaiah 8:20). Then came John the Baptist, who was identified as "the voice of one crying in the wilderness: 'Prepare the way of the Lord' " (Matthew 3:3, citing Isaiah 40:3). Luke records that "beginning with Moses and all the Prophets, [Jesus] interpreted to them in all the Scriptures the things concerning Himself" (Luke 24:27). And Jesus Himself said, "It is written: 'Man shall not live by bread alone, but by every word that comes from the mouth of God' " (Matthew 4:4).

Truly great eras of tremendous advancement in the Church always begin with the call "Repent! Return! Come back! Come back to the Bible and the Lutheran Confessions!" These Confessions teach that the Holy Scriptures are completely sufficient for providing all that we need to know and believe to be Christians. The Scriptures are the "pure, clear fountain of Israel,"[17] and "God cannot lie or deceive."[18] Anything that is "fabricated and invented without God's will and Word" is "dangerous."[19] It leads us away from Christ our Good Shepherd. These very Scriptures inform faith and likewise give us courage for the day. "Christian faith is ready to rest completely on God's Word with all confidence and courage, and then to go joyfully on its way," Luther writes.[20]

The faith must be confessed anew for each generation. And each generation faces similar challenges in new circumstances. The Church's biblical confession is an anchor in the storm, a life raft in the morass of postmodern confusion. It is also the battering ram for storming the dominions of darkness as we go to great lengths and into dark places to rescue precious souls with the light of the Gospel. With the Gospel at its center, our confession is the bright beacon of hope and light in a dark world of sin and death that is running headlong toward its demise.

The Scriptures also give us confidence because they tell of our fathers and mothers in the faith who were weak, often faithless, and fearful in the face of trials and challenges to their vocations. Our predecessors in the faith were just like we are. The biblical accounts give us courage in our weakness so that we do not despair in our many sins and failings. God has always been pleased to "do great things" through sinners.[21] Luther writes:

> We see that no one has ever been deserted who has dared to rely upon God's comforts and promises, even though they were the most miserable and the poorest sinners and beggars that were ever on the earth, indeed, even though it were a slain Abel and a swallowed Jonah.[22]

CHRIST HAS A FUTURE SO THE CHURCH HAS A FUTURE

In the morass of today's insane world, who of us has not felt like a "swallowed Jonah"? In 1939, well into the heat of the struggle with Hitler, Sasse wrote an essay entitled "The Presence of Christ and the Future of the Church."[23] At the time, many theologians were predicting the demise of Christianity in Germany. Sasse responded, "To both the fearful friends and the reveling opponents of the church we must hold up the biblical truth proven through so many centuries: that the future of the church nowhere and never has lain in the hands of people."[24]

While these naysayers would appear to be correct (witness the ignominious fall of the Lutheran Church in Europe), the Church is the Lord's, and it is in His hands. We have the promise: "I tell you, you are Peter, and on this rock [that is, Peter's confession of Christ] I will build My church, and the gates of hell shall not prevail against it" (Matthew 16:18). The Church of Jesus Christ has a future and is even now growing—primarily in the southern hemisphere. And it is growing not because of all the programs (effective or not) coming from denominational headquarters, not because of the fabulous skills of a particular pastor, not because of well-organized and well-executed mission programs, not because of diaconal efforts—however vital and necessary all these are because the Gospel is not a ticket to laziness! *The Church ultimately has a future because Jesus Christ has a future.* When our strength is at its end, Christ's strength is just beginning, as Luther writes:

> When the situation is hopeless and all plans and efforts are in vain, then be courageous, and beware of giving up; for God calls all things from the dead and from nothing. When no resource or hope at all is left, then at last God's help begins.[25]

The LCMS will have a future so long as she believes in, confesses, proclaims, and holds to Christ and His Word. Repeatedly Jesus tells His disciples and us, "Don't be afraid!" So don't be afraid, but "go therefore and make disciples of all nations, baptizing them in the name of the Father and of the Son and of the Holy Spirit, teaching them to observe all that I have commanded you [including mercy: "This is My commandment, that you love one another," John 15:12]. And behold, I am with you always, to the end of the age" (Matthew 28:19–20). And it is this very "Word of God alone that makes learned, ready, and courageous men."[26]

This sure Word of God grabbed and salved the troubled consciences of our fathers in the faith. It rescued them from doubt, united them, and propelled them all over the world with the message of Christ and His Gospel. Friedrich Wyneken (1810–1876), the second president the LCMS, remains the greatest missionary pastor in the history of the LCMS. In 1855, at a crucial moment in the Synod's history (its division into an Eastern and a Western district), Wyneken preached about God's Word and courage in the Church:

> Then why, beloved brothers, do we stand by each other? Why can't we leave one another? It is because we cannot let go of the one truth, which we, in fellowship with all the saints, have acknowledged, do believe, and confess, as it is in the Confessions of the Lutheran Church. These Confessions bear witness to the truth clearly, plainly, and powerfully on the basis of the Holy Scriptures, against all the desires of Satan, to the whole world. And why do we hold so firmly to our confession, that we happily endure the hatred of the world and also of the rest of Christianity, which is difficult to bear?

Why, with God's help and grace, would we suffer persecution and death before we would give up even a small part of that confession? We do so because we have come to make the truth set forth in that confession our own, not in times of good leisure and rest, like we might appropriate other natural or historical truths. The Holy Spirit has revealed this truth to us, in the midst of the burdens of troubled consciences, as our only salvation. The Spirit has through the Word borne witness to the truth in broken and troubled hearts. Our consciences are bound to the Word, and, therefore, to the confession of the church. As poor, forlorn, and condemned men, we have learned to believe in Jesus Christ our Lord and Savior. The peace of conscience, the peace of our souls, the hope of eternal blessedness, our very being and life hang on this truth. To surrender it would be to surrender our salvation and ourselves for time and eternity. Therefore neither can we let go of the most insignificant portion of the confession, because the entire series of the individual teachings of the faith are for us one chain. This chain not only binds our understanding in the truth, it also binds our consciences and lives. The loss of an individual part of the same would break this chain and we would be torn loose from Christ, tumbling again into the abyss of anxiety, doubt, and eternal death.

Therefore we hold fast to our confession, as to our very life's life.[27]

Perhaps our greatest challenge today is that we have never known the kind of crisis of conscience our predecessors in the faith experienced. Thus the Word of God and the Confessions do not yet mean to us what they meant for them. Is this why our missionary zeal is often lacking? Are our consciences still "bound to the Word of God"? If so, then "the only thing that need concern us is that we be sure of the Word and diligently teach it."[28] In Christ, eternity is ours. And Jesus is with us until we arrive there.

There is a world before us, and it begins at the very doors to each of the more than six thousand congregations in the LCMS. It is time to be who we are—uncompromising Lutherans!—and to dare to step in courage and with mercy across the threshold into the world. As we do so, we will find the Lord Himself granting the courage needed for the task and blessing the outcome. With Luther, we can say, "Let him who has a sure Word of God, in whatever vocation he may be, only believe and have courage, and God will undoubtedly grant a favorable outcome."[29] We have a sure Word of God and all its promises. Let's dare to do something! Christ, have mercy.

THE LUTHERAN CHURCH IS THE CHURCH OF COURAGE BECAUSE IT IS THE CHURCH OF SACRED VOCATION

You are a chosen people, a royal priesthood, a holy nation, a people for His own possession, that you may proclaim the excellencies of Him who called you out of darkness into His marvelous light. Once you were not a people, but now you are God's people; once you had not received mercy, but now you have received mercy. *1 Peter 2:9–10*

For it is most certainly true that when anyone in his vocation is convinced in his heart that God desires and has commanded in His Word what he is doing, he will experience such force and effectiveness of that divine command as he will not find in the oration of any orator, either of Demosthenes or of Cicero. . . . It points out and suggests to the heart that God has in view unlimited designs far above our understanding. And when the heart has been provided with this confidence, it proceeds boldly and is not anxious about the possible or the impossible, the easy or the difficult, as St. Paul has magnificently described this confidence and security of the godly in Rom. 8:35ff.[30] *Martin Luther*

God calls us to be Christians. The word *call* or *calling* is often misunderstood. The word *vocation* comes from the Latin *vocare*, which means "to call." Every Christian is called, and the call first comes in Baptism when God places the name of the Holy Trinity on you. He calls you by name and marks you as one redeemed by Christ the crucified. From that moment on, this spiritual vocation touches all you do. The rest of your life is a call to repentance and absolution, and, in turn, a call to serve others. This calling makes you a "spiritual priest" (see 1 Peter 2:9). As such, you are forever called to speak God's Word to your neighbor; to live a life of the sacrifice of praise to God in word and deed (which is love and service for the neighbor); and to offer prayers for yourself, your neighbor, and the world. Lutherans have a view of the call that extends into the daily life of the Christian (Romans 12:1–3), and this brings great consolation and confidence.

At the time of the Lutheran Reformation, it was believed that some vocations in life were holier than others. Monks, priests, and nuns could live more holy lives and earn their way out of purgatory and enter heaven more quickly than laypeople.[31] Laypeople had only the Ten Commandments to keep. But those in these holy church vocations had to commit to poverty, chastity (celibacy), and obedience (to the church hierarchy). Luther rejected it all as contrary to the Bible. Everything needed for ethical direction of life in one's vocation is in the Ten Commandments, which are the true and holy counsels of God Himself. Life is not to be lived "hidden in some corner," in contemplation. Instead, for Luther, "each one is concerned to live a life, so he is also to be concerned that he lead an *actual life*," that is, a life that "sees [the] neighbor suffering need [and] serves and helps him."[32] Common to all vocations are two things: (1) the "common order of Christian love"[33] by which everyone is taught and directed to serve his or her neighbor in the context of vocation; and (2) the need for certainty that what we do in our vocations is acceptable to God because our sins are all forgiven in the Gospel.[34] The Gospel gives us the courage to carry out our callings by which we love our neighbor.

By virtue of our Baptism, all of us are called by God to live as Christians. How do we live out this calling? We do so in our specific vocations. What is the difference between a call to the office of pastor or that of teacher, deaconess, doctor, plumber, mother, and so on? On one level, there is no difference at all. The calls are equally holy and equally important according to God's will. It is the *office and the particular duties of each* that are different and unique. The pastoral office is not the office of deaconess. The office of teacher is not the office of the pastor. The office of father is not the office of janitor. The office of executive director of LCMS World Relief and Human Care is not the office a grade school student. However, God works through each and every one of these offices to mercifully serve His people, to see that they are cared for in both spiritual and physical needs.

The Lutheran view of vocation is very much directed to the external, to the neighbor. Our propensity—especially in a subjective culture and context—is to define our calling only in internal terms. What do *I* like? What am *I* good at? What makes *me* happy? What would *I* like to do with *my* life? These are all important questions, but they are all directed inward and ignore the vocations set before us in our relationships with others. By its very nature, vocation is directed outward, to our neighbor's need. Gustaf Wingren writes:

The incomparably clearest sign in God's providence is the fact that we have the neighbor we actually have. In that fact lies . . . evidence of a definite vocation. Uncertainty as to whether one is called is often due to regarding oneself as an isolated individual, whose "call" must come in some inward manner. But in reality we are always bound up in relations with other people; and these relations with our neighbors actually effect our vocation, since these external ties are made by God's hands.[35]

DIVINE STATION, DIVINE COURAGE

God calls us to have courage to be _____. You fill in the blank! God has placed you in your vocation(s). Luther called them stations or offices in life, and he divided them into three main categories: (1) home/economic, (2) state/government, (3) Church. We all have many different offices at the same time. God's call for me now is to the office of executive director of LCMS World Relief and Human Care. It is quite distinct from His call to me to the office of father, pastor, husband, basketball coach, employer, employee, and so on. Many different offices, many different functions—yet the call into these offices is God's own, and it is holy.

God's callings are high, blessed, and important according to their place in or outside the Church. Each specific office and its duty is unique. God does not call me, a father, to be a mother. For me to seek that office (mother) is impossible and completely contradicts God's will as revealed in creation and Scripture. We have so much to do in the vocations in which God places us, our time is too short, all our space too narrow, and all our energies too limited. God calls us to various duties in life, and He gives us courage to fulfill the offices He gives to us. According to Wingren, "Vocation means that those who are closest at hand, family and fellow-workers, are given by God: it is one's neighbor whom one is to love."[36]

It takes courage for a man to be faithful in his calling to the office of father. Fathers must balance the pressures of the workplace with the need to be present for their children. A father's calling into the office of fatherhood is a call to sacrifice for his wife and family, even as Christ made willing sacrifice of Himself for the children of His heavenly Father. And it doesn't take long for a new father to realize that his call to sacrifice increases tenfold upon the birth of his child. Now he doesn't sacrifice his life only for his bride but also for his children. There is no nobler calling on earth, and to carry it out so that one's wife and children love one another and Christ is a task beyond human ability. However, the task is aided by divine blessing. It takes courage and commitment to make time for family.

It takes courage for women to be faithful to their call into the office of mother. The sacrifice starts with morning sickness and the numerous physical changes that follow. Then there is the sacrifice involved with giving birth and caring for the child and often a needy husband. The vocation of mother grows and changes as a woman passes through every sorrow and blessing of life.

It takes courage to be a wife when you are a mother, to be a husband when you are a father. The offices are difficult and become more so with the arrival of children. Children require so much time and energy that the office of father or mother crowds out the office of spouse. It takes courage and commitment to be faithful to your marital offices while focusing on children. Satan loves to build walls between husbands and wives while they are trying to be fathers and mothers; it's a favorite ploy of the devil to pit one God-given vocation against another. But the courage to face the tasks comes from knowing that the duty is sacred, no matter how it's viewed by the world.

> Now observe that when that clever harlot, our natural reason . . . takes a look at married life, she turns up her nose and says, "Alas, must I rock the baby, wash its diapers, make its bed, smell its stench, stay up nights with it, take care of it when it cries, heal its rashes and sores, and on top of that care for my wife, provide for her, labor at my trade, take care of this and take care of that, do this and do that, endure this and endure that, and whatever else of bitterness and drudgery married life involves? What, should I make such a prisoner of myself? O you poor, wretched fellow, have you taken a wife? . . . What then does Christian faith say to this? It opens its eyes, looks upon all these insignificant, distasteful, and despised duties in the Spirit, and is aware that they are all adorned with divine approval as with the costliest gold and jewels. It says, "O God, because I am certain that thou hast created me as a man and hast from my body begotten this child, I also know for a certainty that it meets with thy perfect pleasure. I confess to thee that I am not worthy to rock the little babe or wash its diapers, or to be entrusted with the care of the child and its mother. How is it that I, without any merit, have come to this distinction of being certain that I am

serving thy creature and thy most precious will? O how gladly will I do so, though the duties should be even more insignificant and despised. Neither frost nor heat, neither drudgery nor labor, will distress or dissuade me, for I am certain that it is thus pleasing in thy sight.[37]

As children, our call is to obey our parents and bring honor to them. Our office requires us to learn from those whom our parents place in authority over us. It takes more courage than ever for children and grandchildren to do the right thing and stand up against peer pressure, premarital sex, alcohol and drugs, and so on. It takes great courage to love and be faithful to the other children in school who are ridiculed or who do not fit the current definition of "cool."

Today, with longer life expectancies (thanks to the blessings of medicine), it takes courage and commitment to be faithful to our vocation as sons and daughters and bring honor to our parents. Luther writes: "We must, therefore, impress this truth upon the young [Deuteronomy 6:7] that they should think of their parents as standing in God's place. They should remember that however lowly, poor, frail, and strange their parents may be, nevertheless, they are the father and mother given to them by God."[38] The sacrifices of a child increase as he or she needs to care for an aging parent. It is our call as children to look out for our parents no matter what they need.

It takes courage as the owner of a business or a farm to fight the barrage of challenges, regulations, equipment failures, needs, employee issues, government programs, IRS issues, fluctuating prices, and numerous other hurdles. It took courage for Dr. Harison Rasamimanana and his wife, Damoina, to radically improve medical care in Madagascar. It took courage for the members of Trinity Lutheran Church, Baton Rouge, to serve their neighbors who were struggling with downed power lines and trees, flooded homes and streets. It took courage for the pastors, church workers, and others in the South to carry on in their vocations after Hurricane Katrina struck. It took courage for prophets and apostles, Augustine and Luther, and the presidents of the LCMS from Walther to the present to be faithful to their offices as church leaders. "Godliness is nothing but divine service, and divine service is service to one's neighbor," Luther writes.[39]

Vocation takes courage, but where do we find such vocational courage? This courage comes from two things: (1) from certainty that God has placed me in this vocation, and (2) from knowing that everything I do in this sacred vocation is pleasing to God by virtue of the forgiveness of the Gospel. Luther found great comfort and courage in knowing God had given him his vocation through the Church. He mentioned this when he wrote against troublemakers in the Church who lacked legitimate calls by God through Christian congregations.

> I have often said and still say, I would not exchange my doctor's degree for all the world's gold. For I would surely in the long run lose courage and fall into despair if, as these infiltrators, I had undertaken these great and serious matters without call or commission. But God and the whole world bears me testimony that I entered into this work publicly and by virtue of my office as teacher and preacher, and have carried it on hitherto by the grace and help of God.[40]

Courage for our vocations comes from confidence that our vocation is pleasing to God and that He Himself has so placed us and helps us in that vocation. That is worth "all the world's gold." How do we know if the vocation is God-pleasing? Simple. Does my vocation accord with God's Word, with the Ten Commandments? If so, then it is pleasing to God. Luther said, "If you are not sure that it is God's Word and command then immediately walk away from it."[41] But are self-chosen vocations also pleasing to God? Certainly! Most vocations are in some sense self-chosen. And we are free to choose and switch vocations (jobs) as long as the choice is not inherently sinful or detrimental to others (such as switching from male to female, or renouncing the vocation of spouse or child for unbiblical reasons, or unduly and negatively affecting one's family). The beauty of the Gospel is that it grants us freedom to make decisions about how we will use our gifts in service to our neighbor. Luther made the choice to enter the monastery (a vocational choice he later regretted), and later he chose to study for his doctoral degree. Yet, for him, the conferral of this degree was tantamount to divine approbation, a divine vocation from the Church to teach and preach the Gospel.

Who of us does not suffer anxiety and doubt about our stations and situations in life? Yet courage is ours when we know that God is pleased with our vocations and confers His blessings on them. God uses us to serve others in a thousand different ways. And because we are His hands, feet, and mouths, we can have confidence and courage that He will not leave us in the lurch. Luther writes: "Now when I show forth such works, then it is a definite sign that Christ's birth has power and a place in me and as He Himself multiplies such works of Christ's love in us, so much Christ enlarges Himself in us."[42] Have courage! God is pleased to have you serving on His behalf, and He is pleased to demonstrate His mercy ("enlarge Himself") through you.

Regardless of your office or call—whether as a janitor or plumber, a doctor or nurse, a stay-at-home parent, a schoolteacher or pastor or director of Christian education, a farmer or engineer—it takes courage and commitment to do to the best of your ability what your office requires. This applies to any job. However, as Christians we understand what a high calling every office is as God uses it to work and to be present in the world and among His people. These offices are God's means to get His work done, because we know that "God does all His works through His servants. Therefore, His works are divine and human at the same time, and whenever He works He soon opens a wide course of mercy for His saints."[43] This is how He has mercy on others in word and deed. Luther said that these vocations are the masks of God, and it is "God's will that under these masks you should serve His ordinance and man's need."[44]

GOD IS IN THE BASEMENT

The sewer pipe at my home became clogged with roots several years ago. What a wretched mess! I watched the sewer man matter-of-factly pull the equipment from his van in front of our home. Burly, a bit overweight, and perfumed from his last job, he loaded each piece of equipment on his person and headed for the basement. He looked the part. He didn't look like God. He certainly didn't smell like God! I might have despised him utterly, ridiculed him and his job—*if* my sewer were not plugged.

I watched in amazement as this man operated the snake and its cutter blade with consummate finesse, feeding foot after foot of rotating cable into the drain. As the metal cord twirled in his hand, his eyes stared into space. He was "seeing" the obstructions in the pipe through his hands. "I just had this done a few months ago," I offered.

"Ya," he replied, "but they didn't use the right cutter head. I'll get you fixed up." His hands were huge and calloused. His clothes were stained from who knows how many previous jobs.

I thought of Luther's quip to the skeptic Erasmus who would not grant that Christ, the God-man, is present everywhere. Erasmus had asked if Christ was everywhere, was He also in a sewer? To this question, Luther replied, "Are we to suppose that if I am captured by a tyrant and thrown into a prison or a sewer—as has happened to many saints—I am not to be allowed to call upon God there or to believe that he is present with me, but must wait until I come into some finely furnished church?"[45] There, in my own basement, I was in the sewer. I had been humbled into recognizing God's vocation and work. Luther pointed out that "everybody must look behind himself and see in what filth and stench he was mired. Then such people will, I suppose, soon forget any pride and arrogance."[46] My pride and arrogance were gone. The rough hands of that sewer man were the very hands of God to serve me. And in fact he had the problem fixed in minutes.

"How long have you been doing this?" I asked.

"All my life. My dad taught me the business," came the response.

Wow! Generations of a divine vocation of helping people out of the muck. Now that was a time when a long Litany with Kyrie turned to a Te Deum! Luther's comment in the Large Catechism never rang more true (even if it was more than a little ironic under the circumstances):

> Know now that the works of this commandment are the true, holy, and godly works. God rejoices in them with all the angels. In comparison with these works all human holiness is just stench and filth [Isaiah 64:6]. And besides, human holiness deserves nothing but wrath and damnation.[47]

THE GOSPEL GIVES VOCATIONAL COURAGE

We can have courage that everything we do in our vocation is pleasing to God because of the Gospel. Anything we do in our vocation—which is not in and of itself sinful—is wholly pleasing and acceptable to God in Christ. According to Gustaf Wingren,

> If one who is mindful of his vocation looks heavenward, he sees only the gospel between God and himself, and not so much as one of his own works. His works, his vocation, involve his relation to his neighbor. His conscience rests in his faith in the gospel, while his love, with body and might, is committed to his vocation.[48]

My sinful motivations, my mistakes, my failures are forgiven. Even my many weaknesses and failings and the crosses I bear help me to be of better service and love to my neighbor. The apostle Paul writes that "we have this treasure in jars of clay" (2 Corinthians 4:7). We can have joyous courage to dare to accomplish something significant in life, to find deep meaning in life in service to others—even in what might appear to be the most mundane circumstances. We can find renewed meaning in our current vocations. We are God's specially appointed agents sent to take care of that little diapered wonder right in front of us. We are God's called servants, sent to care for and love a ragtag bunch of sinners we call relatives. We are God's own divinely called farmers with the sacred task of growing soybeans.

We can have the courage to risk something, to dare something, to serve others. My vocation of supporting institutions of mercy includes travel to exotic places, which might seem extra-divine and God-pleasing. It is not. The man who fixed my drain has a vocation every bit as God-pleasing and necessary. My house would not function without a working sewer! And I would not be traveling internationally if things were backed up at home! As Luther says, "There is nothing which is so bodily, carnal, and external that it does not become spiritual when it is done in the Word of God and faith."[49] Christ, have mercy.

THE COURAGE TO BE LUTHERAN: PASTOR AND PEOPLE JOINED IN MERCY

> For I long to see you, that I may impart to you some spiritual gift to strengthen you—that is, that we may be mutually encouraged by each other's faith, both yours and mine. *Romans 1:11–12*

> Thus God sent you, too, from heaven. You may ask: "How?" You were baptized; at that time you were born as a child of God through Christ. Even though we were all called, however, we cannot all preach; but this does not

relieve us of our obligation to confess Christ publicly. . . . In the rite of ordination the baptized members bestow a special vocation on those whom they select, and those who are called in this way proclaim the Word of God.

Now the point will be made that surely these are not all true priests. . . . Those who are Christians are convinced that they are called to confess God. In Baptism we all receive the chrism and the priestly garb. In the First Epistle of St. Peter, chapter two, we are told that we are called out of darkness into His precious and marvelous light that we may declare all His virtues, His power, and His wonderful deeds (1 Peter 2:9).[50] *Martin Luther*

There are many stunning and stirring examples of Lutheran pastors and people demonstrating extraordinary courage in the face of overwhelming adversity. Cholera raged in St. Louis, Missouri, in 1849. Of 63,471 inhabitants, the disease claimed 8,444.[51] (That is a far higher death rate than is experienced in most of Africa as a result of HIV/AIDS.) At the height of the epidemic, two hundred people a day were dying. Worse yet, the epidemic struck on the heels of a horrendous fire that destroyed much of the city on May 17, 1849 (Ascension Day). More than six hundred buildings and twenty-seven steamships at harbor on the wharf were consumed.

C. F. W. Walther's mother-in-law died of cholera on June 11, his sister-in-law died on June 21, and his nephew succumbed on June 29.[52] In total, Trinity Lutheran Church, Walther's congregation, lost forty-five members that year. Many residents were reeling from the loss of homes and businesses in the fire. The city of St. Louis named Walther as one of the persons responsible for his ward "to use such remedies as necessity demands by supplying the poor with medical devices, having medicines made up for them, and using disinfectants."[53] The Rev. George Schieferdecker of nearby Centerville, Illinois, recounted that when he went to St. Louis during the plague he saw "hearses from morning till night, without ceasing."[54]

Thus when Walther preached in 1862 on the sacred duty of the Office of the Holy Ministry to see that people also are cared for physically, he knew well what he was saying:

Where consolation and help are needed, he [the pastor] shall be the Good Samaritan of the congregation, ready with mercy. Thus the great task of his office is to see to it that no one in his entire congregation is abandoned and suffers need without assistance, be it in external or inner matters, in bodily matters or spiritual matters.[55]

Walther preached repentance courageously amid the St. Louis tragedy:

Rebellions by entire nations against their governments; bloody, destructive wars on land and sea; a contagious epidemic striding across the face of the earth;—these are the awesome preachers to whom God has now issued the command: "Go into all the world and preach repentance to all creatures!"[56]

But Walther also preached faith, mercy, and courage into the hearts of the afflicted. The people rallied and overflowed with mercy for the needy.[57]

Times are no different today. One could write a book on the courage required of Walther to be Lutheran in the chaotic times he faced. It takes courage to be a pastor today and speak the truth as it is in God's Word. It takes courage to call sin what it is and to preach repentance. It takes courage to say *no* to couples young and old who are living together without marriage, to face the wrath of their families, and still to work to assist them in coming to a God-pleasing solution. It takes courage to remain faithful to the biblical and confessional commitments of the LCMS concerning church fellowship. It takes courage to face a member who has become uncharitable (especially to the pastor's family). It takes courage to guide well-meaning congregants in the proper use of the broad freedom in the Lutheran Church when it comes to worship practices. While there is freedom, there is not frivolity or offense[58] nor worship that crosses the line into entertainment. It takes courage for a pastor to preach to himself, to confess his many sins, and to rest in the very Gospel he delivers to others. And it takes courage and wisdom to respond to all these circumstances firmly but charitably, in mercy, and not with a sledgehammer or coercion. It takes courage to gently but persistently hold forth a vision of Christ and His mercy until that vision is grasped and spills forth within the congregation and beyond.

PASTOR FOR PEOPLE FOR PASTOR

The fathers of the LCMS were criticized (especially by European Lutherans) for making the Church into a democratic monster and making pastors mere hirelings. The doctrine of Luther, the Treatise on the Power and Primacy of the Pope, and the position of Walther asserts that the Office of the Keys belongs to the Church as the gathered royal priesthood. The Church confers its privileges on one who in the stead of Christ and the congregation publicly proclaims the Word in its midst. The Church (all the baptized) retain the right and responsibility of speaking the Gospel to one another in their vocations and of wielding the Office of the Keys in their daily lives. They also retain the right and responsibility to judge doctrine and to take part in the governance of the Church.

The early members of the LCMS diligently retained the rights of the royal priesthood and trained the laity to understand these rights and privileges for the benefit of the Church. The result was not that pastors were treated poorly—rather, it was quite the opposite. Pastors and the pastoral office were most often treasured and respected. Friedrich Wyneken spoke eloquently about this at the 1852 synodical convention:

> This office is not about concealing from the so-called laity its sovereignty, patronizing it and defining ever more narrowly the boundaries within which it may move. It does not clip its rights, limit its heart, close its lips, reduce it to timidity that it remain nice looking and subject and not dare in any way to impinge upon the sovereignty of the educated and well-reasoned pastor. In short, the office does not consist in suppression of the laity in order to elevate the clergy and at the laity's expense such that the office boasts of sovereignty that it magnanimously leave the laity to boast of obedience. The dignity, the desire, and joy of the true co-worker of God is to draw ever more his community of believers into their freedom and its worthy use, to encourage them and lead them ever more in the exercise of their rights, to show them how to exercise their duties that they be more and more convinced of their high calling and that they demonstrate that they are ever more worthy of that calling.
>
> He does not live in fear that the laity will overstep its boundaries. For where are the boundaries of true spiritual, heavenly freedom? He fears that they will exercise their freedom as little as the eagle fears its young will

encounter the sun in flight, with the slight anxiety that they might fly too high or above him. For where the flight approaches the boundaries of fleshly freedom, he descends; he does not ascend. There the true watchman of God stands at the boundary with the divine Word, before which the sinking child of God is humbled . . . and turned back. . . .

Our opponents lie when they assert that we are the bondservants of men, leading the congregations of God to fleshly freedom and the despising of the Holy Office. . . . It does not worry us much. We have the testimony of a good conscience. Not only that, the congregations served by us bear witness that we have done our task well. Stubborn opponents are driven by hatred and scorn because we do not allow ourselves to be mere menial servants [*Knechten*]. Those won by the Word of God love and honor us as their teachers ordained of Christ and as shepherds and fathers. They trust us from the heart and are willingly obedient. Instead of jealously guarding their rights over against us, they are diligent to uphold the rights of the office and give appropriate respect to the preacher over against anyone who would hazard to infringe upon the office and forsake it. For they know that we with determination guard their rights and will not suffer infringement upon the grandeur and freedom granted by God to the congregation.[59]

Conviction Not Coercion

"People follow conviction, not coercion," Australian theologian John Kleinig once told me. The pastor's propensity in times of adversity and challenge is to take shortcuts, to act immediately, to command, to legislate, to coerce. When he believes the laity are not respecting the Office of the Holy Ministry and its sacred duties (and it does happen!), there can be an overreaction that denies the laity its glorious vocation, rights, and privileges as the spiritual priesthood. The pastor as undershepherd is called to exercise "authority" as did Christ, that is, in mercy and self-sacrifice. Christ exercised His authority by giving Himself up to death on a cross. How blessed it is to follow Christ our Savior! How sweet is His "authority." Grace does not coerce.

Congregations, submit to your pastors, as to the Lord. For the pastor is the head of the congregation even as Christ is the head of the church, His body, and is Himself its Savior. . . . Pastors, love your congregations, as Christ loved the church and gave Himself up for her, that He might sanctify her, having cleansed her by the washing of water with the word, so that He might present the church to Himself in splendor, without spot or wrinkle or any such thing, that she might be holy and without blemish. In the same way pastors should love their congregations as their own bodies. He who loves his congregation loves himself. *Ephesians 5, slightly amended by author*

How often our anxious and despondent lives require "the powerful plasters of the Scriptures."[60] The route of conviction is slowly and lovingly to teach the laity about its marvelous freedoms, privileges, and responsibilities. The route of conviction teaches the laity the responsibilities of the pastor (perhaps by reviewing the rite of ordination/installation). The hard and slow route of conviction shows the laity how to use the Word of God, the Catechism, the hymnal, and the Book of Concord as their guides in home and at church. Laypeople know a heavy burden is placed on their pastors. Many of them—especially older members—pray for their pastors diligently. They take to heart the apostolic command to "obey your leaders and submit to them, for they are keeping watch over your souls, as those who will have to give an account. Let them do this with joy and not with groaning, for that would be of no advantage to you" (Hebrews 13:17). Because pastors deal with eternal matters ("those who will have to give account"), the devil will work overtime to foul things up. There will be crosses aplenty.

Pastors suffering the crosses of the office do well to take the advice of Luther to Frederick the Wise:

> For many years Your Grace has been acquiring relics in every land, but God has now heard Your Grace's request and has sent Your Grace, without cost or trouble, a whole cross together with nails, spears, and scourges. I say again: grace and joy from God on the acquisition of a new relic! Only do not be terrified by it but stretch out your arms confidently and let the nails go deep. Be glad and thankful, for thus it must and will be with those who desire God's Word.[61]

Such crosses teach us that the results of the work of the Office of the Holy Ministry really are God's. Such crosses are God's way of making us the pastors and people He would have us to be, "conformed to the image of His Son" (Romans 8:29). And if St. Paul required such crosses and afflictions, how much more so will we require them to become the pastors and people God would have us be in this life?

> But we have this treasure in jars of clay, to show that the surpassing power belongs to God and not to us. We are afflicted in every way, but not

crushed; perplexed, but not driven to despair; persecuted, but not forsaken; struck down, but not destroyed; always carrying in the body the death of Jesus, so that the life of Jesus may also be manifested in our bodies. For we who live are always being given over to death for Jesus' sake, so that the life of Jesus also may be manifested in our mortal flesh. So death is at work in us, but life in you. . . .

So we do not lose heart. Though our outer nature is wasting away, our inner nature is being renewed day by day. For this slight momentary affliction is preparing for us an eternal weight of glory beyond all comparison, as we look not to the things that are seen but to the things that are unseen. For the things that are seen are transient, but the things that are unseen are eternal. *2 Corinthians 4:7–12, 16–18*

Christ, have mercy!

NOTES

1 AE 51:391.

2 Peter Matheson, ed., *The Third Reich and the Christian Churches* (Grand Rapids: Eerdmans, 1981), 1.

3 Matheson, *Third Reich*, 1–2.

4 Ap V 384–85 (*Concordia*, 141).

5 AE 46:93.

6 Ap IV 79 (*Concordia*, 93–94).

7 AE 31:25.

8 SA III III 2 (*Concordia*, 272).

9 Carl S. Meyer, ed., *Moving Frontiers: Readings in the History of The Lutheran Church—Missouri Synod* (St. Louis: Concordia, 1964), 66.

10 C. F. W. Walther, *The Proper Distinction Between Law and Gospel*, trans. W. H. T. Dau (St. Louis: Concordia, 1929), 80.

11 AE 1:180.

12 AE 5:131. See also AE 12:319.

13 See Martin Brecht, *Martin Luther: The Preservation of the Church, 1532–1546* (Minneapolis: Fortress, 1999), 262ff.

14 Vergil, *Aeneid* 6.95, in Theodore G. Tappert, ed. and trans., *Luther: Letters of Spiritual Counsel*, Library of Christian Classics 18 (Philadelphia: Westminster Press, 1955), 161.

15 C. F. W. Walther, *The Word of His Grace: Occasional and Festival Sermons*, trans. and ed. by Evangelical Lutheran Synod Translation Committee (Lake Mills, IA: Graphic Publishing Co., 1978), 164.

16 AE 32:112.

17   FC SD Rule and Norm 3 (*Concordia*, 508).

18   LC I 46 (*Concordia*, 363).

19   SA II II 5 (*Concordia*, 264).

20   AE 30:28.

21   AE 5:28: "And we should read the accounts of the fathers in such a manner that the examples of faith strengthen us and give us courage. But the examples of weakness should comfort us, lest we despair or become proud. And we should also comfort others."

22   AE 35:267.

23   Hermann Sasse, "The Presence of Christ and the Future of the Church," in *The Lonely Way*, trans. Matthew C. Harrison et al. (St. Louis: Concordia, 2001), 1:461–69.

24   Sasse, "Presence of Christ and the Future of the Church," 1:461.

25   AE 4:361–62.

26   AE 3:284.

27   *Der Lutheraner* 11, no. 22 (June 19, 1855): 169–73 (*author's translation*).

28   Theodore G. Tappert, ed. and trans., *Luther: Letters of Spiritual Counsel*, Library of Christian Classics 18 (Philadelphia and London: Westminster Press and SCM, 1955), 168.

29   AE 4:104.

30   AE 4:103–4.

31   AE 24:70: "In brief, they have introduced a special, self-devised sanctity, apart from and contrary to the common Word and order of God and the ordinary godly vocations."

32   Joel R. Baseley, trans., *Festival Sermons of Martin Luther: The Church Postils, Winter and Summer Selections* (Dearborn, MI: Mark V Publications, 2005), Winter Section, 168, 173 (*emphasis added*).

33   Luther, cited in Paul Althaus, *The Ethics of Martin Luther*, trans. Robert C. Schultz (Philadelphia: Fortress, 1972), 40.

34   Althaus, *Ethics of Martin Luther*, 41.

35   Gustaf Wingren, *Luther on Vocation*, trans. Carl C. Rasmussen (Philadelphia: Muhlenberg, 1957), 72.

36   Wingren, *Luther on Vocation*, 172.

37   AE 45:39.

38   LC I 108 (*Concordia*, 371).

39   Tappert, *Letters of Spiritual Counsel*, 239. "Divine Service" can be used to mean God's service to us (Word and Sacrament) or our service to God (love for neighbor).

40   AE 40:387.

41   Baseley, *Festival Sermons*, Winter Section, 143.

42   Baseley, *Festival Sermons*, Winter Section, 119.

43 See Holger Sonntag, trans., *Löhe on Mercy*, ed. by Adriane Dorr and Philip Hendrickson (St. Louis: LCMS World Relief and Human Care, 2006), 19.

44 AE 7:184.

45 AE 33:47.

46 AE 28:87.

47 LC I 198 (*Concordia*, 381).

48 Wingren, *Luther on Vocation*, 180.

49 Luther, as cited in Wingren, *Luther on Vocation*, 70.

50 AE 22:479.

51 August R. Suelflow, *Servant of the Word: The Life and Ministry of C. F. W. Walther* (St. Louis: Concordia, 2000), 78.

52 Suelflow, *Servant of the Word*, 79.

53 Suelflow, *Servant of the Word*, 79.

54 Suelflow, *Servant of the Word*, 80.

55 See note above in the section on mercy and office.

56 Walther, *Word of His Grace*, 167.

57 Walther, *Word of His Grace*, 173.

58 See FC SD X.

59 *Sechster Synodal—Bericht . . . vom Jahre 1852. Zweite Auflage* (St. Louis, 1876), 200–207 (author's translation).

60 Tappert, *Letters of Spiritual Counsel*, 83.

61 Tappert, *Letters of Spiritual Counsel*, 139.

Conclusion
IT'S TIME TO DARE SOMETHING FOR MERCY'S SAKE!

THE TIME AND THE WORD OF GOD DEMAND THIS

So we are always of good courage. . . . For we walk by faith, not by sight.
2 Corinthians 5:6

Hence it is up to you to dare something in this matter, since you see that
time and the word of God demand this.[1] *Martin Luther*

There is something else striking about the great missiological eras of
Christianity: they have been marked by mercy! It was so during Jesus'
lifetime. It was so also in the Book of Acts and during the ministry of
St. Paul. It was so in those fabulous and expansive early centuries of
the Church. It was certainly so in the case of the apostolic fathers and
during the time of the great third- and fourth-century bishops
Ambrose and Augustine. Adolf von Harnack's great *Mission and
Expansion of Christianity*[2] has some sixty pages of documentation on
the Early Church's ministrations of mercy at a time when the entire
Mediterranean world was streaming into the Church. Luther and the
Reformation brought a revolution in *diakonia*, care for the needy, hospitals, and so on.[3] The period of Pietism—for all its weaknesses,
errors, and excesses—was both missiologically productive and diaconally active.[4] The great nineteenth-century period of Lutheran
Awakening produced Wilhelm Löhe,[5] the greatest mission- and
mercy-minded Lutheran in history. Löhe was instrumental in the
founding of institutions of mercy, including a deaconess training
institution (Neuendettelsau) that is even now in existence and has
produced thousands of deaconesses for the German church and
which gave impetus in large measure to the work of deaconesses in the
United States. Löhe defined mission in terms of mercy: "Evangelizing
to the Gentiles is the great work of mercy in the New Testament."[6]

So the cry goes up, "Repent! Return to the Scriptures and the
Lutheran Confessions! Have courage! Dare to have mercy!"

Along with the concern confessional Lutherans share over the future of the LCMS, it must be asserted that there has never in history been a better or more opportune moment to be a confessional Lutheran. While passing through Singapore on the way to Medan, Indonesia, I attended Sunday services in a beautiful Singapore Lutheran congregation. After the service, this congregation that exhibited a definite international flare was abuzz with interest in its LCMS visitors, a group that included several faculty members from both seminaries who were visiting tsunami sights in India and Indonesia. One local man approached me and asked with a pronounced Southeast Asian accent, "You live in St. Louis?"

I was smiling a bit smugly, thinking, *He's seen my picture in* . . . Just as I was ready to talk about myself, he asked a second question, "You know Tahd Wiwkin?"

"Who? You mean *Todd Wilken*?" I responded, and the man nodded eagerly.

Todd Wilken hosts "Issues Etc.," a radio program that originates in St. Louis at KFUO, the radio station of the LCMS. Todd's program is a thoughtful, no-holds barred talk show that is intensely doctrinal, intensely Lutheran, even as it explores contemporary issues. It turned out this man, half a world away, was a regular listener via the Internet. And he is hardly alone.

It really is a whole new day. We are witnessing the greatest free flow of faithfully Lutheran information in the history of the Lutheran Church. Concordia Publishing House produces fantastic and faithful materials for a world hungry for solid Lutheran teaching about Christ and the faith—and it is thriving financially. Lutheran Heritage Foundation has now produced Luther's Small Catechism in fifty languages. *Good News Magazine* is in many languages and finding its way all over the world. Lutheran Hour Ministries is broadcasting in country after country, "bringing Christ to the nations and the nations to the church." What a fabulous mission! I see the harvest of this work wherever I travel. It is the worldwide moment for confessional Lutheranism. It is Missouri's moment.

We Are Still Here

Whatever the weaknesses of the LCMS, whatever the weaknesses of her partners around the world, whatever the challenges of the numerous faithful Lutherans within the Lutheran World Federation (and God knows we all have sins and warts and challenges), we are all still here. That is an amazing, wonderful, unfathomable gift of God. Almost five hundred years after the Lutheran Reformation, faithful Lutherans are still confessing Christ! The LCMS still takes seriously its commitment to the Word of God and the Lutheran Confessions— and the world is set before us, a world in which we are hardly alone. In fact, the number of our friends grows steadily. As much of European and U.S. Lutheranism apart from the LCMS and her partner churches becomes increasingly at odds with historic Christianity (particularly concerning issues of sexuality), Lutherans in Africa, Asia, Eurasia, Russia, Southeast Asia, and Central and South America are more and more open to and seeking relationships with the LCMS. And this will continue to be the case.

It is a complex world. We pray for renewal for our friends and fellow Christians in church bodies that are slipping away from the New Testament faith, even as we humbly pray for the Lord's patience and mercy with us. We also thank God that true faith exists wherever the name of Christ is proclaimed. We have many friends, and sometimes we have friends in surprising places.

We have myriad opportunities, and by God's gracious giving, the LCMS has access to unfathomable wealth and resources. In many instances, foundations, individuals, and congregations are wealthier than ever before—and more generous than ever before. We have a $25 million yearly world mission effort and dedicated missionaries. We have a $1 billion pension fund and Lutheran Church Extension funds. We have two world-class seminaries that are faithful examples of what such institutions can and should be. We have ten colleges and universities with untold capacity and resources for training leaders for private and churchly vocations. This *is* Missouri's moment.

MERCY'S MOMENT

And this is a moment for mercy: "The time and the word of God demand it." If we are to regain our missionary vibrancy; experience a renewal in stewardship; if God is to grant renewal, rebirth, and even growth to the LCMS, He will have to grant us repentance, mercy, and courage. His mercy shall beget our mercy. We should not carry on ministrations of mercy to grow the Church. However, if we are to be what Christ has called us to be and made us to be, then we will be His merciful Body. God grant us the mercy to be merciful to one another, to speak well of one another, to be clergy faithful to our ordination vows, as members of the Body to be rigorous in our vocations, to stand together where we need to confess Christ, and to grant freedom and flexibility where the Gospel and its articles are not in jeopardy. God grant us to "be steadfast, immovable, always abounding in the work of the Lord, knowing that in the Lord your labor is not in vain. . . . Stand firm in the faith . . . be strong" (1 Corinthians 15:58; 16:13). In his calling as a Christian (Baptism) and in his vocation as a pastor and teacher of the Church (call and ordination), Luther found courage and comfort:

> For I would surely in the long run lose courage and fall into despair if . . . I had undertaken these great and serious matters without call or commission. But God and the whole world bears me testimony that I entered into this work publicly and by virtue of my office as teacher and preacher, and have carried it on hitherto by the grace and help of God.[7]

LET'S DARE SOMETHING!

It is time to "dare something" in the name of Christ. The LCMS has gifted laity by the thousands. The LCMS has capable and consecrated deaconesses and others ready and willing to serve and lead in the Church's corporate life of mercy. The LCMS has been blessed with a multitude of small and rural congregations. Even as they face deep demographic challenges, the rest of the Church can learn from them, because mercy seems to come almost naturally. The LCMS has gifted and wealthy large congregations with mission zeal. The LCMS has many congregations that hold the bright beacon of Christ's Gospel in challenging inner-city neighborhoods where there are no easy solutions and crosses aplenty.

The mission for mercy is before us all, and so is our Lord. It is time for the "demons" that have caused us to lose courage for the day to be exorcized, and what was spoken once to a demon-possessed man is now spoken of us, "Go home to your friends and tell them how much the Lord has done for you, and how He has had mercy on you" (Mark 5:19). The LCMS should not be surprised that if what is written of the apostolic Church immediately after it carefully arranged its corporate life of mercy should also happen to us: "And the word of God continued to increase, and the number of the disciples multiplied greatly in Jerusalem" (Acts 6:7).

> In spite of all, we should say: "I believe. I have been baptized. I have been absolved. I have God's promise of grace and mercy. I have enough. Whether night, day, tribulation, or joy befalls me, I shall nevertheless not forfeit His mercy or lose courage."[8]

> God of grace and God of glory,
> On Your people pour Your pow'r;
> Crown Your ancient Church's story;
> Bring its bud to glorious flow'r.
> Grant us wisdom, grant us courage
> For the facing of this hour,
> For the facing of this hour.

> Lo, the hosts of evil round us
> Scorn the Christ, assail His ways!
> From the fears that long have bound us
> Free our hearts to faith and praise.
> Grant us wisdom, grant us courage
> For the living of these days,
> For the living of these days.

> Cure Your children's warring madness;
> Bend our pride to Your control;
> Shame our wanton, selfish gladness,
> Rich in things and poor in soul.
> Grant us wisdom, grant us courage
> Lest we miss Your kingdom's goal,
> Lest we miss Your kingdom's goal.

255

Save us from weak resignation
To the evils we deplore;
Let the gift of Your salvation
Be our glory evermore.
Grant us wisdom, grant us courage,
Serving You whom we adore,
Serving You whom we adore.
(*Lutheran Service Book* 850)

Lord, have mercy.
Christ, have mercy.
Lord, have mercy.

Advance boldly, dear brother. Be of good courage, let your heart be strengthened, and wait on the Lord.[9] *Martin Luther*

NOTES

1 AE 48:359.

2 Adolf von Harnack, *The Mission and Expansion of Christianity in the First Three Centuries*, vol. 1 (New York: Putnum, 1908). See the chapter "The Gospel of Love."

3 Carter Lindberg, *Beyond Charity: Reformation Initiatives for the Poor* (Minneapolis: Fortress, 1993).

4 See Holger Sonntag, trans., *Löhe on Mercy*, ed. by Adriane Dorr and Philip Hendrickson (St. Louis: LCMS World Relief and Human Care, 2006), 56.

5 For Löhe, "the key element of mission is mercy" (David C. Ratke, *Confession and Mission, Word and Sacrament: The Ecclesial Theology of Wilhelm Löhe* [St. Louis: Concordia, 2001], 187, 189).

6 Sonntag, *Löhe on Mercy*, 22.

7 AE 40:387–88.

8 AE 5:59.

9 Theodore G. Tappert, ed. and trans., *Luther: Letters of Spiritual Counsel*, Library of Christian Classics 18 (Philadelphia and London: Westminster Press and SCM, 1955), 190.

STUDY QUESTIONS

BY JOHN T. PLESS

CHAPTER 1: LORD, HAVE MERCY; CHRIST, HAVE MERCY; LORD, HAVE MERCY

1. How does the story of Amy Schneider illustrate our need for God's mercy?

2. "I had witnessed a foreshadowing of the Last Day." How is every death a preview of the final day? See Matthew 24:38 and 1 Thessalonians 5:2.

3. How does death reveal what we desperately seek to deny?

4. Read Matthew 15:21–28. How does the Canaanite woman teach us to pray the Kyrie?

5. Luther says that the Canaanite woman "catches Christ, the Lord, in his own words." What does this demonstrate about Jesus?

6. Read The Litany in *Lutheran Service Book* (pp. 288–89). How does life in our world add intensity to our praying of this liturgical text?

7. What does the title "Lord" tell us about Jesus?

8. What does the Kyrie confess? See Luke 18:13.

9. How did Luther stand "the entire worship of the medieval Church on its head"?

10. "Luther described the Divine Service as a man coming with an empty sack." How is this illustrated in stanza 4 of Luther's hymn on the Ten Commandments (*Lutheran Service Book* 581:4)?

11. How does the "cup of blessing" sustain us when the "cup of suffering" is not taken from us?

CHAPTER 2: FATHER, SON, AND SPIRIT

1. Read Luke 6:36. Why is a denial of mercy "a denial of who God is in Christ, a denial of the Holy Trinity"?

2. How have Lutherans in Kenya expressed the mercy of Christ to victims of HIV/AIDS?

3. How has God revealed His mercy to us according to the following texts?
   Hebrews 1:1–3
   Ephesians 1:3–9
   1 Corinthians 2:2
   2 Corinthians 5:19–21

4. Wilhelm Löhe writes: "Because [Christ's] love and His Father's and the Spirit's love can only be mercy, so our love for the brothers and all men should include nothing but mercy." How does this insight shape the Church's practice?

5. How does God show His mercy to us in Baptism? See Titus 3:5–6; Matthew 3:15; and Mark 1:10.

6. Why is the doctrine of the Trinity the only alternative to agnosticism?

7. How does each person of the Holy Trinity manifest divine mercy? See Mark 6:34; Luke 23:34; and Philippians 2:1.

8. Reflecting on the words of Dietrich Bonhoeffer cited in note 16 on p. 37, how do you think Christians show mercy to the needy, the orphaned, and the suffering?

9. How does the mercy of the triune God flow through us to others?

CHAPTER 3: MERCY INCARNATE

1. What is the meaning of the Greek word *splanchnon*? How does it relate to the visceral nature of mercy?

2. How is God's visceral mercy demonstrated in the following texts?
   Matthew 9:36–38
   Matthew 14:13–21
   Matthew 15:32–39
   Matthew 18:21–35
   Matthew 20:29–34
   Mark 1:40–45
   Mark 8:1–10
   Mark 9:14–29
   Luke 7:11–17

Luke 10:25–37

Luke 15:11–32

3. What is the difference between the Gospel and ethics?

4. Read Philippians 2:5–8. What is the "mind of Christ"?

5. Luther says that we "clothe ourselves in our neighbor's flesh." How is Jesus' incarnation the pattern for our lives of mercy?

CHAPTER 4: THE HEART OF MERCY'S HEART

1. How did modernist interpreters view the New Testament? What did this do to the Christian faith?

2. What happened to the naïve optimism of nineteenth-century liberalism?

3. How are non-Christian religions gaining a foothold in the West?

4. What are the differences between modernism and postmodernism?

5. What happens to the doctrine of justification (Augsburg Confession IV) in postmodernism?

6. How is the need for justification universal? How was this demonstrated in the story of the street boys of Marsabit?

7. By nature, what do we know of God? See Romans 2:14.

8. "Every attempt at self-justification before God is futile and damning." How is this demonstrated in Romans 3:19–20; Galatians 3:10; and 1 Corinthians 15:22?

9. How does the "free gift" stand in contrast to the Law? See Romans 5:15–17.

10. What are the "three persistent paths" of self-justification?

11. Christ Jesus is not a path that we make for ourselves to God; rather, He is God coming to us to save us. What does Acts 4:12 tell us of this salvation?

12. Read Ephesians 2:8–9. How is faith itself a gift of divine mercy?

13. "There is no middle ground. Justification by grace for Christ's sake through faith—or self-justification." How is justification by grace for Christ's sake through faith "the heart of mercy's heart"?

CHAPTER 5: BAPTIZED FOR THIS MOMENT

1. Read Romans 6:4. How is Baptism the "water of life in a world of hurt"?

2. How did the promise of Baptism give courage and confidence to the Lutherans who responded in the aftermath of Hurricane Katrina?

3. Water can work death, but it also bestows life. How is this illustrated in 1 Peter 3:20–22? See also John 3:5 and Matthew 28:19.

4. How is Baptism a "passive activity"? See Galatians 3:26–27 and Ephesians 2:8–9.

5. The Bible never teaches that Baptism is symbolic. Rather, what does Baptism actually give? See Acts 2:38 and Titus 3:4–8.

6. Baptism is the sacrament of justification. How does the imagery of birth in John 3:5 demonstrate that the Lord carries the action of the verbs in the Sacrament?

7. What does Baptism have to do with the Church's corporate life of mercy? See Romans 6:1–11.

8. In what sense is the denial of mercy a denial of the Gospel character of Baptism?

9. Read Galatians 3:27 and Colossians 3:3. What does God do with our lives in Baptism?

10. What does Baptism have to do with the Christian's life of affliction under the cross? See Romans 8:26.

11. Luther said that we should not be surprised that we "bear a splinter or two" of Christ's cross in this life. What are some examples of such splinters? How does Baptism strengthen us for such cross-bearing?

CHAPTER 6: SPOKEN FREE AND LIVING MERCIFULLY

1. What is meant by the statement: "Living mercifully is a high holy art of faith"?

2. How does the Gospel "speak us free"?

3. What does God's Word do? See Genesis 1:3; John 6:63; and Romans 1:16.

4. How does the Law make sin "utterly sinful"? See Romans 7:7–9.

5. What is the Office of the Keys? How does it demonstrate God's mercy? See John 20:23 and Matthew 18:15–20.

6. Pastors forgive sins publicly in the stead of Christ according to His mandate. Lay Christians forgive sins "privately" in what Luther calls "secret" absolution. Where does this happen?

7. Wilhelm Löhe said, "The ears of the pastor become tombs in private confession. What goes in never comes out." How is private confession an expression of mercy for both the pastor and the penitent?

8. "The Lord speaks us free, and He frees us to speak." How does the forgiveness we have received enliven us to speak mercifully to others?

9. What is autonomy? How is autonomy different from Christian freedom?

10. Read Matthew 18:21–35. How do we keep from reenacting the parable of the unmerciful servant?

CHAPTER 7: CHRIST'S BODY AND BLOOD

1. What is the relationship between the Lord's death on the cross and His Supper?

2. Why did the Early Church call the Divine Service *Synaxis*?

3. Read Exodus 25:10–22. What was the mercy seat? How does Hebrews 9:22 help us understand the significance of the mercy seat?

4. Who is our mercy seat according to Romans 3:25?

5. Read Hebrews 10:19–25. Where do we have access to Jesus?

6. How does Jesus carry the action of the verbs in the Lord's Supper?

7. What is the meaning of the word *communio*?

8. How is the Lord's Supper "the last will and testament of Jesus"?

9. Read Matthew 26:26–28; Mark 14:22–24; Luke 22:19–20; and 1 Corinthians 11:23–26. How are these words "bedrock for this Sacrament"?

10. Read 1 Corinthians 10:15–17. What is the *koinonia* of which the apostle speaks?

11. Why does the Christian Church practice close(d) Communion?

12. How does our vertical unity with Christ Jesus in the Lord's Supper express itself horizontally? See Acts 2:42; Romans 15:26; Galatians 2:9–10.

13. According to Luther, how does the Sacrament bring about a fellowship of love and mercy?

Chapter 8: Christ Cares for the Needy, Body and Soul

1. How did Luther's final note illustrate the stance and posture of Christian faith before God?

2. Which passages of Holy Scripture did Luther recite as death drew near? How did these texts demonstrate the reformer's understanding of God's mercy?

3. How do the Scriptures teach us to pray to the Lord for mercy? See Luke 18:35–43; Matthew 8:1–13; 9:1–8; 9:18–31; 17:14–21; 20:29–34.

4. What is Platonism? How do the miracles of Jesus prevent us from becoming "begging Platonists"?

5. What is Gnosticism and how does it deny the character of the Christian faith? See 1 John 4:2–3.

6. How does the Lord's Supper demonstrate the bodily nature of the Christian faith?

7. What is enthusiasm? How were Adam and Eve enthusiasts? See Genesis 3:5.

8. What do both creation and redemption teach us about the body?

9. What happened when we split apart body and soul in Christian teaching and practice? See James 2:15–16.

10. Read 1 John 5:6–12. What does this tell us about the Sacraments?

11. Read 1 Peter 4:13; Philippians 3:10; 2 Corinthians 1:5; and Colossians 1:24. What do these texts tell us about the connection between the bodily suffering of Christ and the suffering of His Christians?

12. In what sense is mercy a "mark" of the Church?

CHAPTER 9: THE CHURCH: HOLY AND WHOLE

1. How does the use of plural pronouns in the New Testament stand in contrast with our individualism?

2. How do Jesus' actions on our behalf place us into a community of believers? See John 10:16 and 17:10.

3. What New Testament images for the Church point to its communal character?

4. In the Divine Service, we sing the Sanctus. See Isaiah 6:3 and Revelation 4:8. How does this liturgical text confess the unity of the Church?

5. What is the "communion of saints"?

6. In what sense is sanctification corporate? See 1 Corinthians 3:16–17 and 1 Peter 1:14–25.

7. How is the Church "outwardly nothing but a priestly, royal institute of mercy" (Wilhelm Löhe)?

8. Read Acts 2:44 and 4:34. How is the communal nature of the Church pictured here? What are the implications for life of the congregation today?

CHAPTER 10: GOD AGAINST GOD

1. Luther writes: "He deserves to be called a theologian, however, who comprehends the visible and manifest things of God seen through suffering and the cross." What does this mean for the way that we react to tragedy?

2. The Father reveals Jesus as His Son in the Baptism in the Jordan (see Mark 1:11). After that no one in Mark's Gospel recognizes who Jesus is, except the demons, until He is crucified (Mark 15:37–39). What is going on here?

3. What is the distinction between God's hidden will and His revealed will?

4. Recall Luther's statement: "We must take hold of this God, not naked but clothed and revealed in His Word; otherwise certain despair will crush us." How does Luther's insight help us address questions that arise out of suffering?

5. Read the story of Abraham's near sacrifice of Isaac in Genesis 22:1–19. How does this narrative reveal "God against God"?

6. Recall the Genesis account of Joseph, who was sold into slavery by his brothers. Read especially Genesis 45:4–8 and 50:20. How did God use Joseph's affliction for good?

7. Read Job 2:9; 3:23; 6:4. What do these passages tell us about God's role in Job's suffering?

8. Read Job 13:15. What does Job confess? What does this tell us about faith?

9. Read 2 Corinthians 12:7–10. What is God's answer to Paul's plea?

10. How would you respond biblically to the popular notion "God does not want us to suffer"?

11. Read 2 Corinthians 5:21. How is the cross both Law and Gospel?

12. How does God use crossbearing and affliction for His children?

13. "When we shun our suffering neighbor, we shun a 'living relic' of the cross." How is euthanasia a shunning of the suffering neighbor?

14. Luther refers to the "happy exchange" whereby Christ takes our sin and gives us His righteousness. How is this "happy exchange" reflected in the way that Christians relate to the neighbor in need?

15. Read Romans 8:20–30. How is the suffering that even our sinful actions bring upon us used by God to conform us to the image of His Son?

CHAPTER 11: MERCY, MONEY, AND MISSING THE STEWARDSHIP BOAT

1. Read Galatians 6:10. How does Paul describe the movement of the mercy practiced by Christians?

2. What is the relationship of works of mercy to missions or evangelism? See Luke 5:17–26.

3. How is the Church's life of mercy characterized in Romans 15:26; 2 Corinthians 1:8; 8:4–6; 9:1; 9:5; 9:12?

4. What are the four elements of congregational life according to Acts 2:42?

5. Read 1 John 1:3–7. How is fellowship (*koinonia*) both vertical and horizontal in this text?

6, What does this fellowship mean for those in need? See 1 John 3:15–17 and Acts 4:34.

7. Based on your reading of Acts 11:19–30 and Galatians 2:9–10, comment on the statement: "Where the Church is in motion there is mission, mercy, and money."

8. Read carefully 2 Corinthians 8–9. What do these two chapters tell us about "mission, mercy, and money"?

9. How does "unity in the faith entail unity in love"? See 1 John 4:11–21.

CHAPTER 12: MERCY AND THE CHURCH'S CONFESSION

1. What are the two versions of the Reformation?

2. What was John Calvin's basic philosophical principle? How does this undermine the Gospel?

3. How did Margrave George of Brandenburg confess the faith?

4. How was Lutheranism weakened in Luther's homeland?

5. What was the Prussian Union? How is its spirit still seen today?

6. Why is the right confession of the Lord's Supper necessary?

7. How did C. F. W. Walther respond to the Prussian Union?

8. What does the right confession of doctrine have to do with mercy?

9. What does the New Testament teach us about the content and act of confession? See Mark 8:29; Romans 10:9–13; 1 Corinthians 12:3; Philippians 2:11.

10. The Greek word *homologeo* lies behind our English word *confession*. What is the literal meaning of this Greek word? How do 1 John 1:9; Matthew 11:25; and Romans 10:9–10 show three dimensions of confession?

11. "The Church which cannot curse cannot bless either." What does this statement tell us about the nature of confessing the faith? See Galatians 1:8.

12. How do the assertions "deeds not creeds" or "doctrine divides, service unites" destroy both confession and mercy?

13. How does the Lutheran World Federation actively and aggressively promote the nullification of the binding authority of the Lutheran Confessions? What implications does this have for our life together in the LCMS?

14. What does a rejection of Scripture's authority as rule, judge, and norm entail?

15. How are we freed by the truth of the Lutheran Confessions?

16. What do the Lutheran Confessions teach us about works of charity?

CHAPTER 13: MERCY AND OFFICE

1. What do we learn from Luther's St. Stephen's Day sermon on Acts 6–7 about the "spiritual government's" concern for both body and soul?

2. What are the purposes of the office of deacon?

3. What does Martin Chemnitz have to say about the Office of the Holy Ministry in relationship to care for the needy?

4. According to Johann Gerhard, what are the seven duties of the Office of the Holy Ministry?

5. How did C. F. W. Walther see the pastor's responsibility for the poor? How did he understand Romans 12:6–12?

6. What are "almoners"?

7. What function do deaconesses have according to Wilhelm Löhe?

8. What does Jesus tell us about our care for the poor in Matthew 25:40?

CHAPTER 14: WHAT IS LUTHERAN LEADERSHIP?

1. What is leadership?
2. How might the distinction between the "ministerial" and "magisterial" use of reason apply to the use of "leadership principles" in the Church?
3. What is "First Article fanaticism"?
4. What insights from Jim Collins's discussion of leadership might be helpful in your congregation?
5. How does the mercy of Christ focus and enliven our leadership?

CHAPTER 15: MERCY IN THE CITY

1. How might Lutheran congregations cooperate with congregations of other denominations without doctrinal compromise?
2. How does original sin manifest itself in communities?
3. How do the first six articles of the Augsburg Confession order the priorities in the life and mission of the Lutheran congregation?
4. What does Luke 10:16 teach us about the office of the pastor?
5. What is the problem with the description of Lutheranism as a "confessing movement"?
6. How do the Lutheran Confessions understand poverty?
7. How is the Church's concern for the well-being of the poor a natural consequence of the Gospel?
8. What are the two kingdoms or realms? How does this distinction help Lutherans navigate life in this world?
9. What rights and responsibilities does the Church have in the kingdom of the left?
10. How is "two-kingdom theology" different from the distinction between church and state?
11. How does the episode of Pastor Harrison and Father Delaney illustrate a genuine ecumenism without doctrinal compromise?

Chapter 16: Repentance, Word, Vocation, and the Courage to Be Lutheran and Merciful

1. Read 1 Corinthians 16:13. Where does the courage of which Paul speaks come from?

2. How did Hermann Sasse find the courage to confess against Adolf Hitler?

3. Luther says, "Hearts are given courage through trust in mercy" (AE 1:180). What three things gave Luther both consolation and courage?

4. According to Luther, what does repentance entail?

5. Carefully read 1 Corinthians 11–12. How does God give us courage in weakness so that we "do great things"?

6. Read Romans 15:4. How do the Scriptures give us hope?

7. "The Church ultimately has a future because Jesus Christ has a future." How does Matthew 16:18 help us understand this truth?

8. What is our vocation according to 1 Peter 2:9–10?

9. What three things are spiritual priests called to do?

10. Read Romans 12:1–3. What does our calling have to do with daily life?

11. What is special about an "office"?

12. According to Gustaf Wingren, how is the neighbor evidence of the fact that I have a vocation?

13. What are the three main stations or offices in life according to Luther?

14. How is courage expressed in the context of an office?

15. What does Luther mean when he says that God is with us even in the sewer?

16. Read 2 Corinthians 4:6–7. What promise does God give here that enlivens our courage in vocation?

17. How did C. F. W. Walther serve God's mercy in St. Louis in 1849 amid epidemic and fire?

18. What courage is required of both pastors and laity in our day?

19. How do the Lutheran Confessions understand the relationship of pastor and people?

20. "People follow conviction, not coercion." How might these words shape pastoral leadership?

21. Read Hebrews 13:17. What does this text tell us about the responsibility of the congregation to its pastor?

CONCLUSION: IT'S TIME TO DARE SOMETHING FOR MERCY'S SAKE!

1. How have the great missiological eras of Christianity been marked by mercy?

2. What are the special gifts that the LCMS brings to the world today?

3. How is this present time "a moment for mercy"?

4. Read 1 Corinthians 15:58. How does this text shape our stance toward the future?